AMERICAN HISTORY STORIES VOLUMES I-IV

By

Mara L. Pratt

Cover Photograph: PhotoAtelier (Glen)

ISBN: 978-1-78139-347-5

© 2012 Benediction Classics, Oxford.

Contents

AMERICAN HISTORY STORIES, VOLUME I

AMERICAN HISTORY STORIES, VOLUME II

AMERICAN HISTORY STORIES, VOLUME III

AMERICAN HISTORY STORIES, VOLUME IV

AMERICAN HISTORY STORIES, VOLUME I

SHIPS OF THE NORSEMEN

LONG AGO

Many, many years ago, O, so many that I fear you could not count them even, this country in which we live was one vast expanse of woodland and fields, mountains and swamps.

There were no cities, no villages, not even a single house to break the view across the wild fields.

The whole country looked as it does now in those places which have not yet been built up.

Did you ever stand on a high hill and look off across the country where not one house was to be seen? How broad the fields looked and how strange it was to see the sky dipping down and seeming to rest upon the hills and trees away off at the horizon line! Well, that is the way it looked to the little boys and girls here so many years before the white people came to this country.

We do not know very much about these little boys and girls, and their fathers and mothers; for they knew nothing about writing, and so left no books to tell us about themselves.

We know that they used to live in tents, which they called wigwams; that they called the women squaws, and the baby boys and girls papooses; and that they were all called Indians by the white men.

These Indian people, according to our ideas, were very rude and wild. The fathers spent their time in hunting and fishing. The mothers stayed about the tents, kept the fires going, tilled the ground, raised the corn, cooked the food, such as it was, and loved their children just as mothers do the world over.

The little boys and girls had no schools, no books, no toys to keep them busy; so they spent their time playing about the tent or learning to fish and hunt and build canoes.

Perhaps you think they had lovely times with nothing to do; but I am afraid they some-times had very hard times too.

If I were to tell you the way the tribes of In-dians used to pounce down upon their homes, and slay the fathers, burn the moth-ers, and steal the children; and the way the children used to huddle into their tents dur-ing the cold, cold winters, I think you would not envy them at all.

EARLY DISCOVERIES

Little indeed did the people of Europe know of this country across the water or of the strange copper-colored people living here.

Lately there has been raised in Boston a monument in memory of Lief, the brave Northman or Norseman, who in the year 1000 sailed from his home in Iceland and came to the coast of America.

The vessel in which this Norseman came was odd-looking enough. Sometimes it moved along by the aid of its sails, sometimes each man would take an oar and so help it to move over the water.

STATUE OF LEIF ERICSON, BOSTON

The first land these hardy Norsemen found was flat and stony near the sea; but inland high mountains could be seen from the shore. This was Newfoundland. Then on the Norsemen sailed farther south, pleased with the warmth of the sun and the green trees, the song birds and the rich fruits. At one place, supposed to be on the shores of Massachusetts or Rhode Island, one of their company found such delicious wild grapes and in such abundance that Lief gave to the country the name of Vinland.

So delightful was the climate and so rich the fruits that the little band built huts and planned to spend the winter in the beautiful Vinland. It was all very strange to them, the swiftly changing day and night; for in their own land they had only one long day and one long night in a year.

Spring came, and Lief hastened back to Iceland to tell of the wonderful new land. Other Norsemen came, and, later still, a Norwegian nobleman with his beautiful young wife, Gudfrida. A colony was formed and the people lived very happily here for three years or more.

Then for some reason the colony died out, and little is known of them except what has been found in old chronicles in Iceland.

In Newport, Rhode Island, is a strange old tower which was once believed to have been built by these Norsemen. Certainly it is old enough and strange enough; but as to the true story of the Norsemen in America, I suppose we shall never know it.

ROUND TOWER, NEWPORT

They were a brave, sturdy people and very fond of adventures. No people were ever so brave upon the sea as these Norsemen, and it is a great pity we do not know all about them.

These Northmen were the only Europeans who ever ventured far away from home. The people of the southern counties of Europe would look out across the sea and wonder; but they dared not venture out a great ways upon the ocean.

In fact, the ships in those days were small and frail, hardly more sea-worthy than a simple pleasure yacht to-day; and therefore very little had been learned of the oceans.

"There is," sailors of southern Europe would sometimes say, "an island far out at sea,—a beautiful sunny island with rich fruits and beautiful flowers and great purple mountains. Rich gems and gold and silver sparkle about its shores, and in the centre on a gentle slope of ground stands the palace of the sea-god."

But although the southern sailors talked of it and the poets sang of it, no one had ever seen this land. Sometimes on a clear day, standing upon the shores and looking away out to where the sky seemed to dip down and meet the earth, some imaginative person would think he saw the island, and would call to his companions; but before they could come, behold, it always disappeared.

There was living at this time a good man whom the people called Saint Brandon. He was always trying to help others to do what to him seemed right and good; and when he heard of this island, he with another good priest sailed away towards it, hoping to find an opportunity to help the people who might be living there.

He never found the island, however—the Atlantis, as it was called, but he did find, so he said, another island, afterwards called the island of St. Brandon. But the wonderful part of the story is that even this island could never again be found. Whether St. Brandon was fond, like the other adventurers of his day, of telling a big story, or whether he did honestly find an island which, by and by, sank below the level of the water, as sea-islands sometimes do sink, no one could ever tell.

Once in the history of Spain there was a terrible war between the Moors and the Spaniards. Seven Spanish bishops, pursued by these Moors, took to their ships and sailed out upon the sea. "Better by far drown than be overtaken by our cruel foe," said they; and they sailed out into the great sea, beyond all sight of land, into the very sunset, so they said.

These bishops came at last upon an island,—a beautiful sunny island, rich in fruit and flowers and the most wonderful trees.

Here they built seven cities, each bishop placing himself at the head of his own city and governing such natives as lived in his part of the island.

By and by, when the cities were prosperous, the seven bishops returned to Spain and told of their wonderful discovery. Strange to say, however, no one was ever able again to find this island; and no one has ever found it yet.

Of one other island we must speak—and that is the island of Bimini. This island was not only rich and beautiful, but there was upon it a fountain of sparkling water whose waters could restore youth and strength to the weakest and oldest of men.

Such an island as that was certainly well worth searching for; and, in 1512, long after Columbus had sailed to the new world, an old man, Ponce de Leon, sailed away in search of this wonderful "Fountain of Youth."

Remember this was the childhood of the modern world, a time when wise old men and women would listen to stories that to-day only a baby could be made to believe. It does not seem possible that they believed these tales; yet they must really have thought them true, for the books they made in those days tell us so. And who knows, after all, that the things we believe to-day may not, hundreds of years later, seem just as strange to the people who will be living then.

Christophe Colomb

CHRISTOPHER COLUMBUS

But all these stories, foolish as they may seem, proved in the end a good thing. They kept the people wide awake, and on the look out for any new discovery far away upon the mysterious ocean.

By and by, there was born in the little village of Genoa, Italy, a baby boy who was destined to do more than guess and dream about the land beyond the sea. He was really to go and explore it and bring back proofs of its existence.

This baby boy, as every American school-child knows, was Christopher Columbus, the man whom now we are proud to honor as the discoverer of America.

Living as he did in this little sea-port town, he was generally, when not at school, to be found standing about the wharves watching the great ships come in, and listening to the marvellous stories that the sailors told.

Genoa at this time was a very rich town, and it sent ships to all parts of the known world. The little boy, eagerly drinking in all the wonderful stories the sailors were so fond of telling, thus learned much of the far away countries—much that was true and much also that was purely imaginary.

"I shall be a sailor!" he would say to himself as he listened; and then, like all other small lads, he longed to grow big and strong and old. "When I'm a man, I shall be a sailor! When I'm a man I shall go to all these wonderful countries and gather these beautiful things and bring home ships loaded with silver and gold."

The parents of Columbus were poor people. His father was a wool comber; but they were wise, and they tried to give their boy a good education. He was taught to read and write; and when, by and by, he was old enough to know what he should most enjoy, his father sent him away to a school where he could study arithmetic and drawing and geography.

To Columbus there was no study so fascinating as geography. He had listened eagerly

to the sailors' stories in his very early boyhood; and so now he eagerly devoured every
book and drank in every story he could find
about the wonderful countries so far away.

And he would say to himself, "I must be a
sailor! I must be a sailor!"

One day his good father said to him, "My
boy, I have watched you for a long time; and
since you have made up your mind to be a
sailor, and since you like best those studies
that have to do with navigation, I am willing
to send you to the University of Pavia where, I
am told, geography, astronomy, map-drawing
and navigation are wisely taught."

Columbus was a happy boy, you may be
sure. "Now indeed I may be a sailor!" cried
he—"A wise one! An explorer and a discoverer perhaps!" And seizing a book, he ran down
to the wharf to watch the ships and dream of
the happy time when he should have learned
all the wonders of navigation and be able to
guide for himself one of these great ships.

Columbus improved every hour of his term
at the University, learning so fast and showing so much eager interest and real
thoughtfulness, that the teachers were very
proud of him and predicted a great future for

their pupil. But even they had little idea of how great that future was to be.

Columbus was only fourteen years old when he made his first voyage out upon the great blue sea with some traders bound for the East Indies. From that time on his life was like that of all sailors, I suppose, full of adventures, narrow escapes, and marvellous experiences.

When he was thirty-five years old he went to Lisbon, the capital of Portugal. He was a quiet, dignified, thoughtful man now—his hair already white,—and here and there on his face were lines of care and trouble. For Columbus' life had not been an easy one; neither had he been satisfied to drift along contented with whatever he had been taught, whatever he had heard and read.

The stories of the great flat earth borne upon the back of an elephant or upon the shoulders of a great giant, the tales of the sea-gods and wind-gods,—all of which were believed in those early days,—had long since ceased to amuse or satisfy him. "They are not reasonable," he would say to himself. "They are like the stories one tells little children.

There must be something different from all this."

And so, year after year, Columbus pondered and pondered upon these questions. He read every account of travels, every story of adventure, every theory of the earth's size and shape that he could find. But none satisfied him. "It's easy enough to guess and to guess about these things," he would say; "but there must be some natural law, some real fact, that, if discovered, would give us the truth."

On account of the smallness of the ships, together with the superstitious fears the sailors had of the unknown sea with its angry and revengeful gods, no one had ever sailed very far out upon the ocean, and so had little thought of what might be found far out beyond the horizon.

"There may be land away out there," Columbus would say; "at any rate, I am convinced that this earth is round, and that by sailing straight out to the westward, we should come to the East Indies, a much easier and more speedy route than we now have."

"Hear him! hear him!" the people would say. "He is crazy! he dares say the earth is round, when we and all our ancestors before us have *known* that the earth is flat." "Ha, ha," laughed others; "let him sail westward as far as he pleases. When he has reached the end of the great sea and the sea-gods have cast him over, then he will learn how foolish he is, and Portugal will be well rid of him!"

But John II., then King of Portugal, was convinced that these notions of Columbus, as the people were pleased to call them, were not so absurd as they seemed. "The man knows what he is talking about, I believe," said he; "I will get his plans from him, pretend to favor them, pretend to be willing to aid him— then—then—well, we'll see who will have the honor of the first expedition, Columbus, the Genoese wool-comber's son, or John II., King of Portugal!"

And so this mean king led Columbus on to tell his plans and his reasons for believing the earth to be round. The king was wise enough to see that there was sound common sense and reason in these plans. Then when he had learned all, and had obtained the maps and charts which Columbus had made, he secretly sent out a vessel and ordered the captain to follow closely the route Columbus had marked out.

This was a mean trick, and I am glad, and you will be, that it did not succeed. No sooner was the vessel out of sight of land than the ignorant captain and the superstitious sailors began to be frightened.

"We are surely sailing off the edge of the earth!" cried they. "What shall we do when the sea-gods learn that we have dared come out of our home into their sacred waters!"

Then a great storm arose; the waves rolled and tumbled and broke above them mountains high. The thunder rumbled and the lightning flashed. Terror-stricken, the sailors turned the vessel homeward. "The gods are angry with us! They are punishing us for our boldness!" cried the ignorant sailors.

A more frightened and miserable crew never sailed back into Lisbon harbor than this one sent out by King John II.

And when Columbus heard of it, angry and disgusted with the meanness of the king, he would have no further talk with him; but, taking his little son Diego with him, he left the country and went to Spain.

Friendless and without money, Columbus with the little Diego travelled from place to place, always seeking some one who would understand and help him to an audience with the king or queen of Spain. If only somewhere a person of wealth could be found who would fit out for him a fleet, Columbus had not a doubt or a fear but that he could return with news of new lands or, at least, of a short route to India.

Years and years rolled by; and Columbus had gained nothing but a world-wide name of being a fool or an insane man. Men sneered at him, boys hooted at him in the street. Surely it was a brave man who could endure all this for the sake of right. But it is always so; as you grow older and read larger histories than these, you will find that seldom has a great man or woman brought to the world any great new truth, that ignorant and superstitious people did not scoff at it and make the life of the brave discoverer one of wretchedness and persecution.

"I will go to France," said Columbus at last, "and see if I can get the help of the French king." And he started with his little son, Diego, to walk the long distance.

One day, while on the road, Columbus stopped at the gate of a great gray convent in the town of Palos and asked for food.

COLUMBUS AND DIEGO

As the gate-man brought them bread, one of the monks passed by. Struck with the dignity and the courteous, refined appearance of Columbus, he said to himself, "Whom have we here? This is no ordinary beggar. I will speak with him."

So, going up to Columbus, he saluted him kindly and asked him to stop and rest. Glad enough were both Columbus and Diego to accept this hospitality, and together they entered the great halls of the convent.

Now the monk was a man of great learning for those days. More than that, he was a man who thought and who was always ready to accept any new theories, providing they seemed reasonable and honest proofs of their truth could be presented with them.

The intelligence and conversation of Columbus attracted the monk at once. "This man knows what he is talking about," thought he. "Surely I must bring him to Queen Isabella. She, if any one, will give him patient and intelligent hearing."

SPAIN — TIME OF FERDINAND AND ISABELLA

At that time the Spanish king and queen were busy with a great war against the Moors, so that it was a long time before either could listen to Columbus; but after long weeks of delay, he was summoned before them. There, before the king and queen and a large body of "wise men," as they called themselves, Columbus told his story.

All listened attentively. It was like a wonderful dream or a grand fairy story; and people were very fond of wonder stories of any kind in those days. But when the "wise men" were asked their opinion of the story as one at all likely to be true, they roared with laughter.

"The earth round!" cried they. "It is absurd! If a fleet were sent out upon the ocean it would certainly sail over the edge and fall down—down into unknown space."

COLUMBUS BEFORE THE WISE MEN

"And if the earth *were* round," said others, "and if this crazy man *could* sail down and stand upon his head on the other side of the sphere, how, pray, could he ever get back again? Has he learned to sail up hill?"

This was indeed unanswerable, so they all thought. Of course he could not, and of course he was a fool to think of such a thing. And so Columbus was sent away in disgrace, while the "wise men" entertained their friends for days after with the absurd story the crazy Genoese had told them.

"I will go to France," said Columbus to the good monk, when, discouraged and weary at heart he returned to the convent with the story of his defeat. "There is no hope for me in Spain."

"Wait, wait," said the monk. "I myself will go to the queen. I cannot bear that this honor should pass into the hands of the French. I will go to Isabella and beg her again to give you a hearing."

And so it was that once more Columbus waited and was led at last into the presence of the only one in all Spain who seemed to be kind enough at heart and to be far sighted enough to know that Columbus was neither foolish nor crazy.

After long hesitation—for it was not an easy matter in those days to fit out a fleet, nor was it a politic thing for Isabella to move in opposition to all the advice of her country-men, she sent this word to Columbus: "I will undertake this enterprise for my own king-dom of Castile; and I will pledge my jewels, if need be, to raise the funds."

THE DEPARTURE OF COLUMBUS FROM SPAIN

THE VOYAGE

With Isabella's aid and a little money which Columbus himself had, three ships were fitted out. These were not tall, stout ships such as you see lying at our wharves with their broad sails, huge wooden sides and wide decks. They were small, frail craft, not so large as those you may see to-day sailing up and down rivers and small lakes.

On Friday, August 3, 1492, three small vessels, the *Santa Maria*, the *Pinta* and the *Nina* with twenty men on board set sail from Spain.

They sailed for weeks across the unknown waters, keeping all the time to the west, until at last the sailors began to be frightened at the thought of their distance from home.

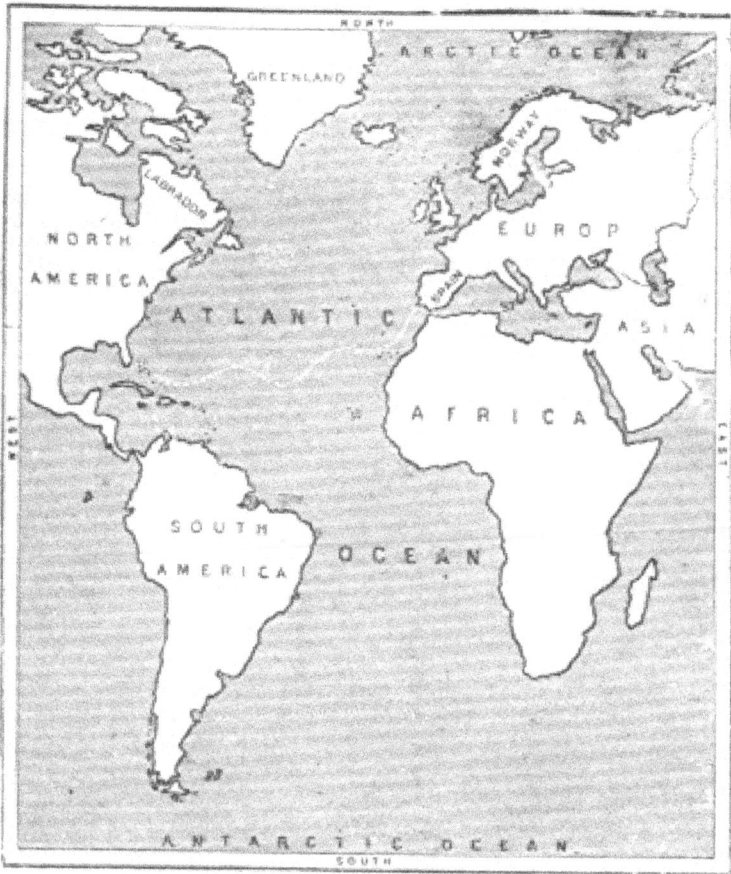

They threatened to throw Columbus overboard if he did not turn back; and at length

Columbus promised them that if they did not see land in three days he would return to Spain. You can imagine how anxious Columbus must have been during those three days. He felt that land was near, although he could not prove it to the sailors. To turn back now would have been a terrible disappointment. But fortunately for Columbus signs of land began to appear. Birds came and rested on the masts of their ships; a large branch of a tree floated by; and even the dullest sailor could not fail to believe these signs.

At last, one morning at daybreak, the cry of "Land! Land!" was heard from the foremost ship; and in a few hours more they reached the shores of a small island, which they called San Salvador.

THE SHIPS OF COLUMBUS

When Columbus set foot upon the dry land, he at once set up the Spanish flag and took possession in the name of Spain. A few days later they set sail for a larger island in the distance, and safely anchored in one of its harbors. They named this island Hispaniola, but it is now called Hayti. A beautiful island it proved to be, for the climate was soft and mild; there was an abundance of rich fruit, and there were many strange trees and flowers.

When the natives saw the white sails of the vessels, they rushed down to the shores, yelling with astonishment, for they never had seen a ship before, and of course were terribly frightened. Some thought they were great birds with white wings, some thought the

"Great Spirit" had come. They were glad to see Columbus and his men, and they said to them in their strange language, "Welcome, white men." And from that time they were very kind to Columbus and his men, and helped them not a little in exploring the island and in hunting for food. Columbus at first treated them kindly; and it would have been well had all white men continued to do so.

Columbus, however, soon returned to Spain, and told of his great discovery and of the wonderful copper-colored people, some of whom he had brought back with him, with their straight black hair and head-dresses of feathers and faces streaked with paint. All Spain was filled with wonder; and it was not long before shiploads of men were sent over to the new country; so that very soon the island was settled by Spanish people.

COLUMBUS'S RETURN TO SPAIN AFTER HIS FIRST
VOYAGE

I wish that I could tell you that Spain was so proud of Columbus and so grateful to him for his gift that he was ever after treated with great honor; that he never again wanted for anything which money and favor could buy; and that he died peacefully at last, loved and honored by all. This is certainly what you might expect to hear of so brave a man.

But there were jealous, envious men in Spain, who plotted against Columbus; and when, a few years later, he went again to the islands he had discovered, he was seized by one of these Spaniards who had been sent out to govern the colony which had settled there, was put into chains and sent back a prisoner to Spain.

When they heard of this cruel treatment, the people of Spain were indignant, and insisted that he be restored to his rights. The queen is said to have been moved to tears by his story.

Columbus made two more voyages of discovery, but sickness and disappointment had undermined his health, and he died shortly after at Valladolid, on the 20th of May, 1506.

OTHER GREAT EXPLORERS

But if Columbus discovered America, how did it happen that the country was named America? It certainly seems as if Columbia would have been a better and more fitting title for it, and it would have been but fair to Columbus, after all he had borne, to have had his name remembered in naming the country.

But people were not very careful in those days about being "fair" to anybody or anything; and so, when in 1497 Americus Vespucius made a voyage to the new world and on his return talked much of the great continent he had seen, and wrote a diary about it, people began speaking of this new world as the country of Americus Vespucius; by and by they called it America; and, since Columbus was not the man to whine at injustice, and Americus Vespucius did not seem to object to the honor conferred upon him, it soon became customary throughout Europe to speak of the new world as America.

STATUE OF AMERICUS VESPUCIUS, (PORTICO OF THE UFFIZI)

Americus Vespucius made another voyage a few years later, and this time directing his course farther south, he came upon the continent of South America. He sailed along the coast for several thousand leagues, very carefully noting all changes in the soil, the climate, and even in the stars.

"In these southern skies," reported he, "there is a constellation never seen by us,—a group of four bright stars arranged in the shape of a cross. One cannot imagine how strange these southern heavens look with this great central figure of four bright stars."

The winds grew colder and colder as they sailed along. The nights were fifteen hours long. Before them lay a great, rocky, ice-bound coast. "Let us return," begged the superstitious sailors; "we must be nearing the land of perpetual cold and darkness and we shall all be caught in the great fields of ice and be frozen to death."

So Americus turned his vessel homeward, glad and eager to tell of his discovery of the "Land of the Southern Cross," and of the marvellous sights he had seen. All Europe rang with praises of the explorer. His writings were passed from one to another, and everybody talked about them; Americus Vespucius, and not Columbus, was now the hero of the hour.

But during all these years the Spaniards had been sending over colonists, until now there were flourishing Spanish towns on those islands round about where Columbus had first landed. The Spanish had begun to be very cruel to the poor Indians, and the Indians were not slow to see that it was an unlucky day for them when the great white ships of Columbus came to their shores.

About twenty years after the landing of Columbus, Balboa came over with a small fleet on a voyage of discovery. A few years later Balboa helped to found a colony on the Isthmus of Panama, and was made its governor. He was very angry because the Spaniards treated the Indians so unjustly; and ordered that no man of his colony should treat them as the other settlers had done.

The poor Indians, who had suffered so much from the Spaniards, were very glad to find these new comers so kind to them; and when they found that the great desire of Balboa was for gold, a chief sent him a large box full of the precious metal as a peace offering.

No sooner, however, had Balboa opened the box, than the men all began quarreling over it, snarling and fighting each other like fierce dogs. The Indian chief, looking with scorn upon their greedy wrangle, said, "Shame upon you, Christians! There is a land not far away where there is gold enough for all."

Balboa and his men cared very little for the Indian's disgust, but began at once to beg him to lead them to this land of gold.

One bright morning very soon after, they started toward a ridge of mountain land beyond which, so the Indian said, lay a great ocean and also the land of gold. Balboa, anxious to see this great ocean first, left his men on the side of the ridge and climbed to its top alone. There lay spread out before him, rolling and sparkling so peacefully, the great Pacific ocean, never seen before by a white man. Calling his men to him, he descended the ridge and, arriving at the shore, took possession of the ocean in the name of Spain.

Since I have told you about Balboa and the new ocean, I must tell you about the first voyage around the world. A Portuguese named Magellan started out from Spain with a large fleet, hoping to find a way through this new continent by which he might sail to the Spice Islands. He sailed directly across the Atlantic to America, and looked all up and down the coast for an opening to the other ocean.

BALBOA DISCOVERS THE PACIFIC OCEAN

Finding there was none, he sailed down to the most southern point of South America, and after sailing around that point he came out into the new ocean. When he saw it first, it looked as it did when Balboa first saw it—smiling and peaceful. On account of its calm, sunny appearance, he named it at once the "Pacific," which means peaceful.

They saw some very strange people as they sailed along the coast of South America, who, so Magellan's men said, were ten and twelve feet tall. These people were unusually tall, but it is not very likely that they were quite as tall as the men said. Sailors in those days liked to tell very big stories, I think, just as they do now.

These natives of South America were as surprised to see the white men as the white men were to see them. The natives could not understand how such little men could make such big ships move; and they thought the boats must be the babies of the ships.

They pulled from the ground, and gave to the white men to eat, something which Magellan and his men said looked like turnips and tasted like chestnuts. The sailors ate them eagerly without cooking, and carried some of them home to Spain as great curiosities. Do you guess what they were? Nothing but common potatoes, which are eaten now everywhere, but which then were only known to the natives of America.

THE WHITE MAN'S FIRST INTRODUCTION TO POTATOES

But it was not curiosities nor even gold and silver that Magellan most desired to find. Like most of the explorers, including Columbus himself, he was in search of a short route to the East Indies. And as he sailed down the Atlantic coast, he hoped at every little bend in the shore to find himself able to steer his ship directly west towards the Indies. So onward he sailed, till as we said, he finally reached the southern end of South America, passed through the Straits of Magellan—as they were afterwards called—and came into the Pacific. Here was another route to India, that was sure. But, unfortunately, it was not another but a shorter route the European merchants wanted. However, Magellan sailed straight across the new ocean as far as the Philippine Islands, meaning to return to Spain by the old route around Africa.

He had five ships when he set out from Spain, but one of these had been lost while sailing down the Atlantic coast of South America. When he entered the straits the captain of another vessel, discouraged by the distance before him, turned and went back to Spain. With three ships then, Magellan crossed the Pacific. Then, at the Philippine Islands, two more ships were lost in battles with the natives, and he himself was killed. Only one ship—the Victoria—with but eighteen men, and those sick and half starved, was able to make its way back to Spain to tell the story of *the first voyage around the world*.

ENGLISH EXPLORERS

The Cabots

But what was England about all this time? No more then, than now, was she the nation to sit quietly by and see another country carry off a prize.

England was soon awake to the possibilities of the new world. She, too, sent out explorers and set up her claims of possession. Among those who set forth were John Cabot and his son, Sebastian, Sir Francis Drake, and Sir Walter Raleigh.

It was in 1497 that the Cabots set sail. Sebastian Cabot had lived in his boyhood days in Venice, the beautiful city built so many years ago on little islands off the coast of Italy. The streets of this city are water, and the people ride up and down the streets in boats called gondolas, just as in our cities we ride up and down the streets in carriages.

It must have been here that Sebastian grew to love the sea; for to the Venetian boy a gondola is what a bicycle is to you. Sebastian used often to say, "I think sometimes I am more at home on the water than I am on land; and to go back to my boat is the rest to me that going on land is to other men."

Now, when reports of the discoveries of Columbus began to attract the English people, the Cabots were inspired with a new zeal for exploration; and, in 1497, fitting out the good ship "Matthew," away they went, the English king, Henry VII., having given them permission to sail to all parts of the seas and countries of the East and to take possession of all lands they might visit. Generous king indeed, to give away lands that he had never seen and that he was by no means sure were on the face of the globe!

"We believe," said the Cabots, "that there is a shorter Northwest Passage by which we may sail to India, and we will go in search of it."

Ah, that Northwest Passage! It has proved a sort of Will-o-the-Wisp to sailors ever since; for every now and then, all along the years since 1497, some adventurous seaman has thought he was the man born to find the wonderful short route. But, alas, it was never found, and the fate of the sailors has always been much the same. If they have lived to return at all, it has always been with the same sad story of wretched suffering from starvation and cold.

The Cabots met with little success on this first voyage, but in the following year, 1498, Sebastian Cabot, for his father was now dead, sailed out for the second time on a voyage of discovery, this time full of courage. "We only learned our way about the strange waters on our first voyage," said he, "but this time we shall bring back reports of discovery."

Sailing off towards Iceland, he went on towards Labrador. Here he reports that he passed that island and found the sea so full of codfish as "truly to hinder the sailing of the ships." Salmon, too, came swimming down the rivers in enormous numbers, and bears flocked at the water sides to catch and eat them. There were no fishery bills in those days, and the American bears and the English sailors fished side by side with not a thought of quarreling.

Sailing on southward, Cabot discovered, to his great astonishment, that the coast was continuous for miles and miles, from Labrador to Florida!

"This is not India," said he, "it is a continent, a New Found Land, lying somewhere between Europe and India." And so, while we remember that it was Columbus' daring that set all this zeal for search into motion and brought about all these wonderful discoveries and opened up to Europe the grand New World, let us give to the Cabots the lesser honor—but the honor due them—of being the first to bring back the report that out beyond the waters lay a new continent—a New Found Land.

SIR FRANCIS DRAKE

But of all the gay, brave knights of Queen Elizabeth's court, none was so gay and brave as Sir Francis Drake!

Like Sebastian Cabot, Drake had, as a boy, been as much at home on the water as on land. Indeed, perhaps it would be the whole truth to say this time that the boy was *entirely* at home on the water, inasmuch as his father had, when Francis was quite a little lad, moved his whole family, twelve children in all—into an old hull of a ship which lay wrecked off the coast of Kent. There they lived year after year—a jolly crew you may be sure—until, one by one, the boys grew up and pushed off for themselves to join some cruising party up and down the coast.

In all the years since Columbus had discovered America,—for it was now 1577—the Spaniards had been pushing on across the new continent and up and down the coast, until there seemed a fair prospect of their gaining possession of the whole of the new world.

EARLY HOME OF SIR FRANCIS DRAKE

More than this, the Spanish navy, growing stronger and stronger as the years rolled on, had for some time been making things generally disagreeable to the vessels of all other nations, even when out upon mid-ocean.

"Does Spain propose to lay claim to the very waters of the ocean?" said Queen Elizabeth.

SIR FRANCIS DRAKE

"We shall see," answered Sir Francis, gallantly. And he did see. Sailing away from England amid the cheers of his countrymen, loaded down with honors and buoyed up with promises of future glory on his return, Sir Francis Drake set gaily forth to teach the Spaniards a lesson—to explore new coasts and conquer new countries should opportunity present,—but above all to teach the Spaniards a lesson.

In 1572, he started for the West Indies, plundering every Spanish vessel he met on the way. He destroyed one whole Spanish town on one of the islands, and even crossed overland with his men the Isthmus of Panama, destroying Spanish shipping on the other side. From the top of a tree, which he climbed while on the Isthmus, he obtained his first view of the Pacific, and resolved, he said, "to sail an English vessel in those seas." And in a very few years he made good his word. Five years later, in 1577, while sailing down the coast of South America, driven blindly on by storm and wind, the *Golden Hind*, Drake's ship, reached one morning a point of high rocky land, the meeting place of two great oceans—the extreme southern point of South America—Cape Horn.

SIR FRANCIS' MEN TOOK THE SILVER

"'Tis an ill wind that blows nobody any good," said Sir Francis (or at least, he might have said it) as he looked with surprise upon the strange view before him, "let us sail up this western coast."

At one place where they landed for water, they found a Spaniard asleep, thirteen bars of silver worth four thousand ducats, lying by his side. "We took the silver," said Sir Francis dryly, when he told his story to the Queen, "and left the man."

At another place they saw a Spaniard driving eight sheep to Peru. Across the back of each sheep were two bags of silver. Without so much as an "if you please," Sir Francis' men took the silver—for they had come, you know, "to teach the Spaniards a lesson."

Again, entering the harbor at Callao, where seventeen Spanish ships loaded with treasure lay at anchor, the Englishmen took possession of all the treasure and sailed away as gaily as mischievous school-boys.

So they went on up the coast, taking the Spaniards everywhere by surprise.

"Very likely," said this daring young captain, "since the two great oceans meet at the southern extremity of this great new land, they will also meet at the northern extremity. We will sail on northward around that point out into the Atlantic to our English coast."

"A very pretty little trip," thought all the crew; especially as, for the best of reasons, anything would probably be pleasanter than sailing back again through Spanish waters and past Spanish forts.

So on they went up the coast, enjoying everything and looking hopefully for the northern point. But it grew so very cold and the days grew so short and the ice was so threatening, they were forced to turn back and take their chances among the Spaniards, who by this time were pretty sure to have recovered from their surprise and to be on the lookout for the returning vessel.

"But what need of sailing around Cape Horn?" said Drake. "We can sail far out into these Western waters, and, the earth being round, we can sail through the Indian sea, around the Cape of Good Hope, up the European coast."

And this he did, reaching England November 3rd, 1580,—the first Englishman to sail around the world! How the church bells rang out as the ship entered the harbor! how the guns thundered and how the people cheered!

And Queen Elizabeth herself, delighted indeed at his success, conferred the honor of knighthood upon him, gave him the title of Sir Francis, and presented him with a coat of arms—a ship on a globe.

The *Golden Hind* she ordered to be lodged in the Deptford dock as a monument to the courage and daring of the brave sailor. For years it stood there; and when its timbers began to decay, a chair was made from it and presented to the University of Oxford. And in the college building it still stands, as grand and as important as ever, ready to tell always its wonderful history.

SIR WALTER RALEIGH

There was another gallant Englishman who made a great name for himself upon the sea.

Did you ever hear of the young Englishman who, when one day Queen Elizabeth, taking her daily walk, came to a muddy place in the road, threw down his rich plush coat, and with a profound bow begged her Queenship to do him the honor to cross upon it?

Well, that young Englishman was the Sir Walter Raleigh of whom we hear in the stories of the earliest discoveries.

Sir Walter had made a voyage with his older brother, Sir Humphrey Gilbert, who had tried again and again to find the Northwest Passage of which the Cabots so long before had talked and written.

And now a time had come when England was very anxious to get a colony founded in

North America before the Spanish should take possession of the whole country.

SIR WALTER RALEIGH

Several attempts were made, but none of them were successful. One colony, called in history "The Lost Colony," was made up of a hundred families. They settled upon the beautiful island of Roanoke in Albemarle Sound, Virginia.

When their rough houses were built and the people had planted their fields and seemed comfortable and prosperous, their governor, John Whyte, returned to England to report their success and to bring back provisions for the colony.

The governor did not like to leave the colony, for there were hostile Indians round about. His people depended on him for guidance, and then, too, there was a little baby girl, his grand-daughter—little Virginia Dare, the first English baby born on American soil—who had a wonderful hold on the heart-strings of the rough old governor, and made him wish that he might stay there on the beautiful island to protect her from all danger.

But the colonists needed provisions, so the brave governor sailed away.

On reaching England he found the country in such commotion and the queen so busy with the war going on between Spain and England, that it was three long years before he could get together the provisions and the help he needed to carry back to the little colony.

When at last he did set sail, it seemed to him that the ocean must have grown thousands and thousands of miles wider, the voyage was so long and he was so anxious about the little colony and so eager to see the little baby colonist.

ON A TREE WERE CUT THE LETTERS CROATAN

At last the vessel neared the island. Eagerly Governor Whyte looked up and down the shores for some sign of welcome. But only the stillness and the gloom of the forest greeted him. Not a sign of life. The huts were deserted, not a sound was to be heard save the cry of the birds and the moaning of the trees.

On a tree were cut the letters, CROATAN. What did that mean? Was it the name of some place to which the colonists had moved? No one knew. No one ever knew; and not one trace of this lost colony, not one trace of the little English baby, Virginia Dare, has been found to this day.

It was at this time that many reports came of the enormous amounts of gold to be found in Guiana. "Why," said one adventurer, "it lies in lumps about the streets; and in the forests it lies like fallen trees across one's path."

"England must have some of that gold. She needs it to carry on the war," said Raleigh. "It will never do to let Spain capture it all." And so he set forth for the wonderful gold country. Of course, he found no such quantities of gold, but he explored the rivers and brought home most valuable reports of the new world.

Later, in a great battle with the Spanish vessels, Raleigh so contrived to set his own vessel across a narrow channel that the whole Spanish fleet was crippled, and had no choice but to blow up their own vessels or

SIR WALTER RALEIGH BLOWING UP SHIP

see them captured by Raleigh. This victory was a terrible blow to the Spanish power on the sea. Never again did she dare defy the powers of other countries as she had done, or proudly proclaim herself "mistress" of the seas." From that day the power of Spain was broken.

Queen Elizabeth was proud indeed of her brave knight, and all England rang with praises of their bold deliverer.

But, by and by, the Queen died. King James of Scotland became King of England. Now the skies grew black indeed for Sir Walter. King James hated him, was jealous of him, and felt he was a man to be feared. Accordingly he had him shut up in prison, and later condemned him to death. It is a sad, cruel story and we will not repeat it here. Only you may be sure, good, brave man that Sir Walter was, that he died nobly; and that, as the years rolled on, the world grew more and more to appreciate and honor him.

The French, too, and the Hollanders were at this same time sending explorers across the sea to find a short route to India. That was how it happened that Jacques Cartier discovered the mouth of the St. Lawrence, and Henrick Hudson the mouth of the Hudson. Cartier's heart beat fast when he found this great river, and saw it led directly west. Hudson, too, though his river ran so far to the north, still hoped it might somewhere turn towards the west. For, you see, the people of those days did not yet realize that they had discovered a new continent thousands of miles wide, and that no river or system of rivers could extend from shore to shore.

This idea of a vast country came to the people slowly; for first, when Columbus discovered the island of Hispaniola, the people thought of this new western land as merely a series of islands. Then, when Balboa crossed the Isthmus of Panama, he reported the new land as only a narrow strip. But, gradually, when Magellan sailed so far south and Cartier so far north, the people began to realize that the new land was not an island nor even a narrow strip of land. And so the truth of the discovery grew, until, by and by, it was known that great continents had been discovered—continents as large as all Europe and Asia put together. And they named these two great continents North America and South America.

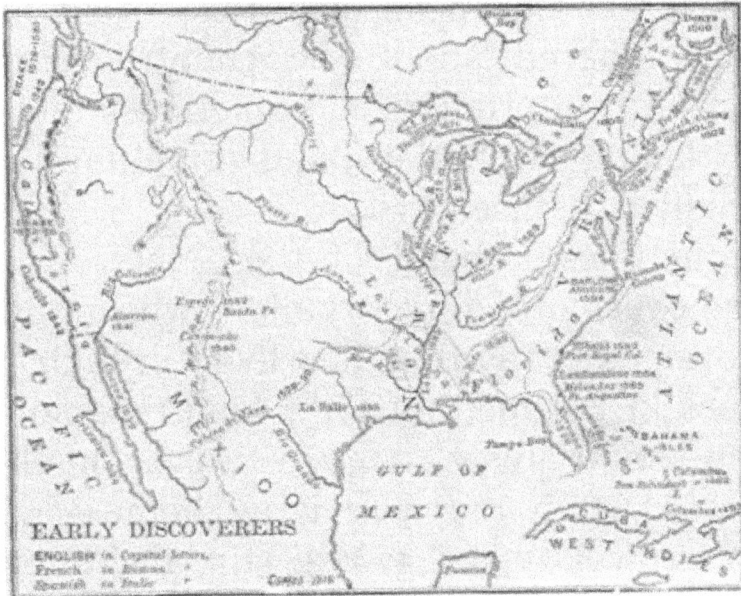

EARLY DISCOVERERS

THE COLONIES

I am going to ask you now to take a long trip with me, out of the period of discoveries over into the period of the colonies. You must not imagine that these few men I have told you about made all the discoveries in the new America.

There were many more, so many, that I think you might read about them every day for a whole year, and then not read the half. Hundreds and hundreds of men had been sent over by England, France, Spain, and many other European countries. These men had wandered about the country, daring much and suffering much, sometimes fighting and killing the Indians, and sometimes getting killed themselves.

Sometimes a band of these men would come over, intending to build towns and live here together, as they had lived in their old homes in Europe; but for a long time something would always happen to prevent their success. Often the men grew homesick, or they grew lazy; or, worse still, the Indians who had now good reason to hate the pale-faces, as they called the white men, would fall upon them and scalp them and slay them with their tomahawks.

But in spite of all the efforts of the Indians the pale-face colonies finally succeeded, and in due time there came to be little towns up and down the sea-coast.

It was as early as 1535 that the French came over to Florida, and built two forts and made a settlement of importance. For some time these French people lived in their settlement, happy and prosperous. But one day some Spanish vessels arrived, and claiming the country because they had first discovered it, they took possession of the French settlement, and massacred the people. There they built a fort for themselves, and made plans for building a town. This they did, and a successful town it proved; for it still stands—the old fort and all—at St. Augustine in Florida. And now people go to visit it, and wander about the old fort, and up and down the quaint narrow streets, and say, "This is the oldest town in America!"

It was not until 1607, however, that settlement by the English began in real earnest. At that time a number of men, having permission from the English government to come to America and found a colony, set sail from London. They reached the mouth of a river in Virginia, which they named the James, in honor of their English king. The town they began to build they named Jamestown.

One of the leading men of this company was John Smith. He was a very wise and able man, and seemed always to do the right thing at just the right time.

The story of his life is as interesting as a novel. If there were time I would tell you some of his strange adventures at sea and on the battlefield.

CAPTAIN JOHN SMITH

One adventure of his in Jamestown colony will show you what a brave man he was, and how a little Indian girl saved his life. John Smith had started up the river on an exploring expedition. Some Indians had been watching him, and when Smith left his boat they seized it, scalped the men he had left with it, and then ran to overtake Smith himself.

When he saw them coming he turned and fought them so furiously that, although there were many of them, they had much trouble to secure him. They led him to their camp. Here he entertained them by showing them his compass, and told them how the needle always turned to the north. This amused the Indians so much that they allowed him to live some weeks in peace. They decided at last that he was too wise, and therefore dangerous to have about; and that the sooner he was killed the safer it would be for them. So, when they had held a long council, and had performed some wonderful war dances around him, they led him forth to be killed.

Poor Smith could see no way of escape; and, as he used to tell afterwards, he was more frightened than he had been when in his younger days he was thrown overboard from a ship or when he fought the Turks.

POWHATAN

Held this state & fashion when Capt. Smith: was delivered to him prisoner. 1607

(From an Old Print)

He was brought out, bound hand and foot, and a savage had already raised his war-club to dash out his brains, when just then up rushed little Pocahontas, the daughter of the great Indian Chief, Powhatan, threw her arms around John Smith's neck, and begged the chief to spare his life. Strange to say, the cruel old chief seemed moved by the child's pleading, and the prisoner was released, and even allowed to return to Jamestown.

For some time John Smith remained in the little white settlement, guiding the affairs of the colony. As long as he was there all went well, for Smith was a very wise man, and not afraid to work hard with the other men in making the settlement a pleasant home. At last, however, having met with a severe injury, he was obliged to return for a time to England.

You would suppose that after he was gone the men would have been wise enough to keep on tilling the ground and building their houses. But, instead, when John Smith returned to Jamestown he found the men quarreling among themselves. They had used up the provisions and were almost starving. Had Smith not returned just when he did, I fear they would have given up the colony and gone back to England. But Smith worked hard

to save Jamestown; and for a time he pre-
vailed upon the men to stop their foolish
quarreling, and to go to work to build up the
colony and protect it from the Indians.

POCAHONTAS

Later he made many voyages along the American coast, exploring the shores as far as Canada.

The Indians, however, were never quite friendly; and after years and years of continual quarreling with them, the Jamestown colonists determined to have peace in some way. One of them, Captain Argall, thought it would be a good plan to steal Pocahontas, and then send word to the Indians that they would do her no harm so long as the colony was not troubled. Pocahontas was now a young woman nearly nineteen years old and was said to be very beautiful. At any rate, soon after coming to the colony she won the heart of a young Englishman named John Rolfe, and he took her to his old home in England.

Pocahontas was received in England with much honor, and came to be greatly loved by all who knew her.

It was Rolfe's plan to spend a few months in England and then to return to the colony in America, and make for himself and Pocahontas a home in which they hoped to live the rest of their lives. But Pocahontas began to fail in health. Probably the change from her free forest life to the close house life of an English city was more than she could bear. Day by day Pocahontas grew weaker and at last she died.

BAPTISM OF POCAHONTAS

She left a little baby boy who was as beautiful, it is said, as his mother had been. John Rolfe took the little one to America, and there he grew up in the colony. Some of the good families in Virginia to-day are proud to say that they are descendants from the little son of Pocahontas.

PLYMOUTH COLONY

The next English colony was settled in Massachusetts. One stormy day in December, 1620, there sailed into Plymouth harbor a queer little vessel named the *Mayflower*. On board this little craft were a hundred brave men and women, who had come from England in order to escape "religious persecution." These are rather large words for young folks; but I think it better for you to learn them just here, because they seem, somehow, to belong to these particular people. Why, you will understand later.

Now, it seems rather cruel to leave these wanderers out in the cold storm; but we must for a few moments, while we hurry over to England to learn what had happened there to force these men and women across the ocean at this stormy time of the year.

Many years before, King Henry the Eighth of England had had a great quarrel with the Pope at Rome. The Pope, being the head of the Catholic Church, sent certain orders to King Henry; for all England at that time was Catholic, and always obeyed the Pope in every point. But King Henry had made up his mind that he would obey no one and that he would be the head of the Church himself. So he announced to his subjects that no longer were they to pay any attention to the Pope's orders, but that they were to obey him instead. And so came about the English Church.

This seemed a fearful thing to some of the people. They believed God would send some terrible punishment upon them. Still, there were very many people in England who were glad of the change, and who, therefore, took the king's side in the trouble that followed.

King Henry died before the people had all grown used to the change, and left the throne to his son Edward, who believed as his father had done and held to the English Church.

Edward died very soon after he came into power, and his sister Mary took the throne. Now, Mary was an earnest Catholic, and as you would suppose, began at once bringing back the priests and doing everything in her power to restore the old religion.

But Mary's reign, too, soon came to an end, and Queen Elizabeth took the throne. Elizabeth was as strong an English Church woman as Mary had been a Catholic; and so again the country was thrown into confusion; places of worship were destroyed; priests were displaced, and all who were Catholics were expected to join the English Church, just as in Mary's reign all who were of the English Church had been expected to turn Catholics.

Queen Elizabeth was followed by James I., the king, you remember, who so cruelly caused Sir Walter Raleigh to be put to death. James was meaner than any of the Kings or Queens who had gone before him, and persecuted all, Catholics or Protestants, who opposed his ideas.

But you will begin to wonder what all this has to do with the men and women we left in Cape Cod harbor. As you will see, it has everything to do with them.

During all this trouble there, a class of people had been rising in England who believed neither in the Catholic Church nor in the English Church as it was then.

These people dressed very strangely, and acted even more strangely. Now, it was the fashion in those days for gentlemen to wear their hair long, and to dress in very elegant clothes; but these people who hated both the Churches, dressed in the very plainest of clothes, wore their hair so short that they were nick-named, "Round Heads," would not allow music in their churches, would not have the old church service, and, in short, would have nothing but the very barest and plainest of everything.

These people were called Puritans, Round Heads, Separatists, and many other names by the English Church people, who looked upon them as fools and lunatics.

You may be sure the Puritans, or Separatists, did not have a very enjoyable time in England under King James.

At last, in 1608, a little band of Separatists, from Scrooby, in England, unable to bear their persecutions any longer, went over into Holland. There they lived happily enough, but they longed for a home of their own, where they could teach their own religion and make it *the* religion of the country.

DEPARTURE OF THE PILGRIM FATHERS FROM HOLLAND, 1620

For this reason they went back to England, obtained permission to found a colony in the new world, and with their hearts full of hope and courage, started out—in the *Mayflower* and the *Speedwell*,—for the unknown land. The *Speedwell*, however, was obliged to put back into port because it was found to be un-

AMERICAN HISTORY STORIES, VOLUME I

seaworthy. Thus it was that the *Mayflower* alone came into Cape Cod harbor.

You will often hear these Puritans, who came first to America, spoken of as Pilgrims, or the Pilgrim Fathers. This was a name given them because of their *pilgrimages* to Holland and to America in search of a home. Try to remember this,—these plain, honest, God-fearing people were all called Puritans in England, while the few who wandered about and finally settled in Plymouth were given the name of Pilgrims.

Let us go back to Cape Cod harbor now, and see what these Pilgrims have been doing all this time. It was one of those snowy, windy days that we, who live in the North Eastern States, expect to have now and then in the winter time. Not a pleasant sort of day to spend on the ocean even in the snuggest and warmest of vessels. Much less pleasant it must have been to these wanderers in their rudely built vessel, drifting about at the mercy of the wind and tide.

The Pilgrims had intended to land much farther south, where it was pleasanter and warmer; but the storm was so severe that the captain of the *Mayflower* said he must make port wherever he could.

I am afraid they were not over-pleased when their vessel came into Cape Cod harbor; for there they found only a sandy, desolate shore awaiting them; and, as it was in the dead of winter, you can imagine how cold and bare it looked. The trees were leafless, the ground was frozen, and the waters about the shores were covered with sheets of ice.

But they were brave and sturdy; and, although they would have been glad to be welcomed by the pleasant warmth of the southern lands as they left their weather-beaten vessel, still they bravely accepted what was before them, perfectly sure that they had been guided to this shore by Divine Providence.

As soon as they had all landed, they gathered together about that large rock at the water's edge, known now as Plymouth Rock, and kneeling down, thanked God for their safe deliverance from the perils of the sea.

Then they went sturdily to work. These men were not idle, lazy good-for-nothings, as many of those first colonists in Virginia had been. They did not need a John Smith to urge them to be industrious. They were all terribly in earnest. They had left their native land and, with their brave wives, had come over to this wilderness to build homes for themselves.

Can you not fancy their axes ringing in the still winter days, as they felled the trees for lumber with which to build their rude houses?

Can you not fancy the brave, tender-hearted wives and mothers working cheerfully on in the bitter cold of their old, uncomfortable houses, washing, ironing, baking, brewing, pounding the corn, spinning the cloth, and making the homes comfortable and even cheerful, in the thousand ways which only mothers and wives can understand?

And the little boys and girls, too! There were not very many of them to be sure; but you may be sure the children of such noble men and women would bravely bear the cold and hunger without a tear, and would try in all their little ways to do their part toward helping their fathers and mothers to build up their village.

A HOUSE WITH PALISADES

And there were two little babies, too; little baby boys, who were born during the voyage from England to America. I am afraid these little babies didn't have all the beautiful little dresses, puffs and powders that our babies have. I should not wonder if the little strangers were wrapped in very ordinary shawls and blankets, and that the mothers were very thankful they could keep them from the cold. Nevertheless, I suspect these little babies had a very warm welcome from all these sturdy, hard-working men and women, and were the pets of the whole colony. Can you not see the women coming every day to look in upon the new babies, and the men, each glad to stop and amuse the little ones for a minute as they went to and fro; and the children only too happy to be allowed to take care of them?

A STREET IN OLD PLYMOUTH

THE LANDING OF THE PILGRIM FATHERS

The breaking waves dashed high
    On a stern and rock-bound coast,
And the woods against a stormy sky,
Their giant branches tossed;

And the heavy night hung dark
    The hills and waters o'er,—
When a band of exiles moored their bark
    On the wild New England shore.

Not as the conqueror comes,
    They, the true-hearted, came;
Not with the roll of stirring drums,
    And the trumpet that sings of fame;

Not as the flying come,
    In silence and in fear;—
They shook the depths of the desert's gloom
    With their hymns of lofty cheer.

Amidst the storm they sang,
    Till the stars heard, and the sea;
And the sounding aisles of the dim woods rang
    To the anthem of the free.

The ocean-eagle soared
    From his nest by the white wave's foam,
And the rocking pines of the forest roared;
    This was their welcome home.

There were men with hoary hair
Amidst that pilgrim band;
Why had they come to wither there,
Away from their childhood's land?

There was woman's fearless eye,
Lit by her deep love's truth;
There was manhood's brow serenely high,
And the fiery heart of youth.

What sought they thus afar?—
Bright jewels of the mine?
The wealth of seas? the spoils of war?
They sought a faith's pure shrine.

Ay, call it holy ground,
The land where first they trod!
They have left unstained what there they found,—
Freedom to worship God!

—Mrs. Hemans.

THE PURITANS

ANOTHER MASSACHUSETTS COLONY

The colonists worked hard during the whole winter and spring and summer, so that by the time the next winter came they had quite comfortable homes.

The Indians had been very kind to them, probably because they had been kind and honest in their dealings with the Indians.

Soon, encouraged by the success of the Pilgrims, there came other bands of English men and women to the shores of Massachusetts. Some sailed into Salem harbor, settling there; others went to Boston, Roxbury, Dorchester, Charlestown, and several other places.

These later bands of colonists were larger than the earlier; besides this, they were quite wealthy people. They were Puritans—like those who had come to Plymouth; but they had not been persecuted very severely, and did not come, therefore, because they were driven from England. They had come hoping to find new homes for themselves, where they could enjoy greater freedom in their manner of worship, to be sure; still, I want you to keep distinctly in your mind the difference between these colonies.

NEW YORK IN 1673

THE DUTCH IN AMERICA

In Europe there is a small country called Holland. It is a strange little country; it is flat, and so low that the whole country would long ago have been swallowed by the ocean had not the sturdy people built great walls of mud and stone to keep back the water. Holland is sometimes called the land of windmills, because there are so many of these great wheels whizzing and whirring about the country.

Now, the merchants and workmen of this little country were far ahead of those of England in these days of which we are reading. Although there was hardly a stick of timber in the whole land, yet Holland built more ships and did more trading than England had thought of.

It was not long, therefore, before some of these enterprising Dutch merchants became interested in the long sought for short route to China and the Indies; and in the autumn of 1693 they engaged Henry Hudson, an Englishman, to search for the passage for them.

In the spring of the following year, Capt. Hudson, with a crew of about twenty men, set sail from Holland in the *Half Moon*, and following a map and letter sent him by his friend, Capt. John Smith, he arrived on Sept. 31 at the fine bay now known as New York Harbor. As he entered the bay, the Indians came hurrying out from the shores in their canoes, paddling up to the *Half Moon*. They were friendly—as Indians generally were until some act of treachery or cruelty on the part of the white men put them on their guard—and they freely traded with the sailors of the strange *Half Moon*.

Then Hudson sailed as far up the beautiful river as he could with his vessel, and then sent boats up as far as what is now Albany. "Perhaps," said he, "this river cuts through the continent to the other ocean, and will prove to be a short route to the Indies."

But, as you and I know now, he was disappointed in this. The river grew less and less navigable as it neared its source, and Hudson was obliged to sail back into New York bay. But so beautiful had the country seemed to him, and so valuable were the furs which the Indians offered in trade, that Hudson, on his return to Holland, gave a most glowing description of the opportunities for making wealth in this new world—so glowing, indeed, that it was not very long before the wide-awake, enterprising little country sent traders to settle upon the banks of the river, and to build up villages for themselves.

Holland, accordingly, now claimed the whole country around the river, and named it New Netherland. The Dutch colonists went to work at once trading with the Indians, cultivating the land and building their mills with the great whirring sails. The Indians were terribly afraid of these monsters, which were able to grind corn or saw boards. They would sit for hours staring at the strange things, wondering if they were alive. Often they would set fire to them, believing an evil spirit must be in them.

But on the whole the Dutchmen got along very well with the Indians, and it was not many years before they bought from the Indians the whole island of Manhattan and began the building of their city—New Amsterdam; or, as it is now called, New York.

Some of the very first governors of this Dutch colony are said to have been rather remarkable men in one way or another. There was Peter Minuit, an enterprising man, I am sure you will believe, when you hear that one of his first acts was to buy the whole of Manhattan Island from the Indians for twenty-five dollars, and that, too, paid mostly with beads and trinkets, of which the Indians were very fond.

Minuit was followed by Van Twiller, the second governor. Of this man I will give you Washington Irving's own description. He says, "Van Twiller was exactly five feet six inches in height and six feet five inches in circumference. His head was a perfect sphere, and of such dimensions that Dame Nature, with all her ingenuity, would have been puzzled indeed to construct a neck capable of

PURCHASING MANHATTAN

supporting it. Therefore, she had declined to try and had settled it firmly on the top of his backbone just between his shoulders. His body was oblong. His legs were short but sturdy in proportion to the weight they had to sustain; so that when erect he had much the appearance of a beer barrel on skids."

Then, by and by, came gallant old Peter Stuyvesant. He was a grim old fellow, battle-scarred, and no more movable when his mind was made up than a wall of solid granite. How he did puff and steam as he stumped around on his funny old wooden leg, shouting his orders and telling of his own wonderful feats in battle! But for all this he was a good governor; and his love for the colony, his pride in it, and his honest desire to see it all and the best it could be, will never be quite forgotten by the New York people. They say that sometimes the bump, bump, bump of the old wooden leg even now is to be heard dark nights moving as of yore up and down the aisles of St. Mark's church, near where his bones lie buried. Well, if this is so it only goes to prove that he still loves old Manhattan Island as he loved it in those early days when he was its ruler and its governor.

It was while brave old Peter Stuyvesant was governor that the English first sailed into the harbor of New Amsterdam and demanded the surrender of the city, under the claim that the country belonged to the English, having been discovered by Cabot.

The fact is, the English king, having learned that the Dutch had secured a very valuable fur trade through their friendliness with the Indians, made up his mind that he needed it. He accordingly gave the territory of New Netherlands to his brother, the Duke of York, and sent several ships to capture the city.

The Dutch were too few to resist; and the appeals of Gov. Stuyvesant to defend the city were vain; and so New Amsterdam passed into the hands of the English on August 29, 1664. The city was then named New York; and, although eight years later the Dutch retook the city, Holland finally gave up all title to New Netherlands and it became an English colony. This was in 1674.

New Amsterdam was an odd little city at that time, looking for all the world like a little Dutch city dropped down upon the new continent.

The little wooden houses had gable roofs; the ends of the houses were of black and yellow brick; over the door were great iron

THE DUTCH IN AMERICA

figures telling when the house was built; and on the roof there was sure to be a gay-looking weather vane whirling around in the strong wind, trying, so it seemed, to keep pace with the whirling windmills that stretched their great arms over the city.

Inside the houses you would have found great, roaring fire-places, with pictured tiles up and down the sides. Such funny pictures! telling all about Noah and the Ark, or perhaps about the children of Israel crossing the Red Sea. Can you not fancy just how the older brothers and sisters used to sit by these great fireplaces pointing out the wonderful pictures to the little children?

I am always glad to think of these little children of the Dutch colonists. They were all so much happier and freer than the little Puritan children. Their homes were so much more cheerful, their parents so much less grim and severe, and there was so much more love and joy everywhere about them.

Such fairy stories as these Dutch people could tell as they sat about their great fires in the long winter evenings, or out upon the doorsteps in the warm summer nights! Not a forest nor a dale, not a single peak of the

Catskill Mountains but had its legend or mysterious story for them.

When the thunder rolled, the people would say, "Hark! that is Henry Hudson and his companions playing at nine pins up among the mountains." And the children would shout and laugh and say, "Good Henry Hudson! Good Henry Hudson! the wicked sailors could not kill you when they bound you and put you afloat on the cold ocean! The little fairies guided you back to your own river and to your own blue-topped Catskills. Kind little fairies! Good Henry Hudson!"

There are so many other stories to tell of this early history of our country that I am going to leave this colony just here. It seems too bad, for these Dutch people were so strange in their dress and customs, and had such odd ideas, that I should like to tell you a score of stories about them. I should like to tell you about Rip Van Winkle, who slept for twenty years up in the mountains; I should like to tell you about old Ichabod Crane, who thought he was pursued by a ghost; of Henry Hudson and his crew playing nine-pins up among the mountains; but you must read Irving's Sketch Book and his Knickerbocker History. There are stories enough there to keep you all busy for a year. But now I must ask you to leave these queer old Dutch people and hurry across to Maryland with me. There is another kind of people there waiting for us.

OTHER COLONIES

You remember the misery of the people of England under Henry, and Mary, and Queen Elizabeth. First they must all be devoted to the English Church to please the king; then they must all turn Catholics to please Mary; then back they must turn to the English Church with Queen Elizabeth. It seems very strange to us now that it should have been considered necessary for a whole country to change its religion to suit the religion of the ruler; but the people in those days had not learned that it is not what a person *believes* as much as what he *is* that makes him a good or a bad citizen.

Thus, at the time the Pilgrims left England, they were not the only people who were being persecuted. The Catholics, too, were having a hard time of it. They also were casting longing eyes towards a free country where they could worship God in their own way.

At last, one of their nobles, Lord Baltimore, obtained from the English King, Charles I., a grant of land and permission to found a Colony, to be called Maryland, on the shores of the Chesapeake Bay.

Lord Baltimore died before he could carry out his good work, but in 1634, his son, Leonard Calvert, came over, bringing with him three hundred emigrants. After a voyage of four months, they reached the mouth of the Potomac, and there built a town, which they named St. Mary's.

The Indians in this part of the country had not seen the white people then; and when they saw them sailing up the Potomac they rushed down to the banks in wonder. Suddenly they gave a great yell, and disappeared in the forests. "Oh," said they, "we have seen a canoe as big as an island, and with as many men on it as there are trees in the forests!"

They could not understand that a ship was built board by board, and they wondered where there could be found a tree large enough to hollow out such a canoe as that.

As soon as these English people were settled in their new home, they made laws for their colony. Their laws were very just and generous, especially in regard to religion. All persons were free to worship as they pleased in Maryland.

On account of this generous law in the new colony, many Puritans from Virginia, who had been persecuted there by the Episcopalians, came to Maryland, Quakers came from Massachusetts, and all classes came from England. Among the latter were many Methodists, who not only desired to worship God in their own way, but sent missionaries among the Indians. Later, John and Charles Wesley, the founders of Methodism, came over to assist in the work; but the bad example of some of the white settlers often did as much harm to the Indians as the missionaries could do good.

During this time colonies had also been settled in North and South Carolina, and they had come to be important and flourishing.

On the southern border of South Carolina there is a large river, the Savannah. When the Carolinas were settled the Indians made great trouble for the white men. They felt that the white men were taking their homes from them, and that something must be done to drive these new comers away. A treaty was at last made with the Indians, in which the white men promised to make no settlements south of the Savannah river. This treaty was not broken for about seventy years. Then there came to be a new king in England, called George II. He gave permission to General James Oglethorpe, a wealthy but brave and charitable Englishman, to found a colony south of the Savannah.

General Oglethorpe's desire was to establish a place in the New World where poor people could obtain a new start in life; for at this time there was much poverty and wretchedness in England.

In November, 1732, his little band, one hundred and sixteen people in all, set sail from England. They arrived off South Carolina in February of the following year, and ascending the Savannah river, chose for their home the present site of that city.

Their leader sent for the Indians soon after their arrival, purchased the land from them and made a treaty with them, which was faithfully kept as long as General Oglethorpe remained in the country.

They named their territory Georgia in honor of the King, and when the laws for this new colony were drawn up, wise General Oglethorpe firmly declared that there should be no rum allowed there, and that any sale of it to the Indians should be punished as one of the greatest crimes. He knew, wise man that he was, that drinking men would not be industrious enough to keep a colony prosperous, and that it would be the very worst thing to allow the Indians to get a taste of the fire-water, as the Indians called it.

For a while the colony prospered, as any colony would under such a wise leader; but these colonists were not all earnest and industrious people as were the Puritans and the Quakers; and though they were helped by the English Government more than were those of any other colony, it was not long before some of them began to grumble bitterly about the hardships of a new country. They also wrote letters to the king of England, making all sorts of complaints against their leader, until, at last, disgusted with them,

Oglethorpe returned to England, saying that he was sick of the very name of colony.

When the twenty-one years had passed for which Oglethorpe and his companions had been granted leave to hold this land in Georgia, their charter was given back to King George. Georgia then became a royal colony; and as the king cared very little what the colonists in Georgia or in any other colony did, they were now free to have as much strong drink as they liked. For a time matters were in a bad state in the colony, and it was not until several years later that the right kind of people came to Georgia. Then Georgia became a very different kind of colony; and when, by and by, the Revolution came on no colony was braver or did more in proportion to its size for the cause than did this of Georgia.

New England Sabbath

CUSTOMS IN THE COLONIES

During all these years a gradual change from the early days of struggle and poverty had been taking place in the older colonies, especially in Virginia.

Hearing of the many advantages in the new world, a number of industrious and even wealthy families had come from England to settle in Virginia. They had obtained from the proprietors great tracts of land, had built for themselves elegant mansions, and were cultivating great fields of cotton and tobacco.

These people were not Puritans nor Catholics, they had not been persecuted at all, and were content with the English Church, but had come to America to found new homes, and to trade and grow up with the country.

Now, in these early days it was very difficult to get laborers to work in the fields; so it had become the custom to ship over criminals and poor people from England, and make them work a number of years before they obtained their freedom. After a time negroes began to be sent from Africa, and thus it became quite common in the South for one to own a number of slaves, and even in the Northern colonies slaves were to be occasionally seen; but here in Virginia where it paid to keep a great many laborers to cultivate the corn fields, the planters owned a great many slaves. These slaves did the work of the fields and received no pay except their food and clothes.

Very likely the masters were kind enough to them, and very likely they worked no harder than men and women do everywhere.

But there is this great difference between slaves and other people who work: The man or woman who goes out to work as we see them doing to-day, goes at a certain hour, works until a certain hour, and receives pay for it. That man or woman has perfect liberty to do whatever he or she wishes with the pay received, perfect liberty to go to another place to work, perfect liberty to do anything and everything proper without asking permission of the employer. But how is it with a slave? His employer owns him just as he owns his horses or oxen.

The slave takes the master's horses in the morning and goes out to work with them wherever the master bids. No matter how much or how little the slave and the horses have earned for the master,—the master takes it all. He would no more think of giving the slave a part of it than he would of giving a part to his horse. The horse receives his bed and supper for his day's work, and the slave receives the same. So you see a slave has no hope (no matter how hard or how well he may work) of receiving anything for it which he can call his own.

Is it any wonder then, as the years roll on and on, bringing him no reward for his labor, that he grows to be stupid and heavy, without ambition or hope, and becomes, as the slave-holders used to say of him, as dumb as the cattle he works with?

But we must remember people did not think of slavery in those days as we do now. Everybody who could afford it owned slaves, just as to-day everybody who can afford servants has servants; and they thought it no wrong so long as they were kind to them and gave them good food and lodging.

In the early days of the Colonies, the need of money was very much felt. There were various ways tried. In Virginia, which was a great tobacco growing country, the colonists used tobacco for money. This, of course, was just as good; for, if a farmer wanted to buy an article worth fifty cents, he gave fifty cents worth of tobacco for it. The dealer who received the tobacco, packed it away with other tobacco until he had a large amount of it. Then he would send it to England and receive for it goods for his store, which he would sell again for tobacco.

At one time in the early history of this colony, when there were very few white women in America, there were sent over from England about a hundred young women, who were sold to the colonists for a hundred pounds of tobacco each. Each colonist then went to the minister with the woman he had bought with his tobacco, had the marriage ceremony performed, and then led her to his home. This would seem a very strange thing now-a-days; but we must remember there was then no other way for these colonists to obtain wives, unless they were sent to them from the old country—and it was no more than right that the future husband should pay the expense.

There were also some very strange laws as well as customs in those early colonial days.

If a woman was a scold she was ducked in running water three times; if she slandered any one, her husband was obliged to pay five hundred pounds of tobacco to the governor of the colony; a husband had a perfect right in those days to whip his wife whenever he seemed to think she needed it.

They had some good temperance laws. No man was allowed to keep a "tavern" who did not possess an excellent character. The names of all drunkards were posted up in the taverns, and no one was allowed to sell liquor to them. In Connecticut no one under twenty years of age was allowed to use tobacco, and no one, no matter what his age, was allowed to use it more than once a day.

One must dress, too, according to law. No one owning land not valued at two hundred dollars or more could wear gold or silver lace; and only the "gentility" were allowed to use Mr. or Mrs. before their names.

There were very severe laws against those who would not attend church. If a man was absent one Sunday, he would not be given his allowance of provisions for a week; if he was absent a second time, he was whipped; a third time, he was likely even to be hanged.

In Virginia, especially, both men and women were sometimes whipped in sight of the whole colony. For some offenses they were made to stand in the church with white sheets over their heads during the service; or they would be made to stand on the church steps, with the name of their crime pinned upon their breasts.

In New England they had an odd way of taking offenders out into a public place and putting them in the stocks or in the pillory, where they were kept until sundown, the subject of the laughter and jokes of every passer by.

Such punishments would seem unchristian now, but they were very common in those days.

STOCKS AND PILLORY

The New England people were also very strict regarding the Sabbath. As soon as the sun went down on Saturday evening their Sabbath began. From that time until sunset on Sunday night no manner of work was allowed to be done; no visiting, no playing, no gayety of any kind was permitted; one man, it is said, was brought to trial and fined for kissing his wife on a Sabbath morning.

Public worship took place in what was called the meeting house, the place where all meetings for attending to the town's business were held.

Slowly and solemnly the families all walked to church, coming sometimes for miles from the country around.

On reaching the church the men took their places on one side of the aisle, and the women took theirs on the other. The children, too, sat all by themselves, and there was a man appointed to keep them quiet.

This man carried a long stick with a hard knob at one end and a little feather brush on the other.

With the knob he knocked the heads of the men if they chanced to grow sleepy, and with the feather tickled the faces of the women.

PILGRIM'S MONUMENT, PLYMOUTH

I shouldn't wonder if he had to use this rod pretty often on men, women, and children all; for the sermons were very long, sometimes lasting whole hours, and they were timed by an hour-glass which stood upon the high pulpit and not until it had been turned three or four times was a sermon considered at all of the proper length. And the singing! For many years it was the custom for the people all to rise and sing. There were few hymn-books; therefore the minister, or some one of the deacons, would read a line of the hymn, the people would sing it, then wait for another line to be read. But, by and by, singing schools began to come into fashion, the "queristers," as the singers were called, began to sit together during the church service, leading the singing, the whole congregation joining with them in rolling out the grand old tunes that were the fashion then.

There were not many tunes that the people knew, but such as they did know they poured forth vigorously and were quite content with them for years and years. The first hymn-book published in the colonies contained twenty-eight tunes.

"Twenty-eight tunes!" cried the people. "We can never learn so many!"

"This book is a sin and a snare," preached one minister from his pulpit. "This new solfa singing is wicked. Singing schools will lead to mischief. Let us have no more of this foolish vanity."

But the "foolish vanity" some way would not go. The young people had begun to learn to sing, and sing they would, until in the course of time both people and ministers became reconciled to it, wicked as it was; and when, in 1764, Josiah Flagg published a book containing one hundred and sixty hymns, no one thought of objecting. On the contrary, every singing youth and maiden hastened to own the book, and it was not long before the churches throughout the colonies rang out the whole hundred and sixty grand old tunes, happy enough that there were so many to sing.

As to the men, as you read in the "Indian Stories," they brought their muskets to the meeting-houses, that they might have them in case of attack.

The meeting-houses were not warmed even in very cold weather; the people had an idea that some way they were better Christians if they bore all these discomforts, without a murmur.

But soon the people began carrying hot bricks and stones to keep their feet and hands from freezing; and, by and by, they carried little foot stoves. These stoves were little tin boxes, with holes in the sides, a cover, a door, and handles with which to carry them. In these boxes were put live coals, and so the fire would last during the whole sermon.

As books were very scarce, the minister read off one line of the hymn, which the people would sing to some old tune; then another line would be read and sung, then another and another, until the whole hymn was sung.

When the service was over, all walked solemnly home again. The fathers and mothers were very strict on this Sabbath day, and I fear many and many a little boy and girl dreaded to have this long, dreary day come, and were very glad when it was over; for you remember there were no beautiful books and magazines in those days; and if there had been, the children would not have been allowed to read anything but the little New England Primer which contained quaint pictures, a few terrible verses, and the Catechism.

I am sure we are glad people have got over the idea that Sunday should be such a dismal, sober day. I am sure the Heavenly Father is much more pleased to see the children spending His day happily in their homes with their fathers and mothers and little sisters and brothers.

Of all the men of rank or office in the colony, none were looked upon with such reverence and respect as the ministers. Though the Puritans hated titles of all kinds, considering them vain inventions, they were willing to honor the minister with "Parson," or "Elder," or "Teacher," and were ready to humble themselves before him. I am afraid, however, that these ministers sometimes received little else than reverence; for their salaries were generally very small; sometimes they had none at all, and depended wholly upon the gifts of the parishioners who supplied them with whatever they had or could spare. "Alas," said one pastor, "my people are very poor; and I am very poor. I have received for salary this year only turnips, there being a generous harvest of that vegetable; but I do not complain. I have always been able to sell them or exchange them, and thus I have been supplied with the necessary things of life."

Time cuts down all,
Both great and small.

Uriah's beauteous wife
Made David seek his life.

Whales in the sea,
God's voice obey.

Xerxes the great did die,
And so must you and I.

Youth forward slips—
Death soonest nips.

Zac-che-us, he
Did climb the tree,
Our Lord to see.

in the branches of an Oak tree in Boscobel wood, where he saw his enemies in full pursuit of him. This Oak tree was regarded, by the friends of the King, with much veneration, after having afforded shelter to the Royal Fugitive.

In *Adam's* fall,
We sinned all.

Heaven to find,
The *Bible* mind.

The *Cat* doth play,
And after slay.

The *Dog* will bite
A thief at night.

An *Eagle's* flight
Is out of sight.

The idle *Fool*
Is whipt at school.

THE NEW ENGLAND PRIMER

Speaking of these little sober-faced children of the colonial times, reminds me of the queer little books from which they learned to read.

I wish you could see one I have. It is very, very old now, its leaves are all yellow and musty, and I fear that before long they will fall in pieces like an old dead leaf.

It is a little square book with blue paper co-vers, on which is an odd looking picture of two children kneeling to say their prayers. In the book are several little verses and hymns and prayers, a long list of questions and an-swers from the Bible, the ten commandments, and then some odd little verses, with pictures which are odder still. On the opposite page are a few of them, which I am sure you will say are very funny.

A NEW ENGLAND HOME IN COLONIAL DAYS

MANNER OF DRESS

You remember how very plain the Puritans dressed at the time of their leaving England. Then the men wore their hair shaved so closely that they were called Roundheads. The women, too, all dressed very plainly, in homespun dresses and stiffly starched white aprons.

There was a time when a fine was imposed on any man who should wear his hair long; and if a woman wore any sort of jewelry, she was looked upon as a most wicked creature, one upon whom the punishment of heaven would surely fall.

As time went on, and the Puritans mixed more and more with other people, these severe styles gave way, and at last the Boston folks of the Puritan colony were as gay in their dress as were the Cavaliers of Virginia.

In a history of America, written for young people by Abby Sage Richardson, there is such a good description of these people as they dressed at this time, just before the Revolution, of which we are going so soon to hear, that I think we must stop and read it.

You remember the rude log cabin in which these first Puritans who came to Cape Cod Bay lived. Compare that rude cabin with Miss Richardson's description of Governor Hutchinson's house in Boston as it looked in the Revolutionary time: "It was a fine brick house, three stories high. If we enter the house we shall find a large hall with massive staircases heavily carved, the floor laid in elegant colored marble or different woods.

"The walls are painted, there are fluted columns supporting the ceiling, and there is heavy mahogany furniture set around in stately grandeur."

Speaking of the dress of the men, she says, "Do you see that elegant looking man? He would hardly be laughed at now and called a Roundhead. The Puritans now dress as the English do. They wear powdered wigs, or else they powder their own hair and tie it in a long queue behind.

"Look at that gentleman standing in his doorway! He has on a red velvet cap, with an inside cap of white linen which turns over the edge of the velvet two or three inches; a blue damask dressing-gown lined with sky-blue silk; a white satin waistcoat with deep embroidered flaps; black satin breeches with long white silk stockings, and red morocco slippers.

When he goes out into the street he will change his velvet cap for a three-cornered hat; his flowered brocade dressing-gown for a gold-laced coat of red or blue broadcloth, with deep lace ruffles at the wrist; put a sword at his side, and wear a pair of shoes with great silver buckles.

"Let us see how the women of the same time used to dress. Here is a lady dressing for a dinner party. First the barber comes and does up her hair in frizzles and puffs and rolls, one on top of the other, until it all looks like a pyramid or a tower. She has on a brocade dress, green ground with great flowers on it, looped over a pink satin skirt. Her dress is very low in the neck, and is greatly trimmed with lace.

"It is very tightly pulled over a stiff hoop which sticks out on both sides so far she has to go in at the door sideways. The heels of her low shoes are very high, and she wears beautiful silk stockings. That is the way she dresses for a party; but how does she dress at home?

"At home she wears a cap and a pretty gown, a neat white apron, and a muslin kerchief over her neck.

"This is the way the rich people dress. Let us take a look at the country people. The farmers' wives wear checked linen dresses in summer, and strong home-spun woolen dresses in the winter with clean white aprons and kerchiefs. The farmers wear stout leather breeches, checked shirts and frocks. Every day but Sunday the working-men wear leather aprons, and are not at all ashamed of them either."

The very early houses of these colonists were rudely built structures, usually of roughly hewn logs from the forests. To keep the houses warm, the spaces between the logs were stuffed with dried leaves, and the whole wall was then plastered over with mud.

Sometimes the houses of the less industrious colonists were very carelessly built, and little pains were taken to fit the logs together.

There is a story told of one colonist who, lying in his bed on the floor against the side of his log house, felt in the dead of the night a sharp bite at his ear, and starting up he saw the fierce head of a wolf pushed in through the space between the logs, close by his head.

It was some little time before there was any window glass used in the colonies. Indeed glass was as yet very rare even in England. "Bring oiled paper for your windows," wrote a Massachusetts governor to his friends in England who were about to sail for the colonies.

"You need not bring oiled paper for your windows," wrote a New York colonist to his friends; "oiled paper is used in Massachusetts colonies, but here we have found in the rocks sheets of mica which make most excellent windows."

But, by and by, when comfortable houses began to be built and window glass had become less rare, we find the dwellings fashioned after the old English style of houses. The more wealthy colonists built great square buildings; the rooms arranged, as it seemed, around a great central chimney in the middle of the house. "They built the chimney," says one writer, "and then fitted the rooms to the chimney." Perhaps they did; it might seem so. At any rate each room had its own great open fireplace, the warm red flames from which leaped and sprang up into the secret places and out of sight—all in this one great chimney. It was a long time before stoves were invented; and a long time again before a kind was invented that would really warm the rooms and be of use. The very first stoves, it is said, were built into the walls; and when wood was to be put on the fire, some one had to go out of doors to do it, the door of the stove being on the outside of the house.

But the old open fireplaces with their cheerful fires were one of the very best features of colonial life. Here in the long winter evenings the families would sit talking and telling wonderful stories, roasting chestnuts and apples, and having just the very best of social times. You will not wonder that they lingered around their cheerful fires and were inclined to make the evening long when you hear what crude beds they often had in these same comfortable houses.

Of course among the very wealthiest of the colonists at this time there were great bedsteads, and warm feather beds, such as one often sees now in country places, where the people are wise enough to still cling to their rich, old-fashioned furniture. But among the less favored classes the beds were not, I am afraid, the most comfortable things in the world, and certainly they were not very handsome pieces of furniture by any means.

One way of building up a sleeping place was to make two holes in the wall and into these to drive two poles. These poles served for the sides of the bed-frame. Then two upright posts were erected, with holes in them into which the side poles were driven. A cross beam from post to post and the bed-frame was complete. Then slats were laid across, or, when possible, ropes were woven in and out, a great bag of hay or straw, sometimes pine boughs, were laid on this—then the bed was complete. But simple and easy to make as these beds and bed-steads were, many strange stories are told of the scarcity of beds in the little taverns here and there at which travelers from town to town must stop over night.

"In England," wrote one colonist, "we were accustomed at the tavern to have a room and a bed and a privilege of bolting our door; it will be so here by and by when we have grown a little more settled in our new land, and have had time and means to make more furniture. At present, however, if we go to bed alone in a tavern, it is by no means sure that some fellow-traveler will not, when we awake, be found sleeping soundly in the same bed, having thrown himself down by our side or perhaps across the foot of the bed."

Furniture, too, of all kinds, was not common in the very first years of colonial life. The wealthiest people had their furniture brought from England; but in those days of slow sailing vessels such importation was far too expensive for poor families. The chairs and tables were accordingly home made, like the bedsteads, and were rude and rough, not very comfortable, but "good enough for now," as the patient, hardworking people would say to each other as now and then they would recall their more comfortable English homes. "Our chairs and tables were better, no doubt, in England," some father would say, "but we can forego all that for the blessed liberty of this country and by and by we shall have them all again."

A few long boards laid across carpenters' horses for a table, some long boards arranged bench-fashion around the room against the walls, and the house was ready for a husking party or a quilting bee or any other good time; and the "time" was nowise any less "good" that the furniture and preparations were so simple.

Carpets were rarely seen then, even in the finest houses. The floors were sanded; and in the best room, as they called their parlors, the sand was lined off into squares or diamonds which suited the proud housekeeper's ambition quite as well as a real carpet with its squares and diamonds.

PINE-TREE SHILLINGS

There is one very pretty story told of these early days of the Massachusetts colony. The only money in use among the people was the gold and silver coins which were made in England and Spain. These coins were very scarce, so that the people had to trade in goods when they wished to make a purchase, instead of being able to pay in money as we do now.

That is, if in those days you had wanted to buy a yard of ribbon, or a top, or a ball, you would very likely have paid for it with butter or eggs—anything that you happened to own that the storekeeper was willing to take.

But as the people were growing more and more in number, and trade increased, this kind of bartering grew very troublesome. The people needed some sort of money; and so a law was passed, a kind of coin was decided upon, and Captain John Hull was made mint-master. The largest of these coins had stamped upon them a picture of a pine tree. This is why they were called "Pine-Tree" shillings.

As payment for his work, it was decided that the mint-master should have one out of every twenty coins he made.

Captain John Hull was an honest man; and although he put aside for himself only one in every twenty coins, his strong boxes got to be very, very heavy.

Captain Hull had a daughter; a fine, plump, hearty girl, with whom young Samuel Sewell fell in love. As Samuel was a young man of good character, industrious and honest, Captain Hull readily gave his consent to their marriage. "Yes, you may take her," he said in his rough way, "and you'll find her a heavy burden enough."

In due time the wedding day arrived. There were John Hull, dressed in a plum-colored coat, with bright silver buttons made of the Pine-Tree shillings; the bridegroom, dressed in a fine purple coat and gold lace waistcoat, big silver buckles on his shoes; and last, but by no means least, the fair bride herself, looking as plump and smiling and rosy as a big red apple.

After the marriage ceremony was over, Captain Hull whispered to his men servants, who at once left the room, to return soon with a great pair of scales. Everybody wondered what could be going to happen.

"Daughter," said the mint-master, "get into one side of these scales." Then turning to his servants, and pointing to a big, iron-bound box, he added, "Bring hither the chest."

The servants tugged and pulled at it, but it was all they could do to get it across the floor. Then Captain Hull unlocked it and threw open the cover.

The guests stood breathless, for behold! the chest was full of bright, shining Pine-Tree shillings.

"Put them into the other side of the scales, lively now," said the mint-master, laughing, as he saw the look of amazement on the faces of the people.

Jingle, jingle, went the shillings, as handful after handful were thrown in, till, big and plump as she was, the fair young bride was lifted from the floor.

"There, son Sewell," said the honest mint-master, "take these shillings for my daughter's portion. Use her kindly, and thank God for her. It isn't every wife that's worth her weight in silver."

EDUCATION IN THE COLONIES

Governor Winthrop, the first Governor of the Massachusetts Bay Colony, had, living in England, a sister, of whom he was very fond. He often wrote letters to her and to her husband, who was also a warm friend of Governor Winthrop, begging them to leave the old country and come with their children to the new colony where there was more than enough of all the good things of life.

The sister, and her husband, too, would gladly have come, and indeed were often almost persuaded to do so; but they were very intelligent people for these times and prized education above all things.

On this account, because there were no colleges in America in which her boys could be educated, she hesitated year after year.

Often she would write to her brother, saying that, by and by, when the little colony should have means for the education of her boys, she would gladly come. Another time she would write that she believed the value of education was above all things, and that therefore she must stay in England until the boys were educated.

GOVERNOR WINTHROP

All these letters set Governor Winthrop to thinking. Would it not be well for the colony to found a college? Surely there were other youth than his nephews who would be glad of a college education.

At last a letter came which seemed to set Governor Winthrop to work as well as to thinking. This letter, written in the early part of 1636, was but another appeal from his sister for a college in Massachusetts. It is a quaintly written letter, spelled after the fashion of the times. In it she says, "If only there were some place of learning for youths, it would make me go far nimbler to New Englande if God should call me to it than I otherwise shoulde; and I believe a colledge would put noe smal life into the plantation."

In October of this very year, Governor Winthrop had convinced those who controlled such things in the colony that a college should be built. The money was raised, and work on the building was begun at once.

The college building, a square, red brick building, with low ceilings and little windows, was considered a very elegant structure at the time. It still stands on the college land in Cambridge, surrounded by the great brick buildings which have from time to time been added to it.

This will show you how much these early colonists thought of education. In fact, as early as 1635, only five years after the settlement of Boston, steps were taken to open a public school for the children of that town.

Salem Witchcraft

No one knows when the belief in witches first sprang up in Europe. There was a time, when James the First was king, that England was wild with excitement over witchcraft. The people believed there were witches in the forests, in the rivers, in the air, and I don't know where else. They stood in mortal fear of them, and believed every strange old woman they saw might be a witch and about to work some evil charm on them.

It is no wonder that, from time to time, witch excitements sprang up in the colonies. They died out soon, however, without much harm being done.

But in the year 1692, there sprang up such a fire of excitement over the witch belief, that no power seemed able to quell it. It seems strange to us, in these days, that grown up men and women could be so foolish. These people believed that the cause of witchcraft was the devil; when a person was bewitched, that meant that the devil had taken possession of that person, and was making him do the most terrible things. The devil, they believed, was an enormous creature, with a long tail, a pair of horns, and terrible hoofs. He could take all sorts of shapes, and was often known to take the form of a goose or a black cat.

The excitement over witchcraft in Salem seems to have started in a minister's family.

One day his little girl began to behave very strangely. The minister, being a strong believer in witchcraft, declared at once that the child was bewitched. He begged the child to tell him who had bewitched her; and the child, frightened half out of her wits by her father's terrible stories, cried out that it was a certain old woman who lived near by.

The poor old woman was brought into the presence of the child. The child, excited as she was now, probably, believed that the old woman had, indeed, afflicted her; and, frightened still more when she was brought before her, the child fell into convulsions. This, the minister thought, was sure proof; and the poor old woman was loaded with chains and thrown into prison.

Soon others in Salem began to declare themselves bewitched. If the butter would not come, the housewives declared there were witches in their churns; if the animals on the farms died, it was said to be the work of witches. Every possible disaster was laid at the door of witchcraft.

Although the excitement over witchcraft was highest and hottest in Salem, there was no small amount of it in all the other towns. In the town of Boston it took such a firm hold upon the people that an educated woman, the sister of one of the governors, one who had, therefore, hosts of friends who used their power and influence to save her, was hanged, as a witch, on Boston Common.

This woman, Mrs. Anne Hibbins, was the wife of a wealthy merchant in Boston. Mrs. Hibbins had, we fear, a very proud, selfish disposition, which caused her neighbors to dislike her most heartily. Being the wife of a wealthy merchant, she rather looked down upon her more humble friends, and was not at all careful to hide her feelings from them. When she and her husband were quite old, there came a long line of business troubles, which swept away their money, leaving them as poor as the poorest of their neighbors.

Mrs. Hibbins' crabbed disposition did not grow any sweeter under this misfortune, you may be sure. She grew to be so ugly and so cruel to the little children that they would run screaming to their mothers if she came towards them. She had very sharp eyes and ears, and seemed to see and hear all that happened in the town. She was, also, very keen, and was sure to ferret out the very boy who stole her apples, or stoned her cat, or broke her windows. At last, the mothers began whispering that they believed she was a witch.

"The Devil himself tells her these things," said they, "else how does she know everything that happens?"

As they grew to fear her more and more, they began really to believe she was a witch. Many a mother would run into her house and hide her baby if the cross old woman was seen coming. Soon her neighbors became so sure that she was a witch that they went to the town officers about it; and in a very, very short time, all Boston was filled with fear of this unhappy old woman, whose selfish, proud heart had made her such a disagreeable object.

This fear of her having broken out, it was not long before the people began to clamor for her death. Every accident in the town was laid to her; every sickness in the homes was laid to her; every trouble in the church was laid to her.

At last she was publicly accused and thrown into prison. Her brother, who stood high in the colony, made no effort to save her; her three sons, whom she loved with all the tenderness of which she was capable, were all away and knew nothing of her arrest. And so the poor old woman, who had once held her head so high, was dragged forth from her prison, tried, and sentenced to be hanged. After she was hanged, the people went back to their homes satisfied that in hanging a witch they had done a good deed, one which the Heavenly Father would reward them for!

It doesn't seem possible that only two hundred years ago people could have been so cruel and so foolish.

By and by not only poor old women were accused, but young people, some of them from the leading families in the colonies. Everybody had accepted this wicked belief, doubting not, so long as no one but poor, friendless old women had been accused. But when, at last, the young people and the wealthy people, who had friends to defend them, began to suffer, then the people began to come to their senses.

"How do we know that this man saw Goody Glover flying on a broomstick? How do we know that he saw Martha Corey turn into a black cat? How do we know that he saw the children ride up the stairs on a white horse?" they began to ask when people came forth at a witch's trial to testify to these wonderful sights.

"We do not know," the judges at last honestly declared; and from that time the witchcraft excitement began to die away.

One of the chief believers in this cruel nonsense was a prominent minister, named Cotton Mather. It is said, however, that when he became old he deeply regretted the part he had taken in it and frankly confessed that he would give years to undo the harm he had done.

COTTON MATHER

KING'S CHAPEL, BOSTON

RELIGIOUS TROUBLES

One might think, after all the Puritans had suffered because of their desire to have their own style of church worship, that they would be perfectly willing to let all other people have the same freedom that they themselves had sought.

But this was not the way people thought in those days.

"Believe what you wish," they would say, "only please do not come among our people."

With all the trouble the Puritans had to contend against, they may be excused for speaking thus. Enemies were on all sides of them, as well as in England, and it seemed absolutely necessary to them that they should be united among themselves.

But there were people of other beliefs who had also found it uncomfortable to live under the strict laws of England, and who preferred to come to a new world where they thought they could do more as they pleased.

Their ways, however, were not the ways of the Puritans, so, naturally, they were not very welcome.

In 1631, a young minister, named Roger Williams, came to the colony, and he soon began to give the Puritan leaders much trouble.

He thought that people should worship where they pleased—and he publicly said so. But, what was still worse, he preached that the early settlers had no right to the very land they lived on unless they bought that land of the Indians.

"Surely," the Puritans said, "we have enough trouble with the Indians without putting this new idea into their heads."

As was the case with troublesome people in those days, Roger Williams was ordered out of the country. Fearing that, if caught, he might be sent back to England, he made his escape into the deep forests.

It was midwinter, but the Indians welcomed and protected him. He gradually made his way to that part of the country now called Rhode Island. Here, in 1636, he purchased land of the Indians, and, before very long, many of his friends in Salem followed him and made a settlement.

They built a town and named it Providence. In this colony, it was declared that every one should be free to worship as he pleased. There, for the first time in the history of the world, all people were allowed to act as seemed to them best in their own churches.

Roger Williams, meanwhile, did not forget the kindness of the Indians. After he had learned to speak their language, he spent much of his time with them, teaching them to read and work.

You may be sure, his people all loved this good, well-meaning man. At one time, when he had been away in England nearly two years, the whole colony crossed the river to meet him as he returned.

The old men and the young men, the old women and the young women, and all the children, met him with flowers and songs and every sign of joy.

OLD NORTH CHURCH, BOSTON

Roger Williams' kind old heart was touched when he saw how his people loved him, and he was not ashamed to let the tears run down his cheeks as he thanked them for their love.

Meanwhile, there had sprung up in England another class of people, under the leadership of George Fox, who went much further in their idea of simple form of church worship than even the Puritans had.

These people, called "Friends," would have no form at all. They believed it was best and most pleasing to God to go into their little churches, with no minister, no singing, no praying, and sit there, perfectly quiet, fixing their minds only on holy things. This, compared with the elaborate form of worship in the English Church, was certainly a great change, to say the least.

The English Church, which thought the Puritans had been foolish enough, thought these last people more than foolish—they thought them mad.

There is a funny little story connected with these Friends, which shows how later they came to receive their peculiar name of Quakers. It is said that one of these people was brought for trial before an English judge.

The English judge having been rather severe, the Quaker turned to him and said, "Dost thou not quake with fear before the Great Judge, who this day hath heard thy cruel judgment upon his chosen people?"

But just then, the Quaker, who was very nervous and excitable, began to shiver and shake and quake to such an extent that the whole court burst into a roar of laughter. From that time these people were nicknamed "Quakers."

In due time the Quakers were driven from England, as the Puritans had been before them. They, too, came over to America, hoping to find freedom to worship God in the way they thought best.

It was about thirty-five years after the *Mayflower* entered Plymouth harbor that the first Quakers came.

There had been many changes in the colonies in that time. The little children had now come to be middle-aged men and women with children of their own.

The men and women who had done the hard work of settling the little home at Plymouth, had now grown to be quite old, and very, very many of them had, long since, been laid away in the quaint little burying-ground.

Many, many other men and women had come over from England, so that now, instead of thinking of a few people living in their huts at Plymouth, you must think of little towns all along the coast, having residences, stores, churches, and schools, all of which were quite fair buildings for the times.

The Old South Church, the Old North Church and King's Chapel, which stand now in Boston, were built in these early times.

The new-comers, the Quakers, were strange in their looks and in their manners, it is true; but so were the Puritans as to that matter. Then, too, in their enthusiasm they often forgot the rights of the Puritans in whose towns they were living.

And so it came about that the Puritans had these Quakers whipped in the streets; they cut off their ears and their noses; they put cleft sticks upon their tongues to keep them from speaking; and they punished them in many other ways.

Until within a few years, there stood on the beautiful Common in Boston an elm tree, to whose boughs the Puritans hanged a woman named Mary Dyer, not so much because she was a Quaker and preached the Quaker doctrines, but because she insisted on preaching on the streets and in direct defiance of the laws of Boston.

OLD SOUTH CHURCH, BOSTON

And surely, we have to admit that the Puritans thought they had a right to enforce their own laws: only of course punishments were very severe; still we must remember they would have used these same punishments on their own people had they broken the same laws.

The one thing that exasperated the Puritans with the Quakers above all other things, was the fact that the Quakers allowed the women to preach and pray as they liked. "A preaching woman," said the Puritans, "is a disgrace to religion! Away with such!"

OLD ELM TREE, BOSTON COMMON

You can imagine, therefore, how annoyed the Puritans were with Mary Dyer when she insisted on preaching.

For a time Mary Dyer lived quietly in Rhode Island; but when she heard of the cruel treatment of the Quakers in Boston, she was determined to go to their aid. Twice was she driven from the town, and threatened with hanging if she came again.

But Mary Dyer was fearless; her one thought was that her friends, the Quakers, were in prison, many of them dying of fever and hunger. A third time she entered the town. She was at once seized, brought before the judge, and condemned to be hanged. Many friends begged that she might be spared, but the judge would not yield.

On the 27th of October, 1659, Boston Common was to witness the hanging of a woman. The streets were thronged with people, all anxious to get even one glance at the unhappy Quakeress. By her side walked two young men, also Quakers, who were to be hanged with her.

It was one of these who first ascended the fatal ladder. As he was speaking of his faith, and his willingness to die, someone in the crowd called out: "Hold thy tongue! Art thou going to die with a lie in thy mouth?"

Soon the other young man was led forth. As the rope was being fastened he cried, "Know all ye, that we die not for wrong doing, but for conscience' sake!"

And then the judge called, "Mary Dyer!"

Her two friends were hanging dead before her eyes. Fearlessly she mounted the scaffold, and quietly allowed the hangman to fasten the blindfold and the rope. All was ready. The great crowd stood breathless.

The hangman raised his hand to give the signal, when there was heard a cry from the distance, "Stop! stop! she is reprieved! The Governor has reprieved her!"

Shouts of joy rang through the Common, mingled with hisses from those who had longed to see her hanged. She was taken back to the prison, where she was received by her brave son, who looked upon her as one brought back from death. He it was who had besought the Governor to save his mother, and at last won from him her reprieve.

Joyfully, the son carried away the mother to their home in Rhode Island. I wish I could tell you that the good woman lived out her days there with her brave boy, happy and free. But it was not so. Before many months had passed, again she was seized with the idea that it was her duty to go again to Boston and speak for her people.

Nothing could keep her from it; even the prayers and tears of her son, who loved her so, could not prevail upon her to give up the dangerous journey.

Hardly was she within the limits of the city before she was seized upon by the officers and again carried before the judge.

The judge, exasperated with her foolhardiness, as he called it, offered her, once more, her choice between hanging and promising to leave the colony forever. She would not accept the chance to escape, and was sentenced to be hanged on the morrow at nine o'clock.

Half wild with grief, Mary's husband begged the judge to save her once more; but the judge, saying that she had made her own fate, would not change her sentence.

At the appointed hour, the officer led her forth from the prison to the Common, and there, before the eyes of a great number of people, she was hanged, declaring, with her last breath, that she was giving her life, not for any wrong act of hers, but for her religion's sake.

WILLIAM PENN

The Quakers of England certainly were in
great need at this time of someone who

would call them together and find for them a place of safety. Such a leader appeared at last.

This leader was William Penn. He was the son of Admiral Penn, of the English navy. Admiral Penn had been brought up to believe only in the English Church, and to hold in contempt all such people as Puritans and Quakers. Imagine that father's astonishment when his son, having returned from college, came before him dressed in the queer garb of a Quaker, and told him that he had resolved to join these much abused people.

The old gentleman was horrified. He scolded and he argued; he raved and he threatened, but not one whit was the son moved by it all. He sent him abroad, hoping that the gay life at Paris and other great cities of Europe would cure him of this foolish freak he had taken.

Penn came back to England still a Quaker. His father's patience was now exhausted; he allowed Penn to live in the house, but he would have nothing to say to him, and for years would not even look at him.

When his father died, Penn made up a large party of Quakers to come to America. On August 31, 1682, he set sail from Deal, England, in the good ship *Welcome*, and after a voyage of two months arrived at New Castle on the Delaware on October 27, 1682, and immediately began a settlement. To this settlement he gave the name, Philadelphia, which means "brotherly love."

In payment of a debt owed to Penn's father, King Charles of England had already granted to Penn that tract of land which we now call Pennsylvania; still Penn was not willing to take the land from the Indians without paying them also for it. He held a council with them under a large elm tree. There he made a treaty with them, and the agreements were made peaceably and honestly. Think what a strange picture it must have made! There was the Englishman in his long-skirted coat, with blue sash and broad hat, while all around him stood the Indians gorgeous in their feathers and war-paint, glittering with strings of wampum, and wrapped about with furs.

Like Roger Williams, Penn was always loved and reverenced by the Indians. The great elm under which the treaty was made has long since decayed and fallen; but in its place to-day stands a monument which tells the story of Penn and the treaty.

REDUCED FAC-SIMILE OF TREATY WITH INDIAN TRIBES.

REDUCED FAC-SIMILE OF TREATY WITH INDIAN TRIBES

This treaty of peace, made between the Quakers and the Indians, had no other than the blue sky, the bright sun and the forests for witnesses. But the Indians were a true-hearted race, and if they were treated with any degree of fairness, whatever, were ready and willing to be honorable in their dealings with the white man. There was a simple gratitude about them that was like a child's; and it is a pity that other white men, not Quakers, had not wisdom enough to deal fairly with these simple-souled people.

The history of this treaty was kept by the Indians by means of their strings of wampum, and long afterwards they would tell the story over to their children, bidding them always in their fights and war-makings to remember their father's promises to the good Quaker, William Penn.

And so it was that, in the years that followed, when war was raging on every side in all the surrounding States, not one drop of Quaker blood was ever spilled.

There is a little story told of how one Quaker saved the lives of many families about him.

One morning, some Indians, incensed at the behavior of certain colonists up the river, fiercely set forth in full war dress, war paint and all, cruelly bent upon revenge.

On the borders of the forest, toward which they strode, lived a good Quaker and his family. As the Indians approached, the Quaker went forth to greet them. Knowing how honorably the treaty with the Quakers was held by these red men, the Quaker had no fear for his own family.

"But they mean bloodshed to the colonists up the river, I am sure," said he to his wife. "I must try to turn them back."

So generous and frank was the Quaker's greeting, that the fierce warriors, thirsting as they were for blood, melted in the warm sunlight of his gentle heart, and turned back to their wigwams, the massacre given up for that day, at least.

As they went away, one of the Indians climbed up on the little porch over the door and fastened there the "white feather of peace," which was a mark among these Indians that the house upon which that was placed should never, under any provocation, be molested.

War raged on every side in the days that followed; many cruel deeds were done, and hundreds of colonists were slain; but the good Quaker and his family dwelt in safety and slept without fear of harm from their savage neighbors.

INDIAN TROUBLES

During these hundred years or more, from the founding of the Plymouth Colony in 1620, there had been continual trouble with the Indians.

The Indians, you remember, were kind to the white men at first; but after the white men began to be cruel and hard to them, they, too, grew hard and cruel, and there seemed nothing too terrible for the Indians to do in revenge.

The newcomers thought that these Indians had very strange ways of carrying on their battles. They never came out and met the enemy face to face in battle array, as the white men were then used to doing, but would skulk around behind trees, in swamps, or in the high grass.

When the white men first used muskets and gunpowder, the Indians were terribly frightened; but it was not long before they, themselves, learned to use them.

One day an old Indian chief begged some gunpowder from a white man and ran away to his wigwam with it.

The white man watched to see what he would do with it. When he reached his wigwam, he called some of his friends about him and, after a long council together, they began to plant the powder. They thought it would grow like corn and beans.

When an Indian killed a white man in battle, he always tried to tear off the skin from the top of the white man's head. These were called scalps. The more scalps he could get the braver he thought he was. After a battle he would show the scalps, with great pride, to the people of his village.

These Indians were a very wandering people, never staying in one place very long at a time. When they made up their minds to move, the women would take down the tents, strap their babies onto their backs and trudge on the best they could, carrying, on their shoulders, the poles and household wares, the mats and the furs. The men would march on ahead, with nothing but their bows and arrows.

Sometimes the poor women would sink under their heavy loads. Then the men would beat them and kick them until the poor things would rise and struggle on.

When the Indians reached a place which looked pleasant for a camping ground, the men would throw themselves down upon the ground, in a sunny place, and lie there smoking and napping, while the women set up the tents and got the camps in order.

The men treated the women like slaves. They expected them to do all the work, such as planting the corn, building the tents, carrying the baggage; while they did nothing but hunt and fish and smoke and fight.

But, in reading of this life of the Indians, let us judge them not too harshly. They were cruel to the women and girl children, that is true; but it was because they knew no better rather than because they meant to be cruel.

Remember they were rude, rough people, accustomed to war and to fighting. Surrounded on all sides by enemies, they grew to regard physical strength and skill in overcoming an enemy as the highest virtue in the world; and, consequently, they had come to look upon women as of very little account— good enough to do the cooking and the drudgery of wigwam life; but that was all.

They had never learned that men and women, boys and girls, were to be judged and valued by something better and higher than mere brute force.

"Good to squaw!" exclaimed an Indian in surprise, when one of the colonists had rebuked him for his treatment of his wife. "She no fight—no scalp!" and I suppose no argument could have convinced the Indian that he was wrong; or that, since she could neither fight nor scalp, it was worth while to make of her anything better than a slave or a servant.

The Puritans, you will remember, landed at Plymouth one cold December day. A few Indians had been seen on the top of the hill when they first landed, but they had fled at the sight of the white men, and were not seen again for some time.

Glad, indeed, were the white men that they did not again appear until they got their log cabins built, in which their wives and children might be safe from the arrows of these strange red men.

Weeks passed by. At last, one morning in March, when the Puritans were holding a town meeting, in stalked a solitary Indian. The Puritans were not overjoyed to see him, you may be sure.

They waited for him to speak. Solemnly he looked about upon them all, and then cried, "Welcome, Englishmen! Welcome, Englishmen!"

These were indeed welcome words; for a minute before the white men had stood breathless, wondering whether this stranger was about to declare peace or war upon them.

Samoset—for that was the name of this visitor—was a tall, straight man, with long black hair, and was arrayed in feathers and furs, and colored with bright paints, as was the custom of these savages.

Samoset was so delighted with the manner in which the white men received him, that he speedily declared his intention of staying with them all night. The white men did not relish that; but, not daring to displease him, they made him comfortable for the night in one of the cabins, and kept watch over him until morning.

At sunrise he was ready to return to his home, and the Puritans gladly bade him farewell.

I am afraid Samoset hadn't very many ideas of what we call etiquette. He did not wait for the Puritans to return his call, but appeared again the very next day, bringing with him five other Indians.

The Puritans were annoyed with this second visit; however, they gave them all food and drink, after which the six Indians danced and sang in a fashion peculiar to themselves.

At night the five Indians went away, but Samoset had made up his mind to stay longer with his new friends.

A few days later, seeing that he had no idea of going home, the Puritans sent him to find Massasoit, who, as Samoset had told them, was the chief of the Indian tribes in that neighborhood—the Wampanoags.

Soon Massasoit, the chief, came, with sixty armed and painted warriors; terrible to look at in their feathers and paint. But Massasoit did not come to fight. He wanted peace between his tribe and the strange people. After a little talk, he sat down with John Carver, the Governor of this little colony, smoked the pipe of peace with him and promised to befriend the colony as long as he should live.

This treaty he always kept, and, as he was a very powerful chief, the Puritans were safe from Indian attack as long as he lived. It was after his death that their real trouble with Indians began.

South of the Plymouth Colony there lived a tribe of Indians who hated Massasoit's tribe. They also hated white men; therefore, you may know that when they learned that Massasoit was protecting these Puritans, they were doubly angry. For a long time they annoyed the colonists in little ways, but there had been no real trouble.

At last, one day, there marched into the village a huge Indian, covered with his war paint, and carrying in his hand a long snake-skin.

This skin he presented to William Bradford, who was now Governor of the colony, telling him that in the snake-skin was a bundle of arrows.

"And what does that mean?" inquired Bradford.

"War, war, war!" yelled the messenger.

"Very well," said Bradford, calmly; "you may take this back to your chief." And as he spoke, he emptied the skin of its arrows and filled it full of shot and gunpowder.

"This means," said Bradford, "that if your chief comes to us with arrows, we will come to him with gunpowder and shot."

The messenger understood, and, snatching the skin, he ran out of the village to his home. There was no more trouble with that tribe of Indians.

One day word came to the Puritans that Massasoit was dying, and that he wished to see the white men once more.

Quickly, one of the Puritans, Edward Winslow, who knew considerable about medicine, hastened to Massasoit's home.

He found the tent, in which Massasoit lay, so full of people that the sick man could hardly breathe. These Indians, both men and women, were howling and dancing around him, trying, so they said, to drive away the bad spirits which were giving him pain.

This was a custom of theirs when an Indian was ill. If the sick man recovered, they believed it was because their noises had scared away the evil spirits; if he did not recover, it was because they had not made a noise great enough.

When Winslow arrived, he set to work to do all he could to relieve the poor chief, who was suffering from high fever.

In two or three days, Massasoit was quite well again. The Indians looked upon the cure as a miracle, and families came from miles and miles around to see the wonderful "medicine man."

No one was more glad of Massasoit's recovery than the white man himself; for all knew that if Massasoit died the tribes of Indians on all sides would at once rush upon the white settlements, burn the houses, scalp the men, and carry away the women and children as captives.

And this did happen within a very few years. After Massasoit's death, the Indians

began to grow jealous of the increasing power of the white men. They were being gradu-
gradually driven from all their hunting
grounds.

KING PHILIP'S WAR

Many tribes of Indians, under the leadership of their chief, Philip, banded together and vowed that they would not rest until every white man was driven from the country. There were so many Indians in this league that it seemed for a time as if their threat would indeed be carried out.

The first attack was made upon the people of Swansea. The people had all been gathered together in their little church, which you remember was more like a fort than a church. As they came out, and were walking slowly homeward, suddenly there was heard the Indian war-whoop; and in an instant there burst out from the forests troops of Indians armed with guns, arrows, clubs, tomahawks—anything with which a deadly blow could be given.

After this, the Indians fell upon all the towns and upon the farms scattered about over the country. If you ever read the history of King Philip's War, you will find it full of terrible stories of the cruelty of these Indians, and of stories, sad, sad stories, of the poor women and children who were cruelly murdered or dragged away to be made slaves of.

The Indians were continually on the watch. When men went out to work, they would be shot down by an unseen foe. The women at work in their homes would be shot by a ball or an arrow coming in through the window.

King Philip's right-hand man in this war was Annawon. He it was, who, in the midst of the fire of battle, could be heard shouting to his men, "I-oo-tash! I-oo-tash!" meaning, "Stand to it! Stand to it!"

At last, in August, 1676, King Philip was surrounded in a swamp at Mount Hope and killed. "Now," said the colonists, "if we could capture or kill Annawon, we should be safe."

Finding that Annawon had made his camp in another swamp near by, Captain Church, one of the bravest of the colonists, set out with a companion and some Indian guides to find it. Soon they came in sight of it—down in a deep recess among the hills. There lay Annawon himself, stretched out before his tent half asleep. Slowly and quietly they climbed down, and before Annawon even knew of their presence, Captain Church stepped across the chief's body and took him prisoner.

Meantime, the followers of Captain Church went to the other Indians lying about before their camp-fires, and told them that their chief was taken, that there were hundreds of white men just outside the camp, and that their lives should be spared, if they would surrender at once.

Captain Church, exhausted with his long march, now lay down close to Annawon and slept, throwing his foot over Annawon, so that the least movement would awaken him. For two hours the captain slept. When he woke, he found Annawon lying with eyes wide open staring at him. At last, Annawon arose and stalked off into the forest. As he had surrendered his arms, Captain Church allowed him to go, wondering what he would do next.

Soon he returned, bringing a war-belt, which had belonged to the Indian chief, King Philip.

Laying it at Captain Church's feet, he said, "Great Captain, you kill King Philip—you capture me—now the war is ended—this belt belong to you."

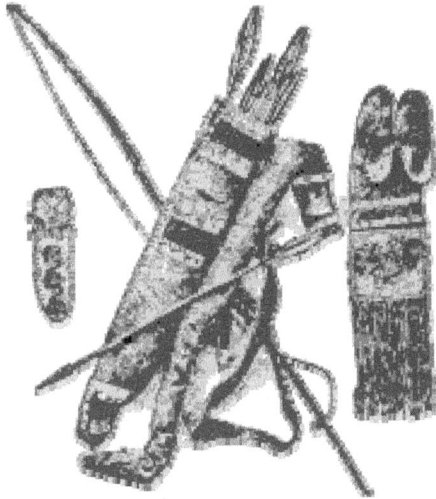

FRENCH AND INDIAN WAR

From 1754 to 1763 there was a bitter war carried on between the French, aided by the Indians, on one side, and the English, aided by her colonies, on the other. We shall pass very quickly over this war, which, though very important, does not chance to have so very many stories for young people in it.

One of the first attacks in this war was made on the French settlement in Acadia. I wish you were old enough to read the beautiful story of Evangeline as it is told by our Longfellow. By and by I hope you will read it, and will learn to love this beautiful Evangeline, who was so cruelly driven from her home in Acadia.

In the beautiful Basin of the Minas was a quiet little French village. The people of this village were peaceful, home loving families, and took no part in the war on either side.

The English colonists, however, fearing that they might, by and by, be persuaded to join the French forces, made up their minds to break up this village and scatter the people.

One bright morning the English officers came into the village and demanded that the people be gathered in the churches to hear a message which the English brought to them.

The people all left their work and flocked to the churches. The farmer left his harvest field, the blacksmith his anvil, the wife and maiden their spinning-wheels.

No sooner were all the people within the churches than they were surrounded by British soldiers, hustled down to the water-side, and crowded on board the ships like so many herds of sheep. O, it was a cruel deed! Families were torn apart; wives lost their husbands; mothers lost their little ones; brothers and sisters, lovers and maidens, were doomed never to meet each other again. Piteous were the cries of these poor people, but the soldiers only laughed at their grief.

As they sailed out from the harbor, they saw the soft September sky all one terrible glare of flame. Then they knew that their last hope was gone; their beautiful homes were burned. This the cruel soldiers had done lest the poor Acadians might try to wander back to their old home in this beautiful Basin of the Minas.

When these vessels reached the New England coast, the unhappy people were put ashore here and there at different places, from New England to Virginia, that there might be no possibility of their banding together again. Very few of them ever met their dear ones again, and many died of homesickness and heart-break.

GEORGE WASHINGTON

GEORGE WASHINGTON IN THE FRENCH AND INDIAN WAR

I suppose every child in America knows about George Washington. Indeed, I hardly dare offer you a story about this man, lest you say, "O, don't bother! we know all about him." And very likely you do; but let's read this one story together.

When the French and Indian War broke out, George Washington was a young man, only about as old as those big boys that you see coming now and then from their colleges to spend their vacations at home.

George Washington, you remember, lived in Virginia. The Governor of Virginia at that time was Governor Dinwiddie.

It became very necessary to get a message to the commander of the French forts on the Ohio river; and, as Washington had already made a name for himself, being a brave, honest, trustworthy lad, Governor Dinwiddie chose him to go on this important journey with the message.

It was a terrible journey, and one that was full of danger. Very likely Washington would have been quite willing to be excused from the task; but as it must be done, and somebody must do it, he bravely and willingly accepted the trust.

It was in the winter time; and his journey lay over mountains, through forests, and across rivers, where very likely, no white man had ever been before.

One night he and his companion worked till daylight, making a rude raft with which to cross a narrow river too deep to ford, expecting every minute an attack from the savages of the forest.

Lossing, in his "Life of Washington," gives the following account of this journey:

"I was unwilling," writes the guide, "that he should undertake such a march; but, as he insisted on it, we set out with our packs, like Indians, and traveled eighteen miles. That night we lodged at an Indian cabin, and the major was much fatigued. It was very cold;

all the small streams were frozen, so that we could hardly get water to drink." At two o'clock the next morning they were again on foot, and pressed forward until they struck the southeast branch of Beaver Creek, at a place called Murderingtown, the scene, probably, of some Indian massacre.

WASHINGTON FALLS INTO THE ALLEGHENY RIVER

"Here we met with an Indian, whom I thought I had seen when on our journey up to the French fort. This fellow called me by my Indian name, and pretended to be glad to see me. He asked us several questions, as, how came we to travel on foot, where we parted from our horses, and when they would be there. Major Washington insisted upon traveling on the nearest way to the forks of the Allegheny. We asked the Indian if he could go with us, and show us the nearest way. He seemed very glad and ready to do so; upon which we set out, and he took the major's pack.

"We traveled quite briskly for eight or ten miles, when the major's feet grew very sore, and he very weary, and the Indian steered too much northeastwardly. The major desired to encamp, upon which the Indian asked to carry his gun; but he refused that. Then the Indian grew churlish, and pressed us to keep on, telling us there were Ottawa Indians in these woods, and that they would scalp us if we lay out; but to go to his cabin and we should be safe.

"I thought very ill of the fellow, but did not care to let the major know I mistrusted him. But he soon mistrusted him as much as I. The Indian said he could hear a gun from his cabin, and steered us more northwardly. We grew uneasy, and then he said two whoops might be heard from his cabin. We went two miles farther. Then the major said he would stay at the next water, and we desired the Indian to stop there; but before we came to water we came to a clear meadow.

"It was very light. Snow was on the ground. The Indian made a stop, and turned about. The major saw him point his gun toward us and fire. Said the major, 'Are you shot?' 'No,' said I; upon which the Indian ran forward to a big standing white oak, and began loading his gun, but we were soon with him. I would have killed him, but the major would not suffer me. We let him charge his gun. We found he put in a ball; and then we took care of him. Either the major or I always stood by the guns. We made him make a fire for us by a little run, as if we intended to sleep there.

"I said to the major, 'As you will not have him killed, we must get him away, and then we must travel all night;' upon which I said to the Indian, 'I suppose you were lost, and fired your gun.' He said he knew the way to his cabin, and it was but a little way. 'Well,' said I, 'do you go home, and as we are much tired, we will follow your track in the morning.' He was glad to get away. I followed him and listened until he was fairly out of the way, and then we went about half a mile, when we made a fire, set our compass, and fixed our course and traveled all night. In the morning we were on the head of Piney Creek." There is little reason to doubt that it was the intention of the savage to kill one or both of them.

The fort on the Ohio was at last reached. Washington delivered his message to the commander there, who sent back a very insolent reply to Governor Dinwiddie.

The journey back was as hard and as dangerous as the journey to the fort had been. It was accomplished, however, and the French commander's reply delivered to Dinwiddie.

I will not try to tell you what these messages had been about, but the one that Washington brought back from the fort was such that the people of Virginia knew that the French were determined to fight, and that war would surely follow.

Quickly the Governor of Virginia prepared for war, and, sending word to the other colonies, bade them be ready too. All the colonies bravely made ready to meet the foe. Even Georgia, settled only twenty years before, was ready to join hands with Virginia and Massachusetts, the oldest colonies of all, to give what help she could.

To help the colonies, England also sent over a large army of soldiers, with General Braddock at the head. Now, General Braddock felt himself to be a great man. Indeed, he had made up his mind that, as soon as he and his army arrived, the whole war would be as good as over. He little knew what sort of people these Indians were with whom he was going to fight. He supposed that, as soon as they caught sight of the great red-coated soldiers with him at their head, they would be so overcome by fright that they would give up at once. "Pooh!" said he, "the idea of Indians daring to fight with me!"

GENERAL BRADDOCK

General Braddock's contempt for the colonists was as great as his contempt for the Indians. How he sneered when the sturdy colonists took their places among the red-coats as he drew up his forces in battle array!

It is a wonder he didn't tell them to go to their homes, while he started off through the forests with his troops alone.

Washington, who was at the head of the Virginia militia, talked long and earnestly with Braddock, trying to show him how impossible it would be to attempt to fight these Indians as he would fight a battle where the armies on both sides were trained soldiers.

He told him the Indian way of fighting; how they never came out in battle array; how they always hid behind trees, in bushes, and in swamps.

But Braddock only sneered. "Do you suppose a General in the King's army needs advice from a boy like you?" thought he. And I shouldn't be at all surprised if he said it too.

Now, Washington and his Virginia troops were used to the ways of the Indians, and when they saw that Braddock was determined to set out upon the journey to meet the Indians in the English fashion, they knew only too well what the result would be. Nevertheless they made no complaint, but were ready to start at Braddock's command.

In the first place, there were the Virginia mountains to be climbed, and the rivers to be forded. The English soldiers used only to their level country, began to give out before the journey was half accomplished.

Still, Braddock had not sense enough to see that it would be well to heed the advice of Washington and the other colonists. "Perhaps the Indians can frighten such soldiers as you are," said he, sneering at the colonists, "but they cannot frighten English soldiers."

So they were marching on, in full battle array, drums beating, and colors flying.

Braddock's head was high in the air, and he was very likely expecting to see the Indians advancing in the same manner.

Suddenly, as his army was ascending a little slope with deep ravines and thick underbrush on either side, they were greeted with the terrible war-whoop of the Indians. Arrows began to fly in every direction, men were falling dead about him; still no enemy was to be seen.

"Where are they?" weakly asked the boasting General.

The terrible war-whoop resounded on every side. Well might the General ask, "Where are they?" They seemed to be everywhere.

The British regulars huddled together, and frightened, fired right and left at trees and at rocks.

The Virginia troops alone, with Washington at their head, sprang into the forests and into the bushes and met the Indians on their own ground. Washington seemed everywhere present. The Indians singled him out as the especial object for their shot. Four balls passed through his coat; two horses were shot dead beneath him. Braddock was mortally wounded and was borne from the field. Then, when the Virginia troops were nearly all killed, the British soldiers turned and fled disgracefully.

Washington and his few men, seeing they were fleeing turned again upon the Indians, and, by keeping them busy returning his fire, prevented them from pursuing the frightened British regulars.

This battle was a terrible one to the British and the colonists. Nearly all of Washington's troops were killed and a great many of the

English; the French and Indians on the other side lost very few.

After this the British were more willing to take the advice of the colonists, who were so much more familiar with the ways of the Indians.

Now in this war it was important that Quebec be taken from the French.

To give you some idea of how Quebec was situated, and how difficult it was to besiege it, perhaps nothing can help you more than the story of how the city came to be named Quebec.

Away back in these early times, when the French were sailing down the St. Lawrence, and taking possession of what they saw, in the name of France, by a turn in the river, they came suddenly into view of a great, sharp over-hanging cliff. *"Quel bec!"* cried one of the sailors, meaning "What a beak!"

Coming nearer, the leader saw that the top of this cliff would make a fine site for a trading-post. It would be difficult for the enemy to attack, and it would be an excellent watch-tower from which to watch vessels passing on the river.

Accordingly the cliff was chosen for the trading-post and remembering the sailor's cry, the explorer gave it the name Quebec. When it afterwards became a city, you can see that it was indeed a watch-tower for the people. If an enemy's vessel was seen approaching, the people were warned long before it reached them, and they meantime had plenty of opportunity to prepare for defence.

"Quebec must be taken!" said the English officers.

"We can do nothing on the river with that city scowling down upon us, ready to attack our vessels as soon as they pass within the shadow of that great beak."

And so it came about that General Wolfe was sent to attack this city of Quebec. Landing at night two miles above the city, the soldiers climbed the steep banks of the river, and stood at daybreak, on the plains of Abraham.

Montcalm, who held the city, was surprised indeed to see the English upon the plain in full battle array. But Montcalm was a brave soldier; and though he knew that in Wolfe he had a "noble foe," he did not shrink from the encounter, which seemed likely from the beginning to be disastrous to the French.

Towards ten o'clock the French advanced to the attack. Two cannons, which, with very great labor the English had dragged up the path from the landing place, at once opened fire upon the French.

The advance was badly conducted. The French soldiers marched steadily on, but the native Canadians, firing as they advanced, threw themselves on the ground to reload, and this broke the order of the line. The English advanced some little distance to meet their foes, and then halted.

Not a shot was fired until the French were within forty paces, and then, at the word of command, a volley of musketry, crashed out along the whole length of the line. So regularly was the volley given, that as the French officers afterwards said, it sounded like a single cannon-shot. Another volley followed, then another and another; and when the smoke cleared away there lay the dead and wounded on every side.

All order had been lost under the terrible fire. In three minutes the line of advancing soldiers was broken up into a disorderly shouting mob. Then Wolfe gave the order to charge, and the British cheer mingled with the wild yell of the Scotch Highlanders rose loud and fierce. The English regiments advanced with levelled bayonets; the Highlanders drew their broadswords and rushed headlong forward.

The fire was heaviest on the British right, where Wolfe himself led the charge. A shot shattered his wrist. He wrapped his handkerchief around it and kept on. Another shot struck him, but he still advanced. When a third pierced his breast, he staggered and sat down. Two or three officers and men carried him to the rear, and then laid him down and asked if they would send for a surgeon.

"There is no need," he said. "It is all over with me."

A moment later one of those standing by him cried out:

"They run, see how they run!"

"Who run?" Wolfe asked.

"The enemy, sir; they give way everywhere."

"Go, one of you, to Colonel Burton," Wolfe said, "tell him to march Webb's regiment down to the Charles River to cut off their retreat from the bridge;" then, turning on his side, he said:

"Now, God be praised, I die in peace!" and a few minutes later he died.

At almost the same moment Montcalm, mortally wounded, said to his surgeon, "Have I much longer to live?"

"No," answered the surgeon; "only a few moments, I fear."

"So much the better," answered Montcalm, "I shall not live to see the surrender of Quebec."

This French and Indian War was carried on for about five years. There were many terrible battles, and thousands and thousands of brave men were killed on both sides. At last the British and the colonists won, peace was made, and England now owned all the land from the Arctic Ocean to the Gulf of Mexico, and from the Atlantic to the Mississippi.

HOW THE COLONIES GREW UNITED

The close of this French and Indian War brings us close upon a period which is perhaps the most important in the whole history of our country.

We are coming upon that great war known as the Revolutionary War. Revolution, you know, means a turning over, a changing about; and you will think, before you get through, that it was indeed a turning over and a changing about.

Before we start upon that great war, let us look over this country and see what sort of people and conditions we are going to deal with.

During this French and Indian War, the people of the thirteen colonies had unconsciously been getting ready for the Revolution which was so near at hand.

Before this war, there had been a great deal of petty jealousy between the different colonies. Each had been jealous of the other's religion and customs. The Swedes didn't care to have much to do with the Dutch, and the Dutch were rather jealous of the Swedes; the Puritans and the Quakers had not quite forgotten the days of persecution; the Episcopalians of Virginia, the wealthy planters with their slaves, looked down upon the northern colonists as a very common sort of people.

But during this French and Indian War all the colonies had fought side by side against a common foe, the Indians and French. They had grown more used to each other's ways; the Virginian Episcopalians had found that the Massachusetts Puritans were, after all, quite as brave and noble as they themselves were; while on the other side these rigid Puritans had found that the Virginians were true and honest-hearted, and could make just as sturdy soldiers as were to be found in any colony. All these bitter feelings were gradually softened down, and at the end of the war many a Puritan, Catholic and Episcopalian had made warm friendships with one another, which no doubt lasted as long as they lived.

Other things, too, had been working to bring them together. The British officers had, throughout the war, sneered at the colonists, and had plainly shown them that England considered them as a very inferior sort of people.

Their wishes and their advice had been thrust aside in contempt, and their best officers had often been pushed out to make room for some young Englishman who knew no more about the work before him than a child.

All these and many other influences had been at work to bring about in the colonists a more united brotherly feeling; while, at the same time, there had been creeping into their hearts and heads a feeling of rebellion against the injustice of England, and a sense of strength in themselves, which by and by, as we shall soon see, broke out in that war between England and America known as the Revolution.

AMERICAN HISTORY STORIES, VOLUME II

CAUSES OF THE REVOLUTION

YOU remember, in the French and Indian War, the colonists began to feel dissatisfied with the way England treated them. Up to that time, England had left them pretty much alone; but as soon as she found they really were beginning to be quite important,

that they were carrying on quite a little commerce and manufacturing, that they were
raising quite a large amount of cotton and tobacco, and were really growing every year in
wealth, and in numbers, and in power, then
she thought it quite time that they be made to
help support the English government.

The colonists, since they considered England their mother country, were quite willing
to do this, and would have done it had England treated them fairly.

Did you ever think where the money comes
from to keep in order the cities or town you
live in—to build its public buildings, to lay
out its streets, and to pay all the officers and
workmen for their work?

Of course you know that every State has a
Governor, who has been chosen by votes of
the people. He stands as the head man in the
State; but of course he could not go about to
every house to ask people what they would
like to have done in their particular cities or
towns.

And so the work is divided; somewhat as
the school system is in large towns and cities.
There is a Superintendent, who has charge of
the teaching in the town or city; but as he

could not teach every child, he engages a principal to take charge of each school building, and each principal, in his turn, has a teacher to take charge of each room in the building.

PATRICK HENRY DELIVERING HIS CELEBRATED
SPEECH, 1765

The government of the State is somewhat like this—in its division at least. All the men of one town go to the "polls," as they call it, and vote for some one man to represent them. They tell him what they want, and he is expected, when he meets at the State House with the representatives from all other parts of the State, to express the wishes of these men who voted to have him fill this office.

The State calls these representatives together, finds what each town wants, and the money which all these property owners in all the towns have paid in, is distributed as these representatives think best.

In the same way, the work is divided in each city or town. The men all go to the polls again for a *municipal election*, as it is called; that is, to elect men to carry on the city affairs. They elect one man to oversee the whole city, much as the Governor oversees the whole State, and as the Superintendent oversees the whole school system. Then there is another man elected to oversee the water supply, another to oversee the roads, another to collect the taxes—and many, many more; so many that, rather than take the time here to try to name them, I think I will leave you to ask your fathers about them; for very likely they can explain it all to you a great deal better than I can on paper.

But all these officers must be paid for working for the city, and they must also have money to carry on the work that is expected of them. And this money is raised by taxation,—that is, every property holder pays in a certain amount of money to help pay the expenses of the town or city. The tax-payers are willing to do this, because they know it will all go to pay the salaries of these officers, to build roads, lay out public parks, support the schools,—all those things that go to help make our cities and towns pleasant and comfortable.

This sort of tax paying is perfectly just; because each town in this way gets its share of the good things which its tax money has bought.

Now let us see what England tried to do,— what it was that made the colonies so angry that at last they rose in arms against the mother country.

She said, "You are getting so wealthy now, you ought to pay tax to us."

The colonists said, "Very well, we shall be glad to do so; for we consider ourselves as little towns belonging to England, and so of course we expect to give our share of the money which the government needs."

"But you are not to have any of this money back again," said England. "The King will do what he pleases with it. Neither are you to send any representative to us, and we will hear none of your prayers."

Then the colonists were angry indeed. "We are not slaves," said they, "and we are not going to pay money to England unless we can have representatives and be treated like the towns in England."

But greedy England only laughed at them, and said, "You shall do as we tell you to, or we will send our soldiers over to whip you into obedience."

England didn't realize that the colonies might prepare to whip British soldiers themselves.

Now I hope from all this,—and this has been a pretty long lesson I fear,—I hope you will understand, and will never forget, that the reason the colonists made war with England was because England was determined to tax them without allowing them any part in the government. As the histories say, the cause of the Revolution was *"Taxation without Representation."*

"Taxation without Representation."

THE STAMP ACT

One of the first things England did to raise money from the colonists, was to issue the *Stamp Act*.

The king sent over a large amount of paper on which had been put a certain *stamp*. This paper the king ordered the colonists to use on all their government writing.

Nothing, so the king said, would be considered of any value unless it was written on this stamped paper. For example, suppose a man owed another man a hundred dollars. When he paid the debt, the receipt would not be considered of any value unless it was written on this particular paper. Suppose a young man and maiden were to go before the minister to be married; the marriage was not legal, so the king said, unless the minister did the writing, which was always given the married bride and groom, on this stamped paper.

Now, as the king had put a very high price upon this paper, you can see how, by compelling the American colonists to buy it, it was but one way of getting a heavy tax from them.

BEHAVIOR OF THE COLONISTS

The colonists all over the country were furious when this stamped paper was sent to them.

The Boston people declared they wouldn't buy one sheet of it; they would buy nothing, sell nothing; the young men and maidens would not get married; they would do nothing, indeed, which should compel them to use this stamped paper. To show their contempt for the whole matter, they made a straw figure of the English officer who had the paper to sell, dressed it in some old clothes of his, and hung it on a big tree on Boston Common.

In New Hampshire, the people paraded the streets with a coffin on which was written, "Liberty is dead." They carried it to the grave, had a "make-believe" funeral and then, just as they were about to bury it, some one shouted, "Liberty is not dead!"

Then they drew up the coffin and carried it through the streets again; crying, "Liberty's alive again! Liberty's alive again!"

In Charleston, South Carolina, stood an old tree, known as "Liberty Tree." It was a great live oak, growing in the centre of the square between Charlotte and Boundary Streets.

During the excitement over the Stamp Act, about twenty men, belonging to the "best families" in the state, assembled beneath this tree to hear an address by General Gadsen.

With vigor he condemned the measure, and urged his hearers to resist to the utmost such abominable tyranny.

This is said to have been the first public address of the kind that had been delivered in the colonies.

The men, after hearty cheers, joined hands around the tree, and pledged themselves to "resist English oppression to the death."

The names of these men are still on record. Most of them were indeed true to their pledge and distinguished themselves in the war that followed, by their courage and patriotism.

This "Liberty Tree" was regarded with such reverence by the patriotic Carolina people, that Sir Henry Clinton, who held Carolina after its surrender to the British, ordered it to be destroyed. It was cut down, and afterwards its branches were heaped about the trunk and the whole burned. A mean act, one would say, to burn an unoffending tree; but perhaps Sir Henry had in mind the old anecdote which, if I remember rightly, runs something like this:

"Why do you kill me, an innocent trumpeter? I have not fought against you."

"Very true," replied the captor; "you may not fight yourself, but you incite others to fight. Hence I kill you."

In Pennsylvania, William Bradford, the editor of the *Pennsylvania Journal*, came out with a "final issue," at the head of which were "skulls and crossbones," pickaxes and spades, all suggestive of the death-blow that had been struck at the press. This number of the journal was deeply embellished with heavy black margins, and was in truth a most dolorous looking affair, as you may see from the picture on the next page.

In Virginia, a young man, named Patrick Henry, so stirred up the people that the old men, angry as they were with England, were frightened, and begged him to be careful what he said.

Benjamin Franklin was sent to England by the colonists to see what could be done. When he reached there, he found that many of England's greatest men were on the side of the colonists.

FAC-SMILE OF THE "PENNSYLVAINIA JOURNAL"
ON THE STAMP ACT

One of the men in the English government rose and made a speech against the colonists, in which he said, "What! will these Americans, these children of ours, who have been planted by our care, nourished by us, protected by us, will they now grudge us their money to help throw off our heavy debt!"

Up jumped Colonel Barre. "Planted by your care, indeed! It was your persecution that drove them to America in the first place!" he cried.

"Nourished by you! When have you nourished them? They have grown up by your very neglect of them! Protected by you! Have they not just now been fighting with your soldiers to protect *you*, rather, from the French and the Indians?"

And good William Pitt of England! He arose and made a speech which, by and by, every boy and girl should learn. He said, "We are told that the Americans are obstinate; that they are in almost open rebellion against us. I *rejoice* that America *has* resisted. I rejoice that they are not so dead to all feelings of liberty as to be willing to submit like slaves!"

Hurrah for William Pitt and Colonel Barre! Don't forget, all you little American men and women, that we had good friends in England then as we have now. There were lovers of liberty in that country, who were as eager as we were to resist all unjust laws.

DAUGHTERS OF LIBERTY

People who write histories always tell how brave and bold and patriotic the men and boys are; but seldom do they think it worth while to tell of the brave deeds of the women and girls. Now, I don't think this is fair at all, do you girls? And you, little boys, if your sisters had done something just as brave as your brothers had done, wouldn't you be very indignant if every body should come to your house and praise your brothers, and cheer them, and all the time shouldn't speak one word to your sisters?

I am sure you would; manly, brave hearted boys are always ready to stand up for their sisters, and are always very angry when some one hurts or neglects them in any way.

Now, of course the mothers and maidens couldn't take guns and swords and go into battle as the men did, although they did even do that in some cases. But let us see what they did do. Somebody must stay home and take care of the children, and the homes, and keep up the farms. So the brave women said to their husbands and sons, "You go into the battle-field, because you are stronger and larger and know about war; we will stay at home and keep the children cared for, that they may grow up strong to help you by and by; we will spin and weave day and night to keep you in yarn for stockings, and in cloth for clothes and blankets to keep you warm; we will plant, and harvest, and grind the corn, and do all your work on the farm that there may be food to send you, and food to keep you from starving when you all come home again."

What, think you, would the brave men in any war do if it were not for the brave women back of them at home to keep them from starving? O, it is a mean, cowardly man who would say that because the women didn't go forth in battle array that they didn't do their half in saving our country from British soldiers!

Let us see who these "Daughters of Liberty," as they called themselves, were.

As soon as the trouble between England and America broke out, the men had formed themselves into societies, and had called themselves "Sons of Liberty." They pledged themselves to do everything in their power to drive back the English rule. The women, too, not wishing to appear to be one step behind their fathers, and husbands, and brothers, formed themselves into societies—"The Daughters of Liberty." They pledged themselves not to buy a dress, or a ribbon, or a glove, or any article whatever that came from England. They formed spinning societies to make their own yarn and linen, and they wove the cloth for their own dresses and for the clothes of their fathers and brothers, and husbands and sons.

The women used to meet together to see who would spin the fastest. One afternoon a party of young girls met at the house of the minister for a spinning match. When they left, they presented the minister with thirty skeins of yarn, the fruit of their afternoon's work. The old women, some of whom were too old to do very much work, pledged themselves to give up their tea-drinking because the tea came to them from England, and because England had put a heavy tax on it. These dear old ladies, who loved their tea-drinking so much, bravely stood by their pledge. They drank catnip, and sage, and all sorts of herb teas, and pretended they liked it very much; but I suspect many an old lady went to bed tired and nervous, and arose in the morning with an aching head, all for the want of a good cup of tea.

At that time, there appeared in the newspapers many verses written by the English officers, no doubt, often making fun of these brave women, old and young. Here is one of the verses:

"O Boston wives and maids, draw near and see,
Our delicate Souchong and Hyson tea;
Buy it, my charming girls, fair, black or brown,
If not, we'll cut your throats and burn your town."

"Within eighteen months," wrote a gentlemen at Newport, R. I., "four hundred and eighty-seven yards of cloth and thirty-six pairs of stockings have been spun and knit in the family of James Nixon of this town." In Newport and Boston the ladies, at their tea-drinkings, used, instead of imported tea, the dried leaves of the raspberry. They called this substitute Hyperion. The class of 1770, at Cambridge, took their diplomas in homespun suits, that they too might show their defiance of English taxation without representation.

THE BOSTON BOYS

Here is a story about the Boston Boys, which is a match for the one you have just read about the Boston girls.

On Boston Common the boys used to skate and coast and build forts, just as other boys do to-day. Perhaps their skates weren't quite so elegant as those the Boston boys have now, and very likely their sleds were clumsy, homemade affairs, not at all like the beautiful double-runners and the toboggans you boys are so proud of; nevertheless those little lads then had just as jolly times, coasting down the same hills and skating the same ponds.

The English had, by this time, become so convinced that the colonists were preparing for war, that they sent over a large detachment of red-coated soldiers. These soldiers made headquarters in Boston, and soon became generally disagreeable to the people.

The boys had been watching eagerly the freezing of the ice on the pond on the common.

"To-morrow," thought they, "the ice will be strong enough to bear; and then, hurrah for the skating!"

Eagerly the boys hastened to the pond in the morning, their skates over their shoulders, their faces bright with the thought of the pleasure before them; but what do you suppose the cowardly soldiers had done during the night? Having nothing else to do, they had broken the ice all over the pond—and just to bother these little boys. Don't you think those great, strong soldiers must have had very mean hearts to go to work to plague little boys in that manner?

I am inclined to think these boys were pretty angry when they learned who had done this cowardly act, and very likely they scolded furiously about it.

Again and again the soldiers did the same thing. At last, one day when the boys were building a fort, some of these soldiers came idling along and knocked down the fort with their guns.

The boys, now angry through and through, determined no longer to bear this mean treatment.

"Let us go to General Gage," said one of the boys, "and tell him how the soldiers are treating us; and if he is any kind of man, he will put a stop to it."

And go they did at once. With eyes ablaze with anger, they marched into the presence of the great English general.

GENERAL GAGE

After they had laid their wrongs before him, he said, "Have your fathers been teaching you, too, to rebel, and did they send you here to show their feelings?"

"Nobody sent us, sir," answered the leader; "but your soldiers have insulted us, thrown down our forts, broken the ice on our pond, spoiled our coasts, and we will not stand it."

General Gage could not help laughing at the earnestness of these plucky little fellows. He promised that the soldiers should not bother them any more; then turning to an officer near by, he said, "Even the children here draw in the love of liberty with the very air they breathe."

A BRAVE LITTLE GIRL

While General Gage held the town of Boston, our people were nearly starved, because of the number of British soldiers that must be fed. Accordingly, men were sent into the surrounding villages to obtain help. "Parson White," of the little town of Windham, urged his people to give all they could; and his little daughter, catching the spirit of loyalty, wondered how *she* could help the suffering Bostonians. Soon after, the villagers prepared to send Frederic Manning to the town with sheep and cattle and a load of wheat. The little girl thought of her pet lamb. *Could* she, *ought* she to part with it? Running to her father, she eagerly asked his advice; but the parson, smiling kindly, said, "No, dear; it is not necessary that your little heart be tried by this bitter strife;" and bade her run away and be happy. But the thought would not leave

her. There in Boston were little girls, no older that herself, crying for food and clothing; she *must* give all she could to help them. At last the day came on which the cattle and supplies of help were to be driven to town. Choking down her sobs, the little martyr untied her pet from the old appletree, and, crossing the fields, waited for Manning, the driver at the cross-roads.

"Please, sir," said she, her lip quivering, and

the tears rolling down her cheeks, "I want to do something for the poor starving people in Boston—I want to do my part, but I have nothing but this one little lamb. Please, sir, take it to Boston with you, but, couldn't you carry it in your arms a part of the way—'cause it—it—it is so little, sir?" Then bursting into tears and throwing her apron over her eyes as if to shut out the sight of her dear little pet, she ran towards her home. Poor, brave little girl! I hope when she told her mamma and papa what she had done, that they took their little girl up in their arms and kissed her many, many times, and told her what a dear, brave little girl she had been. I suspect the tears were in their eyes, too, when she told them; and I have always wished the good parson had sent a fleet messenger to overtake the driver and bring back the little lamb to its loving owner; for I think it took more real courage to give up that one pet lamb, than it did for the Boston boys to go before General Gage when the soldiers had spoiled their fort.

THE BOSTON MASSACRE

SOLDIERS who would be mean enough to bother little boys as these soldiers had done, would be pretty sure to get into trouble with the citizens by their mean acts.

They had entered the town, one quiet Sabbath morning, but instead of coming in quietly and doing whatever was necessary to do in a quiet way, they came in with colors flying, and drums beating, as if, for all the world, they had conquered the city. Then, as if this were not insult enough, they took possession of the State House, and then marched to the Common, where they set up their tents, planted their cannon, and indicated to the enraged citizens, in every way, that they were going to stay.

Frequent quarrels took place between these soldiers and the people. One day they fell into an "out-and-out" fight.

Nathaniel Hawthorne, an author who has written such beautiful stories for you children,—The Snow Image; A Wonder Book; Grandfather's Chair, etc.,—gives the following account of the Boston Massacre:

It was now the 3d of March, 1770. The sunset music of the British regiments was heard as usual throughout the town. The shrill fife and rattling drum awoke the echoes in King street, while the last ray of sunshine was lingering on the cupola of the town-house. And now all the sentinels were posted. One of them marched up and down before the custom-house, treading a short path through the snow, and longing for the time when he would be dismissed to the warm fireside of the guard-room.

In the course of the evening there were two or three slight commotions, which seemed to indicate that trouble was at hand. Small parties of young men stood at the corners of the street, or walked along the narrow pavements. Squads of soldiers, who were dismissed from duty, passed by them, shoulder to shoulder, with the regular step which they had learned at the drill. Whenever these encounters took place, it appeared to be the object of the young men to treat the soldiers with as much incivility as possible.

"Turn out, you lobster-back!" one would say. "Crowd them off the side-walks!" another would cry. "A redcoat has no right in Boston streets." "Oh, you rebel rascals!" perhaps the soldiers would reply, glaring fiercely at the young men. "Some day or other we'll make our way through Boston streets at the point of the bayonet!"

Once or twice such disputes as these brought on a scuffle; which passed off, however, without attracting much notice. About eight o'clock, for some unknown cause, an alarm-bell rang loudly and hurriedly. At the sound many people ran out of their houses, supposing it to be an alarm of fire. But there were no flames to be seen, nor was there any smell of smoke in the clear, frosty air; so that most of the townsmen went back to their own firesides. Others, who were younger and less prudent, remained in the streets.

Later in the evening, not far from nine o'clock, several young men passed down King street, toward the custom-house. When they drew near the sentinel, he halted on his post, and took his musket from his shoulder, ready to present the bayonet at their breasts. "Who goes there?" he cried in the gruff tone of a soldier's challenge. The young men, being Boston boys, felt as they had a right to walk in their own streets without being accountable to a British red-coat. They made some rude answer to the sentinel. There was a dispute, or perhaps a scuffle. Other soldiers heard the noise, and ran hastily from the barracks to assist their comrade.

At the same time many of the townspeople rushed into King street by various avenues, and gathered in a crowd about the custom-house. It seemed wonderful how such a multitude had started up all of a sudden. The wrongs and insults which the people had been suffering for many months now kindled them into a rage. They threw snowballs and lumps of ice at the soldiers. As the tumult grew louder, it reached the ears of Captain Preston, the officer of the day. He immediately ordered eight soldiers of the main guard to take their muskets and follow him. They marched across the street, forcing their way roughly through the crowd, and pricking the townspeople with their bayonets.

A gentleman (it was Henry Knox, afterwards general of the American Artillery) caught Captain Preston's arm. "For heaven's sake, sir," exclaimed he, "take heed what you do, or there will be bloodshed!" "Stand aside!" answered Captain Preston, haughtily; "do not interfere, sir. Leave me to manage the affair." Arriving at the sentinel's post, Captain Preston drew up his men in a semicircle, with their faces to the crowd. When the people saw the officer, and beheld the threatening attitude with which the soldiers fronted them, their rage became almost uncontrollable.

"Fire, you lobster-backs!" bellowed some. "You dare not fire, you cowardly red-coats," cried others. "Rush upon them," shouted many voices. "Drive the rascals to their barracks! Down with them! Down with them!"

"Let them fire if they dare!" Amid the uproar, the soldiers stood glaring at the people with the fierceness of men whose trade was to shed blood.

Oh, what a crisis had now arrived! Up to this very moment the angry feelings between England and America might have been pacified. England had but to stretch out the hand of reconciliation, and acknowledge that she had hitherto mistaken her rights, but would do so no more. Then the ancient bonds of brotherhood would again have been knit together as firmly as in old times. But, should the king's soldiers shed one drop of American blood, then it was a quarrel to the death. Never, never would America rest satisfied, until she had torn down royal authority, and trampled it in the dust.

"Fire, if you dare, villains!" hoarsely shouted the people, while the muzzles of the muskets were turned upon them: "you dare not fire!" They appeared ready to rush upon the levelled bayonets. Captain Preston waved his sword, and uttered a command which could not be distinctly heard amid the uproar of shouts that issued from a hundred throats. But his soldiers deemed that he had spoken the fatal mandate, "Fire!" The flash of their muskets lighted up the street, and the report rang loudly between the edifices.

A gush of smoke overspread the scene. It rose heavily, as if it were loath to reveal the dreadful spectacle beneath it. Eleven of the sons of New England lay stretched upon the street. Some, sorely wounded, were struggling to rise again. Others stirred not, nor groaned, for they were past all pain. Blood was streaming upon the snow; and that purple stain, in the midst of King Street, though it melted away in the next day's sun, was never forgotten nor forgiven by the people.

At once the bells were rung, and the citizens, rushing out to learn the cause, hastened to the fight. The people in the country around, hearing the bells, hurried in with their muskets to help the town. At last the soldiers, seeing that the whole country around was aroused and rushing to the rescue, took to flight.

TABLET ON THE CRISPUS ATTUCKS MONUMENT,
BOSTON

THE BOSTON TEA PARTY

HOUSE IN DANVERS WHERE "THE BOSTON TEA PARTY" PLOT IS SAID TO HAVE BEEN TALKED OVER

THIS Boston tea-party was a very different sort of a party from the quiet little tea-parties to which your mammas like to go. There were no invitations sent out for this tea-party, and the people who attended it behaved in a very queer way, considering they were at a tea-party.

This was the way it came about. The English had put a tax, you will remember, upon nearly everything, tea included.

Now, when they found that the colonists were so furious about it, and seemed so determined to stand up for their rights, the English began to be afraid, and to think that perhaps they had gone a little too far.

So, wishing to soothe the angry colonists, they took off the tax on everything *except* the tea. "We will keep the tax on that," said the English, "just to let the colonists know that we have the *power* to tax them, and that they must obey; but we will not ask them to give us their money on the other things."

Foolish people, to suppose the colonists were going to be quieted in that way. It wasn't the money that they were made to pay that had angered them; they were willing to pay that; but it was the *idea* of their being taxed *without* representation!

"Does England suppose it is the few paltry dollars that we care for?" said they. "No; we will show her that, while we would be willing to pay thousands of dollars if we were treated fairly, we will not pay *one cent* when she treats us like slaves!"

Not many days had passed before word came that a great vessel was nearing the harbor, loaded with tea.

A lively meeting was held in Faneuil Hall, and afterwards in the Old South Church; and the people all declared that the tea should never be allowed to be brought ashore.

At evening the vessel was seen slowly nearing the wharf. Everything was quiet, and you would never have imagined what was going to happen.

Slowly the ship comes in, nearer and nearer the little wharf. Now, with a heavy swash of water and a boom, she touches; out jump her sailors to fasten her ropes.

But hark! what noise is that? It is the Indian war-whoop. And see! down rush the Indians themselves, yelling and brandishing their tomahawks. In an instant they have boarded the vessel. Down into the hold they go, yelling and whooping at every step.

The terrified sailors stand back aghast. Out they come again, lugging with them their heavy chests of tea.

Still they yell and whoop; and over go the chests into the dark water below.

THROWING THE TEA OVERBOARD

And now, when every chest is gone, suddenly the Indians grow very quiet; they come off from the deck; and, orderly, take their stand upon the wharf; then do we see that they were not Indians at all. They were only men of Boston disguised.

This then was the Boston tea-party, which took place in Boston Harbor on the evening of December 16, 1773.

Three hundred and forty-two chests were thrown overboard.

On their way home the party passed the house at which Admiral Montague was spending the evening. The officer raised the window and cried out, "Well, boys, you've had a fine night for your Indian caper. But, mind, you've got to pay the fiddler yet." "Oh, never mind," replied one of the leaders, "nev-

THE BOSTON TEA PARTY

er mind, squire! Just come out here, if you please, and we'll settle the bill in two minutes." The admiral thought it best to let the bill stand, and quickly shut the window.

The Americans had taken one great step towards liberty, and the English had been taught a lesson of American grit. It would have been well for England had she been wise enough to heed it.

REVOLUIONARY TEA

REVOLUTIONARY TEA.

Words by SEBA SMITH.

1. There was an old La - dy, lived o - ver the sea, And
2. "Now Moth - er, dear Moth - er, the daugh-ter re - plied, "I

she was an Is - land Queen; . . Her daughter liv'd off in a
sha'n't do the thing you ax, . . . I'm will-ing to pay a fair

new countrie, With an o-cean of wa - ter be - tween; . .
price for the tea, But nev - er the three-pen-ny tax;" . . .

The old lady's pockets were full of gold, But nev-er content-ed was
"You shall," quoth the mother, and reddened with rage, For you're my own daugh-ter, you

REVOLUTIONARY TEA.

she, . . So she called on her daughter to pay her a tax Of
see, . . And sure,'tis quite pro-per the daughter should pay Her

three pence a pound on her tea, Of three pence a pound on her tea.
moth-er a tax on her tea, Her moth-er a tax on her tea."

3 And so the old lady her servant called up,
   And packed off a budget of tea.
And eager for three pence a pound, she put in
   Enough for a large familie,
She ordered her servants to bring home the tax,
   Declaring her child should obey,
Or old as she was and almost woman grown,
   She'd half whip her life away.
   She'd half whip her life away.

4 The tea was conveyed to the daughter's door,
   All down by the ocean's side,
And the bouncing girl pour'd out every pound
   In the dark and boiling tide;
And then she called out to the Island Queen,
   "O Mother, dear Mother," quoth she,
" Your tea you may have when 'tis steeped enough,
   But never a tax from me,
   No! never a tax from me."

THE PATRIOTIC BARBER

There were some of the colonists who did not approve of this rebellion of the people against the king. Although they knew England had no right to do what she had done, still they dreaded a quarrel; and, since they were pretty comfortable, didn't care much whether England treated them as equals or as slaves. There were some, too, who had such great reverence for England and the king, that they would have considered it an honor to have their ears pulled or their faces slapped, if only it were done by a king's hand.

These colonists who believed in obeying the king, no matter what he demanded, were called Tories, while those colonists who were so ready to fight for freedom were called Whigs.

I am afraid a great many of the Tories were persecuted in those days by the excited Whigs.

There is a story told of a Boston barber, which will show you how bitterly the Whigs hated the Tories.

A barber was shaving a customer one day, and, at the same time, earnestly talking politics with him. One side of the customer's face was nicely shaved, when, by something he said, the barber learned that the man was a Tory.

Quick as a flash the barber threw down his razor, clutched the man by the collar and dragged him to the door.

STREET SCENES

"A Tory! a Tory!" shouted the barber at the top of his voice. In less than a minute a crowd had gathered. A roar of laughter went up at sight of the unhappy Tory, his eyes glaring with rage and fright, his face all lathered, one side cleanly shaven, the other all rough with his bristling beard.

Away ran the man, and after him ran the crowd, hooting and laughing, and shouting "A Tory! a Tory!" The crowd followed him from shop to shop, until at last he found a barber who was himself a Tory, and who willingly rescued him from the mob and finished the shaving for the unfortunate man. This was a very mean act in the Whig barber, but, it will show you very well the spirit of the times.

BATTLE OF LEXINGTON

In the spring of 1775, General Gage was told that the Americans had for a long time been secretly carrying to some place outside of Boston stores of gunpowder, guns, muskets and bullets, that there might be a supply whenever they were needed. He also learned that, in every town and village about Boston, companies were being formed for military drill. These men called themselves "Minutemen," because, as they said, they would be ready to enter battle against the British any time at a minute's notice.

Gage began to watch these signs of fight on the part of the colonists. Into all the towns about he sent spies to learn all they could about these military stores and these minutemen. Soon he learned that it was in the old town of Concord that the colonists were storing their ammunition.

"We will start out some dark night and capture those stores," said Gage.

"We will watch the British soldiers," said the Americans, "and see that they do not start off in the night to capture our stores."

"The colonists will be asleep," said General Gage, "and, if we are quiet, they will know nothing of our departure."

"We will keep our eyes on you, General Gage," said the colonists, "night and day; for we suspect you would like to steal our ammunition."

But as General Gage did not hear the colonists say these words, and had not yet learned that the colonists were fully as sharp as his own soldiers, he knew not that sentinels were pacing back and forth all night long, watching him; and that messengers were standing ready with their strong horses to ride out into the outlying towns with the alarm, if the British troops were seen to show any signs of marching.

At last, on the evening of April 18, 1775, one of these sentinels heard sounds and saw a stirring among these soldiers. Soon he saw them creep quietly down to the water and hurry into boats. There was no doubt now that the British were planning to cross the Charles River and set out for Concord.

In twenty minutes, two mounted horsemen were galloping away to rouse the farmers in all the towns around and warn them to be up and ready for fight. One of these messengers was Paul Revere; and as our own poet Longfellow has told the story of his ride in a way that all readers, little ones and big ones, like to hear, I think that instead of trying to tell it to you myself, I better write you the story of "Paul Revere's Ride" just as Longfellow himself told it.

In the little town of Lexington, a hundred brave minute-men awaited the coming of the British army. Of course there was no hope that a hundred farmer-soldiers could drive back the large army, but they were ready to do what they could.

Up came the red-coats with Major Pitcairn at their head. "Disperse, ye rebels," cried the major; "disperse! throw down your arms and disperse!" But the brave minute-men stood their ground. They neither threw down their arms nor did they disperse. Then one of the British officers, angry that they should dare defy him, discharged his pistol into the little band.

Now the minute-men, who had been told not to fire until they were fired upon, promptly returned fire, wounding three of the British soldiers. This was answered by a fierce volley from the British, and when the army passed on, they left eight brave farmer-soldiers dead upon the green.

Then, on the troops marched straight to Concord, their band playing Yankee Doodle— a song which had been composed by them to deride the colonists.

"Play Yankee Doodle, you old lobster backs," cried some boys from behind a fence; "but look out, Lord Percy, that you don't play "Chevy Chase" when you come back."

Now, as it happens that "Chevy Chase," was an old song of a battle in which this very Lord Percy's ancestors had figured, and had been defeated, you can imagine the young officer didn't enjoy the boy's joke very well; especially when some of his fellow-officers, who could appreciate a good joke even if they couldn't appreciate the courage of the colonists, joined in the laugh against him.

On reaching Concord, the troops took possession of the ammunition, rolled a hundred barrels of flour into the river, and started on, intending to cross the bridge at Concord. But there they found the brave minute-men mustered on the bridge, a hundred and fifty strong.

Immediately the command to fire was given, and two of the minute-men fell dead. Now there blazed back a volley from the little band, which compelled the British troops to fall back. From that moment the colonists had the best of the British troops.

Another volley, and away went the red-coats in full retreat back towards Lexington, the minute-men in full pursuit. On, on, the red-coats ran, while from every house and barn, from behind every fence and bush, rang the quick snap of muskets, shooting down the red-coats at every step. On, on, they ran, panting for breath (their tongues, so an English historian says, hanging out of their mouths), until they came into Lexington again.

STATUE TO THE CONCORD MINUTE MEN

Here they were met by Lord Percy's troops. These troops formed a hollow square about them; and they, breathless and exhausted, sank upon the ground, too breathless even to tell what had happened. Lord Percy's troops thus closed about them, and led them, when they had gained strength enough to march again, back to Boston. But all the way they were pursued and shot at on all sides by the colonists concealed by the roadside, until they were glad indeed, at sunset, to get back under the protection of the guns of the British man-of-war.

PAUL REVERE'S RIDE

PAUL REVERE'S RIDE

Listen, my children, and you shall hear
Of the midnight ride of Paul Revere.
On the eighteenth of April in 'Seventy-five;
Hardly a man is now alive
Who remembers that famous day and year.

He said to his friend, "If the British march
By land or sea from the town to-night,
Hang a lantern aloft in the belfry arch
Of the North Church tower as a signal light,
One if by land, and two if by sea,
And I on the opposite shore will be
Ready to ride and spread the alarm
Through every Middlesex village and farm,
For the country-folk to be up and to arm."

Then he said "Goodnight!" and with muffled oar
Silently rowed to the Charlestwon shore,
Just as the moon rose over the bay,
Where swinging wide at her moorings lay
The Somerset, British man-of-war;
A phantom ship, with each mast and spar
Across the moon like a prison bar,
And a huge black hulk that was magnified
By its own reflection in the tide.

Meanwhile, his friend, through alley and street,
Wanders and watches with eager ears,
Till in the silence around him he hears
The muster of men at the barrack door,
The sounds of arms, and the tramp of feet,
And the measured tread of the grenadiers
Marching down to their boats on the shore.

Then he climbed to the tower of the Church,
Up the wooden stairs with stealthy tread,
To the belfry chamber overhead,
And startled the pigeons from their porch.
On the somber rafters, that round him made
Masses and moving shapes of shade,—
Up the light ladder, slender and tall,
To the highest window in the wall,
Where he paused to listen and look down
A moment on the roofs of the town,
And the moonlight flowing over all.

Meanwhile, impatient to mount and ride,
Booted and spurred, with a heavy stride
On the opposite shore walked Paul Revere
Now he patted his horse's side,
Now he gazed at the landscape far and near,
Then, impetuous, stamped the earth,
And turned and tightened his saddle girth;
But mostly he watched with eager search
The belfry-tower of the Old North Church
As it rose above the graves on the hill,
Lonely and spectral and sombre and still.

And lo! as he looks, on the belfry's height
A glimmer, and then a gleam of light!
He springs to the saddle, the bridle he turns
But lingers and gazes, till full on his sight
A second lamp in the belfry burns!

A hurry of hoofs in a village street,
A shape in the moonlight, a bulk in the dark,
And beneath from the pebbles, in passing, a spark
Struck out by a steed that flies fearless and fleet:
That was all! And yet, through the gloom and the light,
The fate of a nation was riding that night;

It was twelve by the village clock
When he crossed the bridge into Medford town.
He heard the crowing of the cock,
And the barking of the farmer's dog,
And felt the damp of the river fog,
That rises after the sun goes down.
It was one by the village clock,
When he rode into Lexington.
He saw the gilded weathercock
Swim in the moonlight as he passed,
And the meeting-house windows, blank and bare,
Gaze at him with a spectral glare,
As if they already stood aghast
At the bloody work they would look upon.

It was two by the village clock,
When he came to the bridge in Concord town.
He heard the bleating of the flock,
And the twitter of the birds among the trees,
And felt the breath of the morning breeze
Blowing over the meadows brown.

So through the night rode Paul Revere;
And so through the night went his cry of alarm
To every Middlsex village and farm,—
A cry of defiance and not of fear,

A voice in the darkness, a knock at the door,
And a word that shall echo forevermore!
For, borne on the night-wind of the Past,
Through all our history, to the last,
In the hour of darkness and peril and need,
The people will waken and listen to hear
The hurrying hoof-beats of that steed,
And the midnight message of Paul Revere.

In the little town of Lexington, a hundred brave minute-men awaited the coming of the British army. Of course there was no hope that a hundred farmer-soldiers could drive back the large army, but they were ready to do what they could.

Up came the red-coats with Major Pitcairn at their head. "Disperse, ye rebels," cried the major; "disperse! throw down your arms and disperse!" But the brave minute-men stood their ground. They neither threw down their arms nor did they disperse. Then one of the British officers, angry that they should dare defy him, discharged his pistol into the little band.

Now the minute-men, who had been told not to fire until they were fired upon, promptly returned fire, wounding three of the British soldiers. This was answered by a fierce volley from the British, and when the army passed on, they left eight brave farmer-soldiers dead upon the green.

Then, on the troops marched straight to Concord, their band playing Yankee Doodle — a song which had been composed by them to deride the colonists.

"Play Yankee Doodle, you old lobster backs," cried some boys from behind a fence; "but look out, Lord Percy, that you don't play 'Chevy Chase' when you come back."

Now, as it happens that "Chevy Chase," was an old song of a battle in which this very Lord Percy's ancestors had figured, and had been defeated, you can imagine the young officer didn't enjoy the boy's joke very well; especially when some of his fellow-officers, who could appreciate a good joke even if they couldn't appreciate the courage of the colonists, joined in the laugh against him.

On reaching Concord, the troops took possession of the ammunition, rolled a hundred barrels of flour into the river, and started on, intending to cross the bridge at Concord. But there they found the brave minute-men mustered on the bridge, a hundred and fifty strong.

CONCORD BRIDGE — THE SCENE OF THE FIGHT

Immediately the command to fire was given, and two of the minute-men fell dead. Now there blazed back a volley from the little band, which compelled the British troops to fall back. From that moment the colonists had the best of the British troops.

Another volley, and away went the red-coats in full retreat back towards Lexington, the minute-men in full pursuit. On, on, the red-coats ran, while from every house and barn, from behind every fence and bush, rang the quick snap of muskets, shooting down the red-coats at every step. On, on, they ran, panting for breath (their tongues, so an English historian says, hanging out of their mouths), until they came into Lexington again.

Here they were met by Lord Percy's troops. These troops formed a hollow square about them ; and they, breathless and exhausted, sank upon the ground, too breathless even to tell what had happened. Lord Percy's troops thus closed about them, and led them, when they had gained strength enough to march again, back to Boston. But all the way they were pursued and shot at on all sides by the colonists concealed by the roadside, until they were glad indeed, at sunset, to get back under the protection of the guns of the British man-of-war.

THE ORIGIN OF YANKEE DOODLE

THE ORIGIN OF YANKEE DOODLE.

Words by GEORGE P. MORRIS.

1. Once on a time old John-ny Bull Flew in a rag-ing
2. Then down he sate in bur - ly state, And bluster'd like a
3. John sent the tea from o'er the sea With heav-y du-ties

fu - ry, And said that Jon - a - than should have No
gran-dee, And in de - ris - ion made a tune Call'd
rat - ed; But wheth - er hy - son or bo - hea, I

tri - als, sir, by ju - ry: That no e - lec-tions
"Yan - kee doo - dle dan - dy." "Yan - kee doo - dle"—
nev - er heard it stat - ed. Then Jon - a - than to

THE ORIGIN OF YANKEE DOODLE.

should be held, A - cross the bri - ny waters: "And now," said he, "I'll
these are facts— "Yan - kee doodle dan - dy: My son of wax, your
pout be-gan—He laid a strong em - bar - go—"I'll drink no tea, by

tax the tea Of all his sons and daugh-ters."
tea I'll tax— Yan - kee doo - dle dan - dy."
Jove!" so he Threw o - ver - board the car - go.

4 Then Johnny sent a regiment,
  Big words and looks to bandy,
Whose martial band, when near the land,
  Play'd "Yankee doodle dandy,"
"Yankee doodle — keep it up!
  "Yankee doodle dandy!
"I'll poison with a tax your cup,
  "Yankee doodle dandy."

5 A long war then they had; in which
  John was at last defeated—
And "Yankee doodle" was the march
  To which his troops retreated.
Cute Jonathan to see them fly,
  Could not restrain his laughter;
"That tune," said he, "suits to a T,
  I'll sing it ever after."

6 With "Hail Columbia!" it is sung,
  In chorus full and hearty—
On land and main we breathe the strain
  John made for his tea-party.
"Yankee doodle—ho!—ha!—he!
  "Yankee doodle dandy—
"We kept the time, but not the tea,
  "Yankee doodle dandy!"

7 No matter how we rhyme the words,
  The music speaks them handy,
And where's the fair can't sing the air
  Of "Yankee doodle dandy!"
"Yankee doodle—firm and true—
  "Yankee doodle dandy,
"Yankee doodle, doodle doo!
  "Yankee doodle dandy."

THE WOMEN AT LEXINGTON

But what do you suppose the women of Lexington and Concord were doing all this time? They were not idle, you may be sure. Every bit of pewter that could be found, old pewter tea-pots, and sugar-bowls, pewter spoons—many of which were old heirlooms, and were therefore very dear to these women's hearts—all were melted and made into shot. Their very dresses they tore into pieces to furnish wadding for the muskets; and on all sides might the women have been seen loading and reloading the muskets that drove back the British troops.

One woman, Dame Batherick, had taken her musket and gone down into the field to work. Being a "lone" woman, she had heard nothing of the morning fray, and had as usual gone out to work upon her farm.

As the British came fleeing back from Concord, Dame Batherick heard the guns and whistling balls. Pausing in her work and screening her eyes from the sun, she eagerly gazed across the fields towards the village. Nearer and nearer came the sound of battle; she saw the village blaze; she heard the shouts of the soldiers.

"'Tis war," she cried; "war, and blood, and fire!"

Seizing her musket she started forward. Just then a squad of red-coats broke through the bush full upon her sight. In an instant her quick woman's wit took in the whole situation. Drawing herself proudly up, her eyes flashing fire, she cried, "Halt! as ye value life, advance ye not another step."

"Ye are my prisoners, sirs! March on!" she said;
Then dropped her plants and pointing out to them the way,
She drove them quickly on, as she had oft ahead
Driven the kine across the fields, at set of day;
And they, "King George's own," without a word obeyed.

Over the fields so green she marched her captive band,
Her dark eyes flashing still, her proud heart beating high
At thought of England's outrage on her native land!
For women were true patriots in the days gone by,
And scorned the foreign yoke, the proud oppressor's hand.

THE WOMEN AT LEXINGTON

And thus this rustic dame her captives safe did bring
  Unto a neighbor's house; and, speaking fearless then,
In words whose every tone with woman's scorn did ring,
  She said unto King George's brave and stalwart men
"Go, tell the story of your capture to your King!

"He cannot crush our rights beneath his royal hand
  With dastards such as you! And ere this war be done
We'll teach old England's boasting red-coat band,
  We're not a race of slaves! From mother, sire, to son,
There's not a coward breathes in all our native land!"

Thus Mother Batherick's fearless deed was done;
  Long will the tale be told in famed historic page,
How, in this first great victory by freemen won,
  A dame with furrowed brow and tresses white with age,
Captured the grenadiers at famous Lexington.

CAPTURE OF TICONDEROGA

After this battle of Lexington, a Continental Congress met in Philadelphia to talk over this battle and to decide what was to be done. War must follow—of this they all felt sure. And so troops must be raised, a leader appointed, and some plan of action be agreed upon. It was at this time that George Washington was appointed "Commander-in-chief of all the forces raised or to be raised in defence of American liberties."

The news of the battle had been carried throughout the colonies, and in every town the women were knitting and spinning clothes for their husbands and brothers and sons, and making all preparation for war; the men were drilling and forming themselves into companies, ready to march to Boston at the first word of command.

In Vermont, called in your geographies, you remember, the "Green Mountain State," the men had formed themselves into a company under their colonel, Ethan Allen, and called themselves the "Green Mountain Boys." On the morning of the very day of the meeting of this Congress which had made Washington Commander-in-chief, Ethan Allen, with a detachment of these volunteers, set out to surprise Fort Ticonderoga. Arriving there in the early gray of the morning, he found all but the sentries sound asleep. Suddenly, that no time might be given for an alarm, Allen's band rushed into the fort, and, making their way directly to the sleeping apartments of the commander, Allen, in a voice like thunder,— so his followers say,—demanded the instant surrender of the fort.

The commander, frightened, and only half dressed, threw open his door, saying, "By whose authority do you—" But Allen broke in upon him with, "In the name of the Great Jehovah and the Continental Congress do I command you to surrender." No resistance was attempted; and so a large quantity of cannon and ammunition which the English had stored there, and which just then was so much needed by the troops at Boston, fell into the hands of the Americans, without the loss of a single man.

RUINS OF TICONDEROGA

BATTLE OF BUNKER HILL

Great indeed was the excitement throughout the colonies when the news of the battle of Lexington was carried from town to town. Meetings were called in every town, congresses were held, armies formed—for everyone knew now that war had indeed begun. Soon, some fifteen thousand men collected from the different colonies about Boston, and these succeeded in giving General Gage a good scare.

All this time the king of England and his counselors were fretting and fuming because of the obstinacy of the American colonists. They sent over more troops, and when General Gage heard of their arrival he began to grow brave again. He sent out a proclamation, saying that if the colonists would lay down their guns and say they were sorry, he would see that the government of England forgave them and received them into English favor again—all but Samuel Adams and John Hancock; those two men, he said, were past forgiveness, and ought rather to be hanged. It is needless to say that the colonists were not at all moved by General Gage's generous offer of forgiveness. They kept straight on about their plans.

On the 16th of June, a detachment of the American soldiers, outside of Boston, was commanded to go over to Charleston and fortify Bunker Hill.

Under the cover of darkness, the soldiers climbed Breed's Hill, this being nearer Boston, and quietly threw up the earth in such a way as to form ditches and forts. Imagine the surprise of the British the next morning, when they looked across the water and found the Americans working away, busy as bees, finishing up their night's work.

The British cannon were turned upon them, but in vain. "We must march up the hill ourselves," said General Howe; and soon three thousand soldiers were on the way to attack the Americans. Eagerly the soldiers watched from behind their embankment; eagerly the British troops in Boston watched; and eagerly watched the women and children from the house-tops. O it was a terrible day for dear old Boston!

Up the hill climbed the British soldiers, firing at every step. At the top, behind the embankment, crouched the brave fifteen hundred, silent as death.

"Boys," said good Colonel Prescott, "we have no powder to waste; aim low; and don't fire until you can see the whites of their eyes."

And so, I suppose, the British, receiving no shots as they climbed the hill, thought they were going to climb straight over the entrenchments into the American quarters. But, as we know, these Americans had other plans.

The red-coats were nearly up the hill. Their waving plumes were nearly on a level with the hill-top. "Fire," commanded the officer. Bang! bang! bang! bang! went the fifteen hundred muskets. The British soldiers fell, mowed down like grain before the scythe. Then on they came again. Again, bang! bang! bang! went the fifteen hundred muskets; and again the British fell back in dismay. It was a long time before they made their third attack;

and the hearts of the brave men within the intrenchment, and the brave women praying from the house-tops, beat high in the hope that the battle was over.

But soon the British forces rallied, and made one mighty rush over the dead bodies of their fallen brothers, upon the intrenchment. The Americans were now, many of them, without powder; and although they battled hand to hand with clubs and stones, the British reached the summit, and drove the Americans down the hill to Charlestown Neck.

Bunker Hill.   Charlestown.   Breed's Hill.

This was the first regular battle of the Revolution; and although the Americans were defeated, still the defeat brought about so many good results, that, after all, perhaps it was quite as good as a victory; for it showed the British soldiers and the British king that the colonists were not to be subdued by simple threats; while, on the other hand it fired the colonists with courage and zeal. They knew now that there was no escape from war; they had learned that, untrained though they were, they could fight even the British regulars; they knew that, had their ammunition not given out, the day would have been theirs. And so, although they had lost some of their bravest men and although they had been defeated, there was no feeling of discouragement in the hearts of the colonists.

BATTLE OF BUNKER HILL

GENERAL WARREN

We must not leave the story of the Battle of Bunker Hill without speaking of the brave General Warren. He was indeed one of the bravest of the brave. He was a man of wonderful talent, and from the very earliest troubles with England had been one of the staunchest patriots. When he learned that the British were setting out to attack the colonists on Breed's Hill, he started out at once across Charlestown Neck, amid showers of British balls; and, on reaching the redoubt, offered himself as a volunteer.

The poet makes him say to the colonists as the British draw near:

"Stand! the ground's your own my braves!
Will ye give it up to slaves?
Will ye look for greener graves?
    Hope ye mercy still?
What's the mercy despots feel?
Hear it in that battle-peal!
Read it on yon bristling steel!
    Ask it—ye who will.

"In the God of battles trust!
Die we may—and die we must;
But, oh, where can dust to dust
    Be consigned so well,
As where heaven its dews shall shed,
On the martyred patriot's bed,
And the rocks shall raise their head.
    Of his deeds to tell!"

Throughout the battle, Warren was in the thickest of the fight; and at the end, when the British had gained the redoubt, he was one of the last to give up the struggle. He was rallying the few remaining colonists, when a British officer who knew him, and knew what a power he was among his countrymen, singled him out and shot him.

When General Gage heard that Warren was dead, he said, "It is well; that one man was equal to five hundred ordinary soldiers."

He had been an honorable citizen, a skilled physician, a noble senator, and a brave warrior. The loss of no one man, in the whole war was mourned more, perhaps, than the loss of this hero, General Warren.

THE MARCH TO QUEBEC

In 1775, the Americans began looking long-ingly towards Canada. Ever since the success at Ticonderoga, Ethan Allen and Benedict Arnold had been saying, "Send us to Montreal and Quebec! Let us take them as we took Crown Point and Ticonderoga!"

Washington knew what a grand thing it would be for the American army to get possession of these cities; but he also knew something which very few beside himself knew; and that was, that the American army had not enough powder to carry on their work, where they were, much longer unless help came. For this reason he held back some time. Many officers and soldiers heaped abuse upon Washington's head for this, and nearly accused him of being cowardly. He endured their blame however, for he dared not let it be known how low the powder supply was growing.

Finally, in the early fall two armies were ordered into Canada. One under General Montgomery, the other under Benedict Arnold. General Montgomery led his division up through New York and down the St. Lawrence to Montreal, while Benedict Arnold led his division up through Maine.

Montgomery's soldiers were a wretched looking set—ragged and dirty, shoeless and hatless,—but still willing to march on and fight for their loved country. On reaching Montreal they found that the British soldiers had been all called into the colonies, and that the city was therefore without defence. Of course the city was taken with little or no trouble, and in the army marched. It is a terrible thing to ransack a city as this army ransacked Montreal, but as long as wars go on these things must be done; and since it has to be done here, we cannot but be glad that it was our own brave men who fell upon the riches of this city. Such treasures as they did find! not so much money, but food and clothing! Blankets and warm shirts, jackets and trousers, stockings and shoes!

They thought it almost worth while to have marched all this distance just to be once more warmed and clothed and fed. They remembered, too, the other soldiers who were coming up through Maine, and would soon be with them, and they carried off enough of all these good things for them, as well.

Montgomery, leaving a part of his soldiers to hold Montreal, now marched on to Quebec, where Arnold was to join forces with him.

When Arnold came, he had a terrible story to tell. Their march up through Maine had been almost as terrible as the "Winter at Valley Forge," of which you will read later on. The army had come up the Kennebec River in boats, and when they had come to places where they could not push along their boats, they had carried them on their backs until open places again were found.

It had been so bitterly cold! they had marched waist deep through icy water, and had lain down in their wet clothing night after night in the freezing forests. Their clothes ragged enough when they set out, could now hardly be kept together; their shoes, in this five-hundred-mile march, had been worn to nothing, and many a soldier had frozen his feet. Their provisions, too, had given out, and many of the soldiers had eaten the leather of their shoes and knapsacks, so hungry were they.

Many of these poor men, overcome by starvation and sickness, had turned back discouraged. Some of them afterwards succeeded in getting back to Massachusetts, but more died lost in the forests.

Arnold had with him a brave young man named Aaron Burr, who acted the part of a hero in this terrible march, and in the attack that followed. When Montreal was reached, Burr started on another hundred miles to tell Montgomery that Arnold's forces were ready to join him in the attack on Quebec.

It was now December—the last day of the year. A severe snowstorm was raging—a real blizzard, we should call it now—and in the very midst of it, the command came for the attack upon Quebec.

Now there were very few soldiers in the city, and it would have been a very easy thing to take this city—as easy as it had been to take Montreal—only that this city was a "walled city," and more than that, it was situated high up on bluffs or cliffs overlooking the river. You can see how hard it was for the army outside to get up to this city, and how easy it was for the army within the city to sweep them down with their fire.

A terrible, almost hand to hand battle followed. One battery had been taken by the Americans, and they were just attacking the second.

QUEBEC

"Follow me, my brave boys," called Montgomery, "and Quebec is ours!"—but just then, down came a volley of grape shot from the garrison above, striking dead this brave leader and mowing down the soldiers on every side of him. Dismayed at the loss of their leader, the men in the rear turned and fled— and Quebec was lost to our side.

When young Aaron Burr, who was standing beside Montgomery in the foremost ranks, saw his leader wounded, he caught up the falling body, and, staggering under the load, dragged it down the bluffs beyond the reach of the fire of the enemy.

Arnold remained for some time in Canada, hoping to find a chance to attack the city again; but the soldiers in the city were on the watch, and before very long British soldiers arrived to help them; then there seemed nothing for him to do but to march home with the broken army, and so leave Canada to the British.

WASHINGTON AND HIS ARMY

Now that the war had really begun, events followed upon each other thick and fast. Before the summer was over, every colony, from New Hampshire to Georgia, was up in arms.

Washington had gathered his army outside of Boston, and there he held General Gage imprisoned in the city. Washington had now several good generals to help him, one of whom, called "Old Put," was famed far and wide for his pluck. In another chapter you will read about Old Put's wolf hunt—a story you must know; for although it is not exactly a story of the Revolution, still it does no harm to know any story of the heroes of the Revolution that tells of the daring courage of these men.

But we were speaking of Washington's army. In a "History of Our Country," written by Abby Sage Richardson, is the following excellent description of the appearance of the Colonial army.

"You can form no idea what a task lay before Washington and his generals. Here was a great body of men hurried into the field from farms and workshops, with no more idea of military drill than a herd of sheep, with miserable old muskets, scanty supply of powder and balls, and no money to buy any. Then the dress of this provincial army was enough to excite the laugh which the British soldiers raised at them. Some of them were dressed in the long-tailed linsey-woolsey coats, and linsey-woolsey breeches, which had been spun and woven in farm-house kitchens; some wore smock frocks like a butcher, also made of homespun; some wore suits of British broadcloth, so long used for Sunday clothes that they had grown rather the worse for wear; and every variety of dress and fashion figured in these motley ranks.

"When General Washington rode grandly out on horseback, dressed in his fine blue broadcloth coat, with buff colored facings, buff waistcoat and breeches, a hat with black cockade, and a sword in an elegantly embroidered sword-belt, I think his heart must have sunk within him as he looked on his tatter-demalion army, and then glanced over towards Boston, and thought of the British soldiers, gorgeous in their elegant new uniforms, trained to march up to the cannon's mouth like a solid wall in motion."

BRITISH SOLDIERS

But for all that Washington knew that his army was brave, and in dead earnest, for were they not fighting for their own homes, their own mothers and wives and children?

Two brothers in Washington's army, to show what skilful marksmen they were, took a board only five inches wide and seven inches long, fastened a piece of white paper the size of a dollar upon it in the middle, and then shot at it at a distance of sixty yards.

Eight bullets they fired; and every one of them went straight through the white paper. When the lookers on wondered at them, they said, "There are fifty more men in our company who can do just as well." They then offered to shoot apples off each other's heads, as William Tell is said to have done long, long ago; but their commander said they had shown their comrades that they could, beyond a doubt, send a bullet straight through the heart of a British soldier, and that now they had better save their powder till a British soldier appeared.

And so you see, that, although these men were so oddly dressed, and although they knew so little of military training, yet they had clear heads and straight eyes, and, above all, dauntless courage.

THE RED-COATS LEAVE BOSTON

ALL this time, you remember, Washington's army had kept the British imprisoned in the city. They had been unable to get out into the country for provisions, and now they were in real danger of starvation. They were short of fuel too. They had already chopped down several wooden houses, and had even been mean enough to chop down the "Old North Church" for firewood. These cowardly soldiers knew that these simple-hearted Puritans loved their meeting-houses as they loved their homes; and so they took great delight in showing all the contempt they could for these places. They liked nothing better than to break the glass and shoot into the windows as they passed along. The old South Church, which the Boston children know, and which still stands on Washington Street, was turned into a riding school. The pews were

OLD SOUTH CHURCH

torn out, and the floor strewed with litter for the horses. One of the pews in this church, a very beautifully carved pew, they carried away to build a fence for a pig-pen. I could not begin to tell you of the needlessly cruel and insulting things these red-coats did to annoy the people of Boston.

Faneuil Hall, now called "the cradle of Liberty," because throughout the history of Boston, so many liberty meetings of all sorts have been held there, was made into a theatre: and there the British army used to delight to meet and listen to plays and songs which were sure to be full of jokes on the American colonists.

At one time the British were acting a play which they had named the "Blockade of Boston." In this play was an actor intended to represent George Washington. He was dressed in some ridiculous manner, wore a funny looking wig, and carried a rusty old sword.

Just as this character was coming upon the stage, another clownish looking figure with another big rusty sword by his side, an officer rushed upon the stage crying, "The Yankees are attacking our works on Bunker Hill!"

UNDER THIS TREE WASHINGTON FIRST TOOK
COMMAND OF THE AMERICAN ARMY, JULY 3RD,
1775

At first the people thought it was part of the
play; but when General Howe ordered, "Officers to your posts!" they began to realize that
the play had indeed come to a sudden end. I
fancy the hall was cleared quickly, indeed;

and it was not many days before the British troop found that Washington's sword was not so rusty as they had thought; at any rate it was able to flash an idea into the British general's eye which made him think it worth while, not many days later, to take himself and his troops out of the town.

At last the provisions had run so low it seemed to General Howe, who was then in command, that the best thing to do was to leave the city while there was a chance. Then, too, Washington had begun to fortify Dorchester Heights; and General Howe feared that soon his escape would be cut off. And so, after stealing all the blankets and woolen and linen in the city, after spiking their cannon and throwing it into the harbor—doing, in short, all the mischief they could, they marched away from the city of Boston. And even as they marched out, they scattered all about the entrance to the city little irons, with sharp points sticking out in all directions. These irons were called "crow's feet," and they scattered them about that the colonists, when they entered the city, might tread upon them and so disable their feet.

The people of Boston had been shut in all this time with the British and the disloyal Tories; and you can imagine how glad they were when they saw Washington marching in at the head of his army.

DECLARATION OF INDEPENDENCE

SIGNING THE DECLARATION OF INDEPENDENCE

At the beginning of the war the colonists had not expected to be free from British rule: indeed they did not wish to be. All they did ask was that they might be treated fairly. But since they had begun to fight, they grew more and more convinced that now nothing less than perfect independence of the mother-country ought to satisfy them.

Then the leading men of the colonies met together at Philadelphia to draw up a writing, in which they declared themselves no longer subject to English rule. Five men, Thomas Jefferson, Benjamin Franklin, John Adams, Roger Sherman and Robert Livingstone, were appointed to write it out; and when this was done every man in the Congress signed it.

It had been agreed that as soon as the Declaration was adopted the old bell-man should ring the big "Liberty-bell" that hung in the tower of the old State House, in order that the great throng of people outside might know it. This, as I suppose you all know, happened July 4, 1776.

The old bell-man had taken his place up in the tower, and had told his little grandson to tell him when the time came to ring the bell.

Messengers were sent in every direction to tell the news in every village and town; the boys lit fires, the cannons blazed, and everywhere the people—men, women, and children, tried in every way to show their joy that they were now all to stand shoulder to shoulder, *a free nation*.

NAMES OF PERSONS WHO SIGNED THE
DECLARATION OF INDEPENDENCE. COPY OF
THEIR SIGNATURES—CAN YOU READ THEM?

Ask your teacher to let you learn this poem about the bell ringing of that day, to read in concert; and if you are one-half as patriotic as the boys and girls then were, I'm sure you'll read it in such a way that the teacher will think "Independence day has come again."

There was tumult in the city,
In the quaint old Quaker town,
And the streets were rife with people,
Pacing restless up and down;—
People gathering at corners,
Where they whispered each to each,
And the sweat stood on their temples,
With the earnestness of speech.

"Will they do it?" "Dare they do it?"
"Who is speaking?" "What's the news?"
"What of Adams?" "What of Sherman?"
"Oh, God grant they won't refuse!"
"Make some way there!" "Let me nearer!"
"I am stifling!" "Stifle then!
When a nation's life's at hazard,
We've no time to think of men!"

So they beat against the portal,
Man and woman, maid and child;
And the July sun in heaven
On the scene looked down and smiled,
The same sun that saw the Spartan
Shed his patriot blood in vain,
Now beheld the soul of freedom
All unconquer'd rise again.

See! See! The dense crowd quivers
Through all its lengthy line,
As the boy beside the portal
Looks forth to give the sign!
With his small hands upward lifted,
Breezes dallying with his hair,
Hark! With deep, clear intonation,
Breaks his young voice on the air.

DECLARATION OF INDEPENDENCE

Hushed the people's swelling murmur,
List, the boy's exultant cry!
"Ring!" he shouts, "Ring, Grandpa,
Ring, O, ring for Liberty!"
And straightway at the signal,
The old bellman lifts his hand,
And sends the good news, making
Iron music through the land.

How they shouted! What rejoicing!
How the old bell shook the air,
Till the clang of freedom ruffled
The calm, gliding Delaware!
How the bonfires and the torches
Illumed the night's repose,
And from the flames like fabled Phoenix,
Our glorious Liberty arose!

That old bell now is silent,
And hushed its iron tongue,
But the spirit it awakened,
Still lives—forever young.
And when we greet the smiling sunlight,
On the fourth of each July,
We'll ne'er forget the bellman,
Who, betwixt the earth and sky,
Rang out OUR INDEPENDENCE,
Which, please God, shall never die!

THE HISTORY OF OUR FLAG

THE old British flag which had once been so dear to the colonists, and which they now so hated, was pulled down from every place, and the new American flag hoisted in its place. For the colonists had long ago learned that no peace with England was possible. They had once offered a petition to the king, in which they had asked that peace might be restored on certain conditions. This petition, the king would not even hear read; and so the colonists had long known that their only hope lay in face-to-face battle with the English troops.

And now that they had declared their independence of England, surely they would no longer bear an English flag.

At the beginning of the war, there had been in use a variety of flags. One of the very first was the "Pine Tree" flag. This was used first in the Massachusetts colony. It had a white

ground, a tree in the middle, and the motto, "Appeal to Heaven." Next, a flag was made having upon it thirteen stripes of red and white to represent the thirteen colonies. It had, however, the British "Union-Jack," as it was called, in the corner. But when the Declaration of Independence came, then, said the colonists, we must have a truly American flag; for now we are the American nation.

Congress voted, June 17, 1777, "that the flag of the thirteen United States be thirteen stripes, alternate red and white, and the Union be thirteen white stars in the blue field."

The first truly American flag was hoisted by Paul Jones over an American ship-of-war. This flag was made by Philadelphia women, and I am sure they must have been proud to have done their part, in the raising of the first American flag.

It was intended that, as time went on and the country grew, a new stripe should be added for each new State; but later, when the

growth of the country caused the flag to become too wide, it was decided to return to the
thirteen original stripes, and let a new star be
added for each new State, And thus it is that
our flag to-day shows thirteen stripes of red
and white, while in its blue field, where the
"Union Jack" used to stand, are—what little
boy or girl can tell me how many stars there
are on our flag to-day?

THE STAR-SPANGLED BANNER

THE STAR-SPANGLED BANNER.

1. Oh, say, can you see by the dawn's ear - ly light, What so
2. On the shore dimly seen through the mists of the deep, Where the
3. Oh, thus be it ev - er, when free-men shall stand Be -

proud - ly we hail'd at the twilight's last gleaming, Whose broad
foe's haughty host in dread si - lence re - pos - es, What is
tween their loved home and foul war's des - o - la - tion, Blest with

stripes and bright stars thro' the per - il - ous fight, O'er the
that which the breeze o'er the tow - er - ing steep, As it
vic - t'ry and peace may the heav'n-res - cued land Praise the

ram - parts we watch'd, were so gal - lant - ly streaming? And the
fit - ful - ly blows, half con-ceals, half dis - clos - es?—Now it
power that hath made and preserved us a na - tion, Then

THE STAR-SPANGLED BANNER.

OUR FLAG IS THERE

OUR FLAG IS THERE.

This song was written by an officer of the American Navy during the war of 1812.

1. Our flag is there! Our flag is there! We'll hail it with three
2. That flag withstood the bat-tle's roar, With foemen stout, with

loud huzzahs! Our flag is there! Our flag is there! Be -
foemen brave; Strong hands have sought that flag to low'r, And

hold the glorious stripes and stars! Stout hearts have fought for
found a speed-y wa - 'try grave! That flag is known on

that bright flag, Strong hands sustained it mast head high, And
ev - 'ry shore, The stan-dard of a gal-lant band, A -

Oh! to see how proud it waves, Brings tears of joy in ev - 'ry eye.
like unstain'd in peace or war, It floats o'er freedom's happy land.

A PETTY TYRANT

In the early days of the Revolution, there was a British officer, General Prescott, stationed at Newport. Although his name was the same, he was a very different man from the one we heard of at Bunker Hill. He was a mean sort of a man, and seemed to think that frightening children, and threatening women, were quite brave things to do.

He demanded that every man who met him should take off his hat to him as he passed. As the people of Newport were entirely at his mercy, many of them obeyed him.

One day, a good old Quaker came along. "Take off that hat," shouted Prescott.

"I take off my hat to no man," said the Quaker.

"Knock off that old fool's hat," said Prescott to one of his companions. And threatening and swearing, Prescott passed on, resolved to get his revenge in some way on the Quaker.

He could think of nothing that would grieve the old man more than to take away from him a pair of horses of which he was very fond. Beautiful black horses they were, as gentle and loving with the old Quaker as kittens.

The very next morning Prescott sent a detachment of soldiers to take these horses. Of course there was nothing to do but to give them up. Whatever the cruel General did with them was never known, but that afternoon the good old Quaker found one lying by the roadside, dying. The old man knelt down beside him, took his head into his lap, sobbing like a child over his four-footed friend. The poor horse tried to lift his head to look into his old master's face, and, with one great shudder, dropped back dead.

At another time, this Prescott wanted a sidewalk in front of his house; and so, instead of going to work to collect the stones honestly and build his sidewalk, he ordered his men to take up the doorsteps of the houses in the neighborhood and build one for him.

The people of Newport declared they would endure him no longer; and so one night, Colonel Barton, one of the patriots of Newport, planned to surprise the General and take him prisoner. Prescott was then staying at the house of a Quaker a little outside of the town.

Quietly they crept up to the house and entered. "Where is Prescott's room?" said Barton to the Quaker. The Quaker pointed directly overhead, and up the stairs they dashed, a little negro boy Jack, who hated the General well, leading the way. Bang went the tough little woolley head of Jack against the door of the chamber and open it flew.

Prescott sprang up in bed as they entered; but there was no chance for escape. His aid in another room, hearing the noise, jumped out of the window to give the alarm, but was instantly captured by the men below. Barton ordered the General to rise, and go with them. He begged for time to dress. But delay was dangerous. Throwing a cloak about him, they took him in his shirt, telling him that on the other side of the bay he would have time to dress at his leisure. The rest of the party who had remained on guard outside, formed around the prisoners; and as stealthily as they came they made their way back to the boats. Once again with muffled oars they passed by the frigates, the men chuckling to themselves as they heard the sentry's cry of 'All's well!' and thinking how angry they would be when, a little later, they learned that all was ill."

He was carried to Washington's camp and made a prisoner. It is said that while on the way to Washington, he was so rude to the wife of a Connecticut innkeeper that her husband gave him a sound horse-whipping.

THE LEADEN STATUE

There had been so much resistance to the Stamp Act before the Revolution that England repealed it not long after. The colonists were overjoyed at the news, because they thought it meant that the English King had decided to deal fairly with the colonists in the future. The Sons of Liberty in New York City, in an excess of joy, cast a leaden statue of the King, and set it up in the Bowling Green.

Hardly was it in place when news came that the English government had passed another law, more unjust if possible than the Stamp Act; and that they were going to send troops over to take possession of the harbors of the principal cities. And when, in the following spring, troops stationed themselves on Staten Island, the fury of these Sons of Liberty knew no bounds.

Then, when, at last, came the Declaration of Independence, read to them by Washington himself, they thronged through the streets shouting "Liberty! Liberty!"

"Down with the statue of England's King," cried one; and in an instant the air rang with the cries of "Down with the statue! Down with the King!"

Rushing to the Green, they tore it down; and, whooping and dancing like wild Indians, they hacked it in pieces.

"Give us the lead," cried a Daughter of Liberty, "and we women will make it into bullets to shoot these British tyrants."

"Yes! yes!" cried the mob; "give the lead to the Daughters of Liberty."

And so the Daughters of Liberty, without so much noise perhaps, but with just as much patriotism, went to work making the lead up into bullets. It is said that the names of the women who made the largest number were placed on record. Report says that Mrs. Marvin made 6058; Laura Marvin 8370; Mary Marvin 10,790 and Ruth Marvin 11,592.

"FREE AND EQUAL"

When the affair known as the "Boston Tea Party" occurred, Cynthia Smith was five years old. Her home was in Charleston, and she helped in many ways when her father sent all his rice to the North, as he was obliged to, because England had shut up our harbor by what is known as the "Boston Port Bill." Two years later, she saw, with aching heart, four of her brothers go to the war; and, eager to help the cause, she learned in time to spin, to weave, and to knit for the brave soldiers. The only pleasure she had was with a pretty red and white calf that her father had given her; and when the Declaration of Independence was signed she named her pet "Free-'n-Equal." Through all the dreary days and months which followed, Cynthia grew more and more fond of her friend. Still she longed to go herself and fight for her country. Finally her father and one remaining brother left home to join General Gates' army. During this time, great damage was done to the Southern homes by the British soldiers. Cynthia was ready to protect her home and mother, come what might. But one day, on returning home from an errand, she was dismayed to find that the British soldiers had carried off "Free-'n-Equal." It did not take long, however, for Cynthia to decide what she would do. Off she started at once for the headquarters of Lord Cornwallis. Hurrying over three miles of hot, dusty road, she gained entrance to the great General's room. A feast was being held just then; but once in his presence, it would not do to give up; so, summoning all her courage, she told him that his soldiers had stolen her cow, and that she had come to take her back again. Lord Cornwallis was much attracted towards the "sturdy little rebel" as he called her, and promised to have "Free-'n-Equal" re-turned to her at once. Before the little girl went back home with her pet, the General patted her on her head, told her she was a brave little woman, and gave her a pair of silver knee-buckles. These buckles are still in the hands of the descendants of Cynthia

Smith, and they are, and justly too, very proud of them and of their grandmother, once the little Cynthia.

AN ANECDOTE OF WASHINGTON

During the Revolution, George Washington was one day riding by a group of soldiers who did not know him. They were busily engaged in raising a beam to the top of some military works. It was a difficult task, and often the corporal's voice could be heard shouting, "*Now* you have it!" "All ready! *Pull!*" Washington quietly asked the corporal why he didn't turn to and help them. "Sir," angrily replied the corporal, "do you realize that *I* am the *corporal?*" Washington politely raised his hat, saying, "I did *not* realize it. Beg pardon Mr. Corporal; then dismounting, he himself fell to work and helped the men till the beam was raised. Before leaving he turned to the corporal, and wiping the perspiration from his face, said, "If ever you need assistance like this again, call upon Washington, your commander-in-chief, and I will come." The confused corporal turned red, then white, as he realized that this was Washington himself to whom he had been so pompous; and we hope he learned a lesson of true greatness.

LYDIA DARRAH SAVES GEN. WASHINGTON

At one time, General Washington was very near being attacked by the British army, and his army would very likely have been totally destroyed had not a brave Quaker woman, Lydia Darrah, risked her life to warn him of his danger.

One night, one of the British officers who was stationed in her house, ordered her to see that her family were abed and asleep at a certain hour, and to admit General Howe very quietly, show him to the officer's apartment, and be ready to let him out just as quietly, when he should be ready to go.

Lydia was suspicious. She felt that some treachery was on foot. So when General Howe was safely in his officer's apartment, she took off her shoes, crept softly up-stairs, and listened at the keyhole. There she heard them plan to surprise Washington, and take him and his whole army. When she had heard enough she went trembling to bed, and was apparently so sound asleep that the officer had to knock again and again when he came to rouse her to let General Howe out of the house.

Next day good Mrs. Darrah got a pass from General Howe to go to mill and get some flour ground, outside the lines of the army in Philadelphia. Off she walked with a bag of wheat in her arms, to the outposts of the patriot army, twenty-five miles away. Meeting an officer there, she told her story, and begged the Americans to put Washington at once on his guard. When Howe's forces marched toward White Marsh with the greatest secrecy, they found such excellent preparations to receive them, that they turned round and marched back again, without striking a blow.

The officer questioned Mrs. Darrah. "Were any of your family awake the night General Howe was here?" "Not a soul," she answered. "Then the walls of this house must have heard our plans," he said, "for some one reported them to the rebel Washington. When we got to White Marsh, he was all ready for us, and we had the pleasure of marching back like a parcel of fools."

WASHINGTON'S CHRISTMAS SURPRISE

School in concert.

All hail, thou blessed Christmas time,
When joy-bells ring their merry chime!
The time of gifts and sweet surprise,
Of smiling lips and beaming eyes.

(Pupil enters and recites the following:)

Not enough of Christmas joys
Without a Christmas story, boys?
Methinks I've just the one for you,
And what is better still, 'tis true.

Then lend your ears and bright young eyes
While I recount that grand surprise
Of Washington's long years ago,
Amid the Winter's cold and snow.

'Twas in our country's stern old fight
For Independence and the right.
Within your minds the date well fix
'Twas Christmas night of seventy-six.
Our army, footsore, weary, sad,

In numbers few, ill-fed, ill-clad,
And fearing much the English foe,
Were spending days in want and woe.

The Hessian camp was all aglow,
And freely there the red wines flow;
Their caution on this Christmas night
In revellings had taken flight.

To Washington was known the way,
The Germans oft spent Christmas day,
And so, while they were free from cares,
He planned to take them unawares.

The Delaware between them rolled,
The night was stormy, dark, and cold,
The floating ice blocked up their way,
But on they pressed, and morning gray

Beheld them on the Trenton side
Hard-spent but filled with honest pride;
Then on the Hessian camp they fall,
A thousand prisoners take in all.

With booty, prisoners and all,
They follow at their leader's call;
Again they cross the river wide,
And reach the Pennsylvania side.

Voice

A brilliant act! A brilliant thought!
And one with mighty issues fraught!
And unto Washington so wise,
We're debtors for that grand surprise.

Voice

A record of that daring deed,
Just in his country's hour of need,
Will ever live in song and fame,
While lives the hero's honored name,
And memory keeps, in pictures rare,
That "Crossing on the Delaware."

All

When Christmas fires send out their glow
Across the pure, untrodden snow,
Let thought go back to that far time,
When rang the bells no merry chime;
But one brave heart, 'neath wintry skies,
Planned out this Christmas-day surprise.

—M. LIZZIE STANLEY.

WASHINGTON CROSSING THE DELAWARE

WASHINGTON'S CHRISTMAS GIFT TO THE AMERICAN ARMY

Washington's army had for some time had nothing but defeat. This, of course, was very encouraging to the British side. There were only about three thousand men with him, and these were suffering from cold and hunger.

Washington felt that a bold stroke must be made, and that too very soon. He knew that there were encamped just across the Delaware, a body of Hessian troops, who had been hired and sent over here by the English government to fight against the colonists.

Washington knew the ways of these Hessians; and he was quite sure that they would spend Christmas day (1776) in a great celebration, and very likely would be "off guard" in the evening.

It was a terrible night. The sleet and rain were pouring down; it was bitterly cold, and the river so full of broken ice that, in the inky darkness, it seemed almost impossible to get across. But Washington was brave, his soldiers believed in him, and so they struggled on.

It was four o'clock in the morning when the last boat-load of men reached the Trenton shore. They crept silently along the bank to where the Hessians lay, tired out with Christmas revelry, and thus burst suddenly upon their unsuspecting enemy. It was a glorious victory. Hessians were captured almost before they could rub their eyes open. Washington lost hardly ten men in all and captured almost one thousand Hessians, besides cannon, guns, and ammunition. The Hessians were sent off for winter-quarters into central Pennsylvania, where they found many German settlers, who treated them kindly and spoke their own language. They had a very comfortable time there, and always spoke of Washington as "a very good rebel." And so ended with a success at last the year of 1776, which had for some months looked so dark and dismal to the American Army.

VALLEY FORGE

All through the winter of 1777 and '78 the British and the American armies lay only twenty miles apart. The redcoats with their commander, General Howe, were quartered in Philadelphia. There they were entertained by the Tories who gave parties, and balls and dinners, and did all in their power to make the winter a pleasant one for these British soldiers.

Twenty miles away, in a rocky, desolate, mountain gorge known as Valley Forge, Washington had led his army from White Marsh. When he went there in bitter December weather, his men, shoeless and almost naked, had marked their way with blood from their bare feet. They reached the valley, and for want of tents were obliged to cut down trees and build huts of logs for shelter from the cold. Congress had no money to pay the men, no money to buy them food. For days and days together, during this winter, they had no bread and lived upon salt pork alone. They sickened with hunger and cold, and there was no money to buy medicines, no comfortable hospitals where they could be nursed. They were ragged and without shoes.

It was a terrible winter for them all. Washington's brave heart ached, and sometimes was very heavy as he saw his men starving, and freezing, and dying. It seemed almost as if the cause of the colonists must be given up. But you have heard the saying that "it is always darkest just before day." And so it proved just now; for in the spring word came from France that aid was to be sent them from that country. When the British heard this, they would have been very glad to make peace with the colonists. Indeed, messengers were sent over from England with very liberal offers—offers which, before the war, the colonists would have accepted; but that time was past now. Then these messengers tried to bribe some of the officers in the patriot army. One man, General Reed of Pennsylvania, was offered ten thousand guineas and distinguished honors if he would exert his influence to effect a reconciliation. "I am not worth purchasing," said the honest patriot, "but such as I am, the king of Great Britain is not rich enough to buy me."

EMILY GEIGER

'Twas in days of the Revolution,—
    Dark days were they and drear,—
And by Carolina firesides
    The women sat in fear;
For the men were away at the fighting,
    And sad was the news that came,
That the battle was lost; and the death-list
    Held many a loved one's name.

When as heart-sore they sat round the camp-fires
    "What ho! Who'll volunteer
To carry a message to Sumter?"
    A voice rang loud and clear.
There was a sudden silence,
    But not a man replied;
They knew too well of the peril
    Of one who dared that ride.

Outspoke then Emily Geiger,
    With a rich flush on her cheek,—
"Give me the message to be sent;
    I am the one you seek.
For I am a Southern woman;
    And I'd rather do and dare
Than sit by a lonely fireside,
    My heart gnawed through with care."

They gave her the precious missive;
*   And on her own good steed*
She rode away, 'mid the cheers of the men,
*   Upon her daring deed.*
And away through the lonely forests,
*   Steadily galloping on,*
She saw the sun sink low in the sky,
*   And in the west go down.*

"Halt!—or I fire!" On a sudden
*   A rifle clicked close by.*
"Let you pass? Not we, till we know you are
*   No messenger nor spy."*
"She's a Whig,—from her face—I will wager,"
*   Swore the officer of the day.*
"To the guard-house, and send for a woman
*   To search her without delay."*

No time did she lose in bewailing;
*   As the bolt creaked in the lock,*
She quickly drew the precious note
*   That was hidden in her frock.*
And she read it through with hurried care,
*   Then ate it, piece by piece,*
And calmly set her down to wait
*   Till time should bring release.*

They brought her out in a little,
*   And set her on her steed,*
With many a rude apology,
*   For their discourteous deed.*
On, on, once more through the forest black,
*   The good horse panting strains,*
Till the sentry's challenge, "Who comes there?"
*   Tells that the end she gains.*

Ere an hour, in the camp of Sumter
*   There was hurrying to and fro.*
"Saddle and mount, saddle and mount!"
*   The bugles shrilly blow.*
"Forward trot!" and the long ranks wheel,
*   And into the darkness glide:*
Long shall the British rue that march
*   And Emily Geiger's ride.*

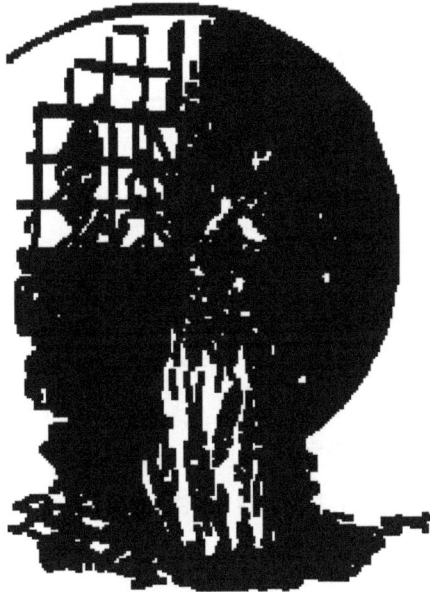

MASSACRE OF WYOMING

One of the saddest events of this sad year, 1778, was the massacre of Wyoming.

Wyoming was a quiet little village in the Wyoming valley along the Susquehanna river. These Wyoming settlers were very loyal people;—hardly a family among them but had sent a dear father or son to the army. All around them were the Tories, who looked upon this peaceful little village with fierce hate.

One summer evening, these Tories got together six hundred Indians, and with howls and yells, shouts and war-whoops, all swept down upon the little village.

The women and children, frightened, hurried within the walls of "Fort Forty," the only stronghold they owned.

One hardly dares think how much more terrible still this might have been had not one

Zebulon Butler, a brave young soldier, chanced to be home on a furlough.

He quickly mustered all the old men and boys into a little army. Then, finding their only hope lay in rushing forth to meet their foe in open field, they left the fort and went bravely out, led by their brave leader.

It was a brief, deadly encounter. The foe, five times their number, broke savagely upon them. When at last the little band gave way, the Indians and the Tories, one hardly less blood-thirsty than the other, pursued them with unrelenting fury.

There is no more brutal picture in all history than this massacre of the peaceful, loyal people of Wyoming. A description of it, even, is too horrible for children's ears. So we will ask you to read Campbell's poem of "Gertrude of Wyoming." It is a famous poem, one you will often come across, by and by, in your school-life; and it is well you should remember what it has to do with the early history of your own people.

MONUMENT ERECTED AT WYOMING

THE SURRENDER OF BURGOYNE

In this war of the Revolution you will always hear a great deal about *the surrender of Burgoyne* and *the surrender of Cornwallis.* These two British generals were at the head of large armies, and had arranged most extensive plans for series of battles, which, had they been successful, would have ruined completely the American army; and instead of the grand history of independence, of progress and of growth which we now have, there would have been I fear, a very sad ending for the Revolution, and a history sadder still of the years that followed.

This General Burgoyne had been sent over from England with an army of "picked men," great stores of firearms, and some of the finest brass cannon that had ever at that time been made.

I fancy the colonists would have been much more afraid of this general and his soldiers, had Burgoyne not done something, as soon as he reached this country, which was so ridiculous that it made the American officers and soldiers roar with laughter when they heard of it.

You see General Burgoyne was a very pompous sort of a man, much given to strutting and bragging. While he was in England, he had written two or three comic plays for the theatre; and had, I suspect, quite a high opinion of his own composition; for as soon as ever he had settled him- self here in America, he wrote out a long, long proclamation, in which he talked to the colonists much as a big bully of a boy might talk to a very little boy.

He promised a great many things to the Americans if they would lay down their arms and surrender at once; but if they did not, there was no end to the awful things he threatened to do;—he would destroy their cities, he would cut their throats, he would let the Indians loose upon them, indeed, he would, judging from his threats, hardly leave the earth for them to walk upon. Now, the colonists believed that the stillest waters run deepest; and so, although Burgoyne was indeed a great general, and had a powerful army, the colonists were sharp enough to see that there was a great deal of wind and bluster about this Englishman after all. Then, too, he wound up this proclamation of his by signing his name with ten or fifteen big sounding titles, expecting that the colonists would surely look with great reverence upon these. But the patriots had now outgrown any reverence they might once have had for English titles, and the newspapers all over the country made all sorts of fun of this proclamation. And said it was a bigger comedy than those he had written in England.

Burgoyne's plan was to come down from Canada into New York State, get possession of the Hudson River, and so hem in the colonies of New Hampshire, Vermont, Massachusetts, Connecticut and Rhode Island, that they would be compelled to surrender.

As you already know, Burgoyne failed in his plan in the end; but it was a terrible campaign for the patriots for all that. For Burgoyne engaged the Indians on his side; and wherever the Indians fought, you know there was scalping, and burning, and murder on every side.

At one time, when General Herkimer was on his way with a company of about eight hundred patriots to help defend a poorly garrisoned fort, a party of these Indians, aided by some cowardly Tories fell upon them and butchered them most savagely. Brave old General Herkimer fought like a tiger. When he had been shot in both legs, and could no longer stand, he sat down upon a stump, still cheering his men on, while with a rifle, he fired at the enemy as long as he could pull the trigger.

At another time, General Burgoyne sent a detachment of his men to attack the colonial army at Bennington. General Stark had just arrived there with an army from the New Hampshire militia. Now, General Stark's wife, Molly, was a patriotic woman, and was well known and highly respected in her husband's army. And so, when the British appeared, General Stark said, "Boys, the British are coming; there's a hard battle ahead; beat them we must, or to-morrow morning Molly Stark will be a widow."

It was indeed a close fight; but success attended the army of the general whose wife's name he had made the watchword.

SARATOGA

There was another terrible battle this time at Saratoga, in which General Gates succeeded in so breaking up Burgoyne's army that this proud British general was obliged to surrender.

Both generals had fought bravely and skilfully; and although they were enemies in battle, they respected each other as men; and when, after the surrender, Burgoyne gave up his sword to Gates, he did so very courteously, saying, "The fortunes of war, General Gates, have made me your prisoner."

General Gates, taking the sword, said with equal politeness, "I shall always be glad to testify, General Burgoyne, that it was through no fault of yours that it happened so."

I am afraid the newspapers again printed many jokes about the defeated Burgoyne, as they recalled the extravagant threats he had made at the beginning of his campaign.

His people, too, in England blamed him severely, which I think was rather unjust; for, in spite of all, he was a brave and skilful soldier; the only trouble was that he was on the wrong side of the truth, and the wrong side seldom succeeds in any battle.

THE HALF-WITTED TORY BOY

At the very beginning Burgoyne was upset in his plans by a half-witted boy. To be sure, this was no credit to the boy, nor was it any discredit to Burgoyne; still, in the later days of the war, when Burgoyne had been conquered by the Americans, and had been made to surrender, the colonists liked now and then to recall this little story as a joke.

St. Leger had been sent by Burgoyne to take a certain fort. Knowing this, Arnold was sent by the American general to hold the same fort against the attack. How the battle might have ended had Arnold and St. Leger met, we cannot tell, but, as the story goes, this is the way Arnold won the fort. He had with him as a prisoner a half-witted boy. He had been taken from some Tory family very likely; for he would not or could not understand that he was in the hands of the Whigs, and so would keep saying over and over in his foolish way, "I Tory! I Tory!"

As the little fellow was homesick and miserable, Arnold was struck with the idea that perhaps he could make some use of him by offering him his freedom. So calling him to him he said, "My young lad, would you like to go home?"

The poor little fellow jumped about and uttered some strange sounds that meant to express his joy at the thought.

Then Arnold explained to him that if he would go to the camp of St. Leger and tell him that a grea-a-at b-i-ig army of Americans was coming to attack him, he should be given his liberty.

The boy understood, and away he went. He cut his clothes full of round holes to represent bullet holes, and rushed breathless into St. Leger's camp.

"What is it, boy? Where are you from? Who are you?" asked the British officers, frightened at his appearance.

I cannot tell you how he did it; but he managed to make St. Leger believe that a terrible army was bearing down upon him and that he had better escape while he could. When St.

Leger asked him how many there were, he pointed to the leaves of the trees, as if to say no one could count them. The result was that St. Leger and his men took to flight, not even taking time to take down their tents or pack their supplies.

They say, "All things are fair in war"—if so, I suppose this must have been fair. How does it seem to you little boys and little girls? You will have to talk this over with your teacher, I think.

GENERAL FRANCIS MARION

THE FOX OF THE SOUTHERN SWAMP

There was one brave patriot working away in the swampy country in South Carolina. This man was General Marion; and so wise was he, and so brave, and succeeded in stealing such marches upon the enemies in this southern district, that he was called the "fox of the southern swamp." I shall not try to tell you of the successful raids he made, and the successful battles he fought, because battles all sound pretty much alike to little folks, and you might grow tired of hearing of them. If I can tell you some of the stories of those times which will help you to understand the kind of men and women these patriots were, how brave they were, and how much they were willing to suffer for the cause which seemed to them right, I know your teacher will be better satisfied than she would be to hear you repeat like parrots the names and dates of all the battles in our whole history.

This General Marion had a camp in a swamp, among the forests and tangled grasses and mosses—a place so hidden and so hard to enter, that no one cared to attempt an attack upon him. From this place Marion and his men used to march forth to battle. At one time a British officer was brought into this camp to talk with Marion about some prisoners. After they had arranged matters, Marion invited the young officer to dine with him. The officer accepted; but when he was taken to the "mess-room," and saw only a pine log for a table, on which were heaped nothing but baked potatoes, he asked in astonishment,

"Is this all you have for dinner?" "This is all," answered General Marion, "and we thought ourselves fortunate in having more potatoes than usual, when we had a visitor to dine with us."

"You must have good pay to make up for such living," said the officer.

"On the contrary," answered Marion, "I have never received a dollar, nor has one of my men."

"What on earth are you fighting for?"

"For the love of liberty," answered the hero. The story says that the young officer went back to Charleston and resigned his position in the English army, saying he would not fight against men who fought from such motives, and were willing to endure such hardships.

SONG OF MARION'S MEN

Our band is few, but true and tried, our leader frank and bold;
The British soldier trembles when Marion's name is told;
Our fortress is the good greenwood, our tent the cypress tree;
We know the forest round us, as seamen know the sea.
We know its walls of thorny vines, its glades of reedy grass,
Its safe and silent islands within the dark morass.

Woe to the English soldiery that little dread us near!
On them shall light at midnight a strange and sudden fear;
When, waking to their tents on fire, they grasp their arms in
      vain,
And they who stand to face us are beat to earth again;
And they who fly in terror deem a mighty host behind,
And hear the tramp of thousands upon the hollow wind.

Then sweet the hour that brings release from danger and from
      toil!
We talk the battle over and share the battle's spoil;
The woodland rings with laugh and shout, as if a hunt were up,
And woodland flowers were gathered to crown the soldier's
      cup.
With merry songs we mock the wind that in the pin-top
      grieves.
And slumber sound and sweetly on beds of oaken leaves.

Well knows the fair and friendly moon the band that Marion
    leads—
The glitter of their rifles, the scampering of their steeds.
'Tis life to guide the fiery barb across the moonlit plain;
'Tis life to feel the night-wind that lifts his tossing mane.
A moment in the British camp—a moment and away
Back to the pathless forest before the peep of day.

Grave men they are by broad Santee, grave men with hoary
    hairs,
Their hearts are all with Marion, for Marion are their prayers.
And lovely ladies greet our band with kindest welcoming,
With smiles like those of summer and tears like those of spring.
For them we wear these rusty arms, and lay them down no
    more,
Till we have driven the Britons forever from our shore.

—BRYANT

THE WOMEN OF SOUTH CAROLINA

The women of South Carolina were not one step behind the men in bravery and patriotic spirit.

In a certain battle at Cowpens—not a very romantic name—a certain General Tarleton was totally defeated by an American officer, Colonel Washington. General Tarleton, who was, I think, not much of a gentleman, used to seize every opportunity to sneer at Colonel William Washington whenever a certain patriotic woman, a great admirer of the brave young Washington, was present.

Now, as Tarleton bore a wound which young Washington had given him, and had, moreover, been chased like a puppy from the battlefield, one would think that Tarleton's good taste would have prevented him from saying much about it; but Tarleton had not very exquisite taste, I think.

"I should like to see this young friend of yours," said Tarleton one day to this lady; "I hear he is a very common, mean-looking man."

"If you had taken time to look *behind* you at Cowpens, General Tarleton, you would have been sure to see him," returned the lady quickly.

One would suppose, after this sharp reply, that General Tarleton would have said no more against Colonel Washington, but only a few days later, at a large dinner, at which this same lady was present, General Tarleton again said, "I understand that this young Washington is a very ignorant man. I am told that he cannot even write his name."

"Possibly he cannot," said the lady, quick-witted as before; "but," continued she, pointing to General Tarleton's wounded arm, "he can make his *mark* as you yourself can testify."

Another story is told of a South Carolina woman who had seven sons in the patriotic army. One day, a British general stopped at her house, and tried to show her how much better it would be for her sons if they would only join the British army.

"Join the British army!" cried she. "Sooner than see one of my boys turn against his own country, would *I* go, this baby in my arms, and enlist under Marion's banner, and show my sons how to fight, and, if need be, *die*, for the freedom of this land of ours."

And these brave women of South Carolina not only encouraged their husbands and sons by brave words, but often acted the part of messengers in expeditions of trust and secrecy. Two brave women, whose husbands were in the army, disguised themselves in the dress of men, and captured two British soldiers, compelled them to give up the messages they were carrying, and bore them to General Greene, whose camp was not far distant.

ISRAEL PUTNAM

This brave general was born in Salem, Massachusetts, in 1718. He was only a farmer boy and so had very little chance to learn the many things about the wide, wide world that you boys and girls are learning every day. He was a plucky little fellow though, and was the leader among the boys of his town in all sorts of things—mischief as well as other things I have no doubt.

At school he learned easily all there was to be taught him; and if he knew nothing but the "three r's," that was not his fault, for that was all little folks were taught in those days.

Do you know what people mean when they speak of the "three r's?" Perhaps I shall not tell you the story just right, but this is something like the way it is told.

Once, in a country village, a school-board was holding a meeting. One man, rather more educated than the rest, arose and said, "I think, gentlemen, we might put a few more studies into our schools. I should like to see our boys and girls studying about the flowers and the stars; I should like to have them know about the different countries and the different people of this world. I move that a committee be appointed to see what can be done about making the course of study bigger, and better, and broader for our children."

Then a hot discussion followed. One man said it was all bosh; another said there was no need of knowing about countries or people that were thousands of miles away; another said he had no money to waste on such foolishness; another said the stars and flowers wouldn't help a boy to earn his bread and butter half as much as potatoes and squashes would. At last one man arose and said, "I don't care nothing about these new fangled notions and what's more I don't want to know about 'em. You and me was brought up in the deestrick school where we learned our readin' and 'ritin' and 'rithmetic. Mr. Chairman, move that we stick to the old way. The three 'r's was good enough for me and it's good enough for my boys. Yes, sir! 'the three r's'—by that I mean readin' and 'ritin' and 'arithmetic."

Well, what has all this to do with Israel Putnam? Not much after all, perhaps. Only to give you an idea of the kind of schools there used to be in those days. It was to this sort of a school where they taught nothing but the "three r's" that Israel Putnam was sent to get his "larnin'" as his old father used to call it.

But, as I said before, he was a plucky boy, and took the lead in all sorts of sports. He could climb like a squirrel, run like a hare, leap like a frog. He could, in short, do all sorts of things that boys admire to do. He was very generous and just; but he wouldn't take an insult from any other boy if he could help himself.

One time, while yet quite a little lad, his father took him to Boston. As he stood admiring this new city, which to the little country boy looked so very, very big, another boy across the way called out, "Hello, country, ain't it about time to milk the caows?"

Quick as a flash, the hot-headed lad fell upon the rude city boy, and gave him a thrashing that lasted him for many a day.

When Israel Putnam was a young man, living on a farm in Connecticut, he was very much troubled by wolf thieving.

Morning after morning he would find the number of his sheep and lambs lessened.

His neighbors, too, often found their chickens and hens gone, and only a few scattered feathers left to tell the story.

One morning finding a lamb which was to the farmer the pride of his flock among the missing, he started forth, gun in hand.

"There is a time," said Israel to his neighbors, "when even a wolf had better be taught that the way of transgressors is hard. I propose that we leave our farm work for to-day, and give this thief a good chase."

Several of the farmers, ready, I suspect for a good time as well as anxious to catch the wolf, joined in a party; and with Israel, who was always full of dry, "cute" sayings as we Yankees call it, at their head, they started out.

They were soon upon the track, and at last, with the aid of their keen-scented dogs, found the wolf's den.

It was a deep hollow in a rock, the opening of which was so small that the farmers could only enter one by one crawling on their hands and knees.

"Now we've lost him," said one farmer.

"Let's smoke him out," said another. So they built a fire of leaves and brush just inside the cave; but no wolf appeared.

"Set the dogs upon him," said another farmer. But the dogs came skulking out yelping with pain.

"We're not going to be beaten in this way," said Putnam; "I'll go in there myself." And so, tying a rope round his legs, that the men might draw him out, he crawled slowly in, his gun in one hand, and a torch in the other.

He soon saw the eyes of the wolf glaring at him from a corner of the cave. Bang! went the gun, and half-blinded by the smoke and half deafened by the noise, Putnam was dragged out by the farmers. Reloading his gun, back he went and fired again—and again was he pulled out.

For the third time he entered, and finding the animal was dead he hauled her out by the ears, while his companions pulled him by the rope round his legs. His clothes were all torn off his back, and his face black with smoke and powder, but he had killed the wolf, and kept her skin as a trophy.

During the whole time of the Revolution, Israel Putnam was one of the foremost in every danger.

After one battle, he found that fourteen bullets had passed through his clothing, not one of which had injured him in the least. At another time when the fort was on fire he would not give up; but worked away at the burning timbers till his hands were burned nearly to a crisp.

At another time, he was taken prisoner by the Indians and bound to a tree. The bullets and the arrows flew on every side of him; one officer shot at him for the fun of it—but neither bullet or arrow struck him, although many of them struck the tree to which he was bound. It seemed indeed, as if he bore a "charmed life."

When the British began to land in New York, "Old Put" led one division of the colonial army out of the city by way of the Hudson River road. He was to meet Washington not far up the river, and then together they intended to retreat.

Now it happened that at just the time Putnam was going *up* the river road, a British division was coming *down*. Mrs. Robert Murray, a good Quaker woman, who, although she did not believe in war and fighting, was nevertheless a staunch friend of the colonists, learned of the danger and resolved to save General Putnam.

The British red-coats, marching nearer and nearer, came until their advanced guard were at her very gate. Going forth to meet them, she saluted the officers and invited them to stop and lunch beneath her trees upon the lawn. The officers, tired and dusty with marching under the hot August sun, gladly accepted her seemingly generous hospitality.

She brought forth fresh bread with sweet golden butter, and gave them plenty of cold, foaming milk to drink, cake and fruits, everything that her house or garden could afford. She talked with them, showed them about her mansion, and in every way attempted to keep them pleasantly occupied until she was sure General Putnam had passed in the road below.

When at length the British division resumed its march, the sun had sunk nearer the west, the air was cooler, the men were refreshed and rested—and, best of all, General Putnam and his division had gone on far up the road and out of sight.

At last, toward the end of the war, this daring general was taken very ill. So strong was his will, that, although helpless and often in great pain, he lived on until the Revolution was over.

He was bold and daring, had no mercy on his enemy in battle, and when fighting, fought, as his soldiers used to say, like a very wild-cat.

Still, for all that, he was generous and had as kind a heart as ever beat. He was not ashamed to be gentle with his friends. Every one who knew him loved him; and when at the good old age of seventy-two, he died, he was mourned by all. Every honor was paid him by the country he had so loved, and for which he had so bravely fought.

BENJAMIN FRANKLIN

One of the wisest men of the times was Benjamin Franklin. You have all heard about him I presume; there are so many stories of his boyhood, which no doubt, you have read in your reading book.

He was a very poor boy; that is, as far as money goes, but he had something in his little head that made him richer than the richest boy that ever scampered with him across Boston Common.

At ten years old he was taken from school to assist his father in his business of tallow-candler and soap-boiler.

"I was employed," he says, "in cutting wicks for the candles, attending the shop and going of errands."

Not liking this trade, however, Benjamin was apprenticed, at the age of twelve, to his brother James, a printer.

Here he stayed for five years, but as he did not get along very well with his brother, he determined to start out and "seek his fortune."

Here is an account of his journey as told by himself:—

"My friend Collins agreed with the captain of a New York sloop for my passage to that city. So I sold some of my books to raise a little money, and as we had a fair wind, in three days I found myself in New York, near three hundred miles from home, a boy of but seventeen, without the least knowledge of any person in the place, and with very little money in my pocket.

"I offered my service to the printer in the place, old Mr. William Bradfod. He could give me no employment, having little to do, but says he, 'my son at Philadelphia has lately lost his principal man; if you go there, I believe he may employ you.'

"Philadelphia was a hundred miles further; I set out, however, in a boat for Amboy leaving my chest and things to follow me round by sea.

"From there I proceeded on foot, fifty miles to Burlington, where I was told I should find boats that would carry me the rest of the way to Philadelphia.

"It rained very hard all day. I was thoroughly soaked, and by noon a good deal tired: so I stopped at a poor inn, where I stayed all night, beginning now to wish that I had never left home.

"I cut so miserable a figure, too, that I found by the questions asked me, I was suspected to be some runaway servant, and in danger of being taken up on that suspicion. However, I proceded the next day and got in the evening to Burlington.

"Walking there by the side of the river a boat came by, which I found was going towards Philadelphia. They took me in, and, as there was no wind, we rowed all the way.

"We arrived at Philadelphia about nine o,clock on Sunday morning, and landed at the Market Street wharf.

"I have been the more particular in this description of my journey to Philadelphia, and shall be so of my first entry into that city, that you may in your mind compare such unlikely beginnings with the figures I have since made there. I was in my working dress, my best clothes being to come round by sea. I was dirty from my journey; my pockets were stuffed out with shirts and stockings, and I knew no soul, or where to look for lodging.

"I was fatigued with travelling, rowing, and want of rest; I was very hungry; and my whole stock of cash consisted of a Dutch dollar, and about a shilling in copper.

"I walked up a street, gazing about, till, near the market-house I met a boy with bread.

"I had made many a meal on bread, and, inquiring where he had bought it, I went immediately to the baker's he directed me to, in Second Street, and asked for a biscuit, intending such as we had in Boston; but they, it seems, were not made in Philadelphia.

"Then I asked for a threepenny loaf, and was told they had none such. So, not knowing the difcrene of money, or the greater cheapness or the names of his bread, I bade him give me threepenny-worth of any sort.

"He gave me, accordingly, three great, puffy rolls. I was surprised at the quantity, but took it, and, having no room in my pockets, walked off with a roll under each arm, and eating the other.

"Thus I went up Market Street as far as Fourth Street, passing by the door of Mr. Reed, my future wife's father; when she, standing at the door, saw me, and thought I made, as I certainly did, a most awkward and ridiculous appearance.

"I then turned and went down Chestnut Street, and part of Walnut Street, eating my roll all the way. Coming round, I found myself again at Market Street Wharf, near the boat I came in, to which I went for a draught of the river water; and being filled with one of my rolls, I gave the other two to a woman and her child who came down the river in the boat with us, and were waiting to go farther.

"Thus refreshed, I walked again up the street, which by this time had many clean-dressed people in it who were all walking the same way. I joined them, and thereby was led into a great meeting-house of the Quakers, near the market.

"I sat down among them, and, after looking round awhile, and hearing nothing said, being very drowsy through labor and want of rest the preceding night, I fell fast asleep, and continued so till the meeting broke up, when one was kind enough to rouse me. This was, therefore, the first house I was in, or slept in, in Philadelphia."

It was this Franklin that made the wonderful first discoveries in electricity; and he made them by means of a kite with a small thread, by which he found that he could "bring down the lightning."

Poor Richard, 1733.

AN

Almanack

For the Year of Christ

1733,

Being the First after LEAP YEAR:

And makes fince the Creation	Years
By the Account of the Eaftern Greeks	7241
By the Latin Church, when ☉ ent. ♈	6932
By the Computation of W.W.	5742
By the Roman Chronology	5682
By the Jewifh Rabbies	5494

Wherein is contained

The Lunations, Eclipfes, Judgment of the Weather, Spring Tides, Planets Motions & mutual Afpects, Sun and Moon's Rifing and Setting, Length of Days, Time of High Water, Fairs, Courts, and obfervable Days

Fitted to the Latitude of Forty Degrees and a Meridian of Five Hours Weft from London, but may without fenfible Error ferve all the adjacent Places, even from Newfoundland to South-Carolina,

By RICHARD SAUNDERS, Philom.

POOR RICHARD'S ALMANAC.

You should know about "Poor Richard's Almanac," children, for the same reason you should know about "George Washington's Hatchet."

A hundred years ago, this was perhaps the foremost book in American literature. It was the work of our lightning hero, Benjamin Franklin. It was an almanac, not unlike the "Old Farmer's Almanac" of to-day. In among the matter that is always to be found in almanacs, Franklin scattered all sorts of "wise sayings" or proverbs. To these, he gave the name "Poor Richard's Sayings," many of them you have heard over and over until very likely you are tired of them. Some of them, I know from the experience of long ago, are very aggravating to children. For example, isn't it enough to make any boy wish Franklin had stuck by his printing press, and his kite, and let literature alone, to have mamma say, just as he is in the midst of the most exciting chapter, "Come, Johnnie, it's time to go to bed.

Early to bed and early to rise Makes a man healthy, wealthy and wise?'"

FRANKLIN AT HIS PRINTING PRESS

"Poor Richard's Almanac" for 1734 says, in speaking of the eclipse for the year: "There will be but two; the first, April 22, the second, October 15 — both of the sun, and both, like old neighbor Scrape-all's generosity, invisible."

Franklin often put into his calendar "weather predictions;" but they were quite as likely to come out wrongly as do "Old Prob's" predictions now.

When he was criticised for the inaccuracy of his predictions, he said good-naturedly:

"However, *no* one but will allow that we always hit the day of the month. As for weather, I consider it will be of no service to anybody to know what weather is to be one thousand miles off; therefore, I always set down exactly the weather my reader will have wheresoever he may be *at the time*. We only ask an allowance of a few days and if there still be a mistake, set it down to the printer."

The almanac of 1738 has a scolding preface, which appears to be the work of Mistress Saunders. She says her husband had set out to visit an old star-gazer of his acquaintance on the Potomac, and left her the almanac, sealed, to send to the printer. She suspects some jests directed against her, bursts the seal, and plays havoc generally with the almanac. She says:

"Looking over the months, I find he has put in abundance of foul weather this year; and therefore I have scattered here and there where I could find room, 'fair,' 'pleasant,' etc., for the poor women to dry their clothes in."

Franklin grew to be a highly educated man, and a very gentlemanly man, too, for all he was so awkward and ungainly on his first morning in Philadelphia. Years later, when he went to England and to France in behalf of his country, his wit and his knowledge and his fine manners were the delight of the Court. And this was a very fortunate thing for America you may be sure and for this reason, these old European countries with all their elegance, and wealth, and "blue blood," and Court society, had formed an idea that Americans were all awkward clod-hoppers; "horny-handed tillers of the soil," they were used to calling them, and they had the idea, I suppose, that the country had not a single cultured, educated person upon its face. And so it was, that when Franklin appeared before them, he carried everybody by surprise; and many an Englishman and many a Frenchman, who had supposed we knew nothing in America except to dig in the earth, turned about and began to think that perhaps we were "somebodies" over here after all.

Franklin was never dizzied by the flattering attention he received in these countries. He never forgot that he was there to plead for America; and plead he did, wisely and well, many a time rendering her a service that she could never repay.

In every position of honor, in every trying time when wisdom and caution were needed, Franklin was sure to be called upon by his countrymen. And never did he fail them.

When at last he died, at the age of eighty-two, not only did twenty thousand of his own countrymen meet to do him honor in America, but in the English and French courts as well, was every possible tribute paid to the memory of this great man.

BENJAMIN FRANKLIN'S TOMB

ARNOLD THE TRAITOR AND ANDRÉ THE SPY

One of the most daring men in the patriotic army for a time was Benedict Arnold. He was brilliant, daring, but cowardly withal, mean-spirited, jealous and treacherous. His meaner qualities had not shown themselves very much in his military life and, as he had really been very brave and had been of great service to the country, Washington put him in command at West Point, one of the most important military posts in the whole country.

But the mean-hearted Arnold had already planned to betray the post into the hands of the British; and Sir Henry Clinton, a British officer, had promised to give him £10,000 in English gold for his treacherous deed.

General Clinton sent a Major André to West Point to visit Arnold and make definite arrangements for the betrayal. He reached the American lines, met Arnold, and received papers from Arnold in which his whole plans were written. Putting these papers within his stockings, he started back to the British camp.

MAJOR ANDRÉ

He had passed the American lines, and had reached Tarrytown on the Hudson. Before night-fall he would be in the camp at New York, and the plan for the surrender would be in Clinton's hands. Almost free from apprehension of danger he rode on. Suddenly three men appeared in his path. Without producing his pass, he asked them, "Where do you belong?"

"Down below," answered one. "Down below" meant New York, and André was thrown off his guard by the answer. "I belong there also," he said. "I am a British officer on important business. Do not detain me." "Then you are our prisoner," answered the men.

André then produced his pass, but as by his own confession he was a British officer, it availed nothing. He offered his watch, his purse, and more valuable than either, he offered to deliver to them next day a cargo of English dry goods if they would let him pass. They were unmoved by his bribes, and already had begun to search him. They searched pockets, saddle-bags, his hat. They even ripped open the linings of his coat. The prisoner stood nearly naked in the road, yet no paper had been found. At length they pulled off his boots. His boots were empty; but they heard the rustle of paper when they were drawn off. The stockings came last, and in his stockings under the soles of his feet were found, in Arnold's handwriting, the treasonable papers, with a plan of the fort, the way to enter it—every thing, in short, that would make it easy for Clinton to get possession.

SEARCHING ANDRÉ

André was at once taken to the nearest officer and given up to him as a prisoner. André, true to Arnold even now, asked that he might be permitted to send a line to him.

As the papers had not been read, André's request was granted; and Arnold received a note which told him of André's arrest.

Of course Arnold knew that his life was now in danger. And so, hurrying from the fort, he leaped a precipice now called Traitor's Hill, and rode to the nearest boat landing. Thus he escaped to the British lines where he put himself under the protection of Clinton.

The unfortunate André was sentenced to be hanged. Clinton did all in his power to save the young man, who was by no means as black-hearted as Arnold; but it was the army law, and nothing could be done. Washington tried to capture Arnold intending then to release André and hang him instead. The plan failed, however, and André was doomed to execution.

André wrote a very manly letter to Washington, asking that he might be shot like a soldier, rather than be hanged like a dog. Washington laid this letter before André's judges, but they would not hear of any other death than hanging for the unfortunate spy.

"Have you forgotten," said they, "how the British hanged our brave Nathan Hale—the noble Nathan Hale, whose last words were, 'I regret that I have but one life to give for my country'? Have you forgotten that they would not allow him to send one word to his mother, would not allow him to speak with his old minister?" "No," said they, "André must die as Hale died,—on the gallows."

André met death like a brave man. He hoped to the last that he might be shot and so die a soldier's death; and so when he saw the gallows awaiting him, he gave a start, shuddered, and said, "I am not afraid to die, but I hate this way of dying."

Seeing that all was ready for him, he stepped into the wagon, bandaged his own eyes, fastened the rope about his neck and said, "I pray you to hear me witness that I meet my fate like a brave man." Thus ended Major André's life, a tragedy which is one of the most touching of this whole war.

Arnold, during the remainder of the war, fought on the English side; and at its close, since no one in America had any respect for him, he went to live in England. Even there he was held in contempt by the very ones to whom he had sold himself; so that, since he was a proud man to the end, we know he must have suffered most keenly for his dastardly act.

At one time, while he was living in England, a gentleman who was about to come to America on a visit asked Arnold to give him some letters of introduction to some of the leading families in America. Arnold's reply shows how bitterly he was paying for having sold his own soul. He said, "Alas, in all that great country which gave me birth there is not one man whom I can call friend."

SURRENDER OF CORNWALLIS

AFTER the surrender of Burgoyne, there was, I think, never quite such deep despair in the hearts of the Americans. Still the British were by no means weak. There were Clinton and Cornwallis with large and powerful armies yet to be defeated.

At last came the final great battle between Cornwallis' troops and those of Washington at Yorktown. Cornwallis had been very busy fortifying this town, into which he had withdrawn his forces. He had dug trenches, and had thrown up earth works all around the city to keep away Washington's army. Cornwallis' army had now grown much smaller than the Americans had any idea of. Indeed he had only 7000 men, 1000 of whom were negro slaves. Washington's army was nearly 16000, all well trained, and 3000 of them were "picked men" from the Virginia militia.

Clinton had promised, however, to send aid in a week's time surely; and so Cornwallis felt sure that if he could hold out until then, he should defeat Washington. On September 28, 1781, the American army marched up and encamped one mile from Yorktown. Cornwallis withdrew all his forces into the city to wait for Clinton's aid.

The Americans, however, had no thought of waiting. At once the batteries began their terrible work against the besieged city. Gun after gun which the British had placed upon their walls fell from the hands of the brave Briton who held it. The ditches were filled with fragments of the shattered walls, and heaped with the bodies of the dead soldiers.

The American forces drew nearer and nearer every night under cover of the entrenchments which they threw up in the darkness. On the evening of the 14th of October, they had come so close that Washington ordered an immediate attack; and accordingly two columns were formed—one French, the other American—to rush upon the city from the right and from the left. A hot battle ensued. Cornwallis, giving up all hope now of aid from Clinton, and finding himself surrounded on every side, declared all defence useless, and gave up the struggle.

The general whom Washington appointed to take possession of the defeated army was one who, at a previous battle, had been defeated by Cornwallis, and had been made to surrender his troops to him. Cornwallis had at that time been very severe with the general; and now he meted out to Cornwallis the same measure of severity.

The French and American armies were drawn up in two lines, and between them the conquered army passed.

When they came to stack their arms, the men, most of them, maintained a sullen silence, shading their faces with their hats. Some threw their guns with violence upon the ground. Some of the officers wept outright at giving up their arms, while others wore a look of haughty defiance, and refused to look upon their conquerors.

Washington and all his officers showed the utmost kindness to their captives. Even Cornwallis, in his report to Clinton, speaks of this, and mentions with great warmth the kindness of the French officers, which he hopes will be remembered in future warfare.

But Cornwallis was so deeply humiliated by his conquest that he could hardly appreciate the courtesy of Washington. Once when they were conversing together, Cornwallis stood with his head bare.

"You had better be covered from the cold, my lord," said Washington, politely.

"It does not matter what becomes of this head now," answered Cornwallis, putting his hand to his brow.

With this surrender of Cornwallis, the war was really at an end. The power of the English army was broken. There were battles in other parts of the country after this, but all felt that peace was at hand; and when, at two o'clock in the morning, the news of Washington's great victory reached Philadelphia, the people were awakened by the watchman's cry, "Cornwallis is taken! Cornwallis is taken!"

Lights flashed through the houses, and soon the streets were thronged with crowds eager to learn the glad news. Some were speechless with delight. Many wept, and the old doorkeeper of Congress died of joy. Congress met at an early hour, and that afternoon marched in solemn procession to church to return thanks to God.

SURRENDER OF CORNWALLIS AT YORKTOWN

As soon as possible, the British army embarked in their vessels, leaving New York once more a free city. Then indeed, there was great rejoicing: There was a great show of fireworks on Bowling Green, where, you remember, had once stood the leaden statue of King George III.

A week later, Washington called together all his officers to bid them farewell, and thank them for their ever ready aid and helpful courage during the terrible war. These brave men who had stood side by side in the bloody battle, facing death together for seven long years, met now together in silence and sadness.

Illumination.

COLONEL TILGHMAN, Aid de Camp to his Excellency General WASHINGTON, having brought official acounts of the SURRENDER of Lord Cornwallis, and the Garrisons of York and Gloucester, those Citizens who chuse to ILLUMINATE on the GLORIOUS OCCASION, will do it this evening at Six, and extinguish their lights at Nine o'clock.

Decorum and harmony are earnestly recommended to every Citizen, and a general discountenance to the least appearance of riot.

October 24, 1781.

REDUCED FAC-SMILE OF THE PROCLAMATION
RESPECTING ILLUMINATION ON THE SURRENDER
OF CORNWALLIS

When all were present, Washington raised his glass, and drank to the health of them all. Then he said—and his voice trembled, and there were tears in his eyes, as he spoke, "I cannot come to each of you to take my leave of you; but I shall be glad if each man will come and take me by the hand."

Then General Knox, a man whom Washington loved, came forward and with tears in his eyes, attempted to speak. Though he could not say one word, Washington understood;

WASHINGTON TAKING LEAVE OF HIS COMRADES

and, with tears in his own eyes, drew his friend's head down upon his shoulder and kissed him. Then each officer came forward to take his leave of his much loved commander; and the bravest men, the most warlike, men who without one tremor had faced the cannon's mouth, men who without a murmur had borne the sufferings of these terrible years, were not ashamed on that day, to let the tears run down their rough sun-burned faces as they said goodby to Washington.

Sometimes I fear we get almost tired of hearing of Washington so much. I confess I often did when I was a child at school. There was the hatchet story of his childhood, the story of his wonderful journey when he was only twenty-one, and the old, old titles of "First President," and "Father of his Country"—yes, I did sometimes say that I was tired of hearing about him; but when I grew older, and I came at last upon a history that told me more, about the real character of the man, rather than so much about the battles he fought, and the victories he won, then I came to respect the great heart of the man. He was so brave and daring, and yet always so gentle, so charitable. Although he could dash into the thickest of the fight, yet when the battle was over, and the enemy were taken, you never hear of his blustering about as Burgoyne did, or bullying those who had fallen into his hands as Cornwallis did at the South, or Colonel Prescott at Newport. When a battle was over, he never thought he must celebrate it by getting drunk and making a brute of himself. No, whether in the camp or the drawing-room, whether with friends or with foes, whether conquered or conquering, Washington always thought it worth while to be a gentleman. I do not mean by that an aristocrat—not that; but a real gentleman,—*a gentle man.*

DATES TO REMEMBER

Revolution began 1775—ended 1781. Battle of Lexington April 19, 1775. Battle of Bunker Hill June 17, 1775. Declaration of Independence July 4, 1776.

ANECDOTE OF BURGOYNE

Nothing, perhaps, helped the colonists on to victory more than the conceit, and consequent unwillingness to learn, of the British generals.

After Bunker Hill, Gen. Gage was, as we know, shut up in the town of Boston by Washington's troops.

As Generals Howe, Clinton, and Burgoyne were sailing up the harbor an outward-bound vessel hailed them, saying, "Your British troops are under seige. Washington's troops surround the city."

"How many are there?" called Burgoyne.

"Ten thousand colonists to five thousand British."

"What!" exclaimed Burgoyne puffing himself like a vain frog; "do you mean to say that ten thousand country clods are keeping under seige five thousand British troops? Just let us get there and we'll make elbow-room!"

Boston people did not forget this boast; and a few months later, when Burgoyne and his army were marched as prisoners of war into Cambridge, an old apple-woman, perched with her basket on a fence, made great sport by crying as he passed, "Make way there! elbow-room! elbow-room!"

You remember that it was Burgoyne's troops that used the Old South as a riding-school. Nothing so angered the Boston people as this. And it is said that when, after his surrender, Burgoyne was walking with other generals along Washington Street, he said, as he came to the Province House, "There is the former residence of the Governor."

"Yes," shouted a voice in the crowd, "and there opposite is the riding-school."

NANCY HART

NANCY HART was known throughout the South in Revolutionary times as "the giantess" and "the heroine of Georgia."

She lived in the wild woods, and supported herself and her children by hunting, fishing, and trapping.

Nancy was not handsome, as she stood over six feet in height, her mop of red hair bundled into a big coil, and her crooked eyes staring and winking as was their custom.

But for all her uncouth appearance, one who knew her said, "Her voice was quiet and soft, and if she had the bravery and courage of a man, she had beneath it all the warm, tender heart of a woman."

She was a fierce supporter of the Whig party from the very outset.

One day six British soldiers, pursuing deserters, came to her cabin for food.

While they were eating, she hid their guns, drove away their horses, locked her doors, and found a way to send word to her neighbors, "I have trapped six Tories. Come and help me."

During one winter, dressed as a man, she used often to go to the British camp; and, with her sharp, clear perception, she would learn what was going on within, and carry the news to the Whigs.

One day she met a little pale-faced British soldier. Taking his gun from him, she marched him on before her into the Georgian camp.

The Georgian colonel had great confidence in her power and wisdom. So much so, that he once put her in charge of a fort filled with women and children.

Nancy proved, before the colonel's return, that she was equal to the occasion. A company of skirmishers attacked it.

Nancy, in uniform, forced the frightened women to put on their husband's clothes and present themselves upon the walls. She, herself, kept up meanwhile a steady firing from the old cannon.

"I understood the soldiers had gone with Colonel Clarke; but the fort seems only too well manned. We may as well march," said their leader.

When the war was over, a few "squatters," as they were called, came into the country, not far from Nancy's cabin. Nancy fled into the wildernesses of Kentucky. "So many neighbors," said she, "leave me no air to breathe."

THE MARQUIS DE LAFAYETTE

LAFAYETTE

DURING this war, the French were our firm allies against the English. One Frenchman, Marquis De Lafayette was so much in sympathy with us, that, nobleman that he was, he left his home and his country to join our army and fight for our cause.

He was young, only nineteen years of age, wealthy and blessed with everything that should bind his heart to his own home. But so great was his sympathy with the struggling colonies that he was willing to give up all and come to America. "I have always held the cause of America dear," said he; "now I go to serve it personally."

When he arrived, the first act of generosity was to supply clothing and arms to the South Carolina troops, then in great distress.

He wrote at once to Washington saying, "The moment I heard of America I loved her.

The moment I heard she was fighting for liberty, I burned with a desire to bleed for her."

Lafayette was so long in this country, and so much heart and soul with us in our fight for independence, that when ever he referred to the Revolution after his return to France, he spoke of himself as an American. One evening, in 1824, while visiting Boston, Mrs. Josiah Quincy said to him:

"The American cockade was black and white, was it not, General?"

"Yes, madam," he replied; "it was black at first, but when the French came and joined *us*, *we* added the white in compliment to them."

At the siege of Yorktown, in the attack which hastened the surrender of Cornwallis, Lafayette and his American division captured one redoubt some minutes before the French carried the redoubt which they commanded.

"You don't remember me, General!" cried an old soldier, pressing through the crowd at the State House to welcome Lafayette on his arrival in Boston. The General looked at him keenly, holding the hand of the old man, who added:

"I was close to you when we stormed our redoubt at Yorktown—I was just behind Captain Smith—you remember Captain Smith? He was shot through the head just as he mounted the redoubt."

"Yes, yes, I remember!" answered Lafayette, his face lightening up. "Poor Captain Smith! *But we beat the French! We beat the French!*"

At the surrender of Cornwallis, the American troops were drawn up on the right, and the French troops on the left of the road, along which the British army marched in solemn silence. Lafayette, noticing that the English soldiers looked only at the Frenchmen on the left, and ignored the American light-infantry, the pride of his heart, and being determined to bring their "eyes to the right," ordered the band to strike up "Yankee Doodle."

"Then," said he, narrating the story, "they did look at us, but were not very well pleased."

THE PUNNING PARSON

At the beginning of the war, the pastor of the Hollis Street Church, Boston, was Matthew Byles.

He was as staunch a Tory as many of his brothers were Whigs. No matter what rebukes or what threats were hurled at him, he would not be crushed. His fire of sarcasm was hot as ever; and his fund of humor never failed him.

At last he was removed from his pastorate, and a guard placed over him.

"Sir," said he, as the officer paced back and forth, "how nobly I am *guarded*."

Later the guard was removed, and then later still replaced.

"See now," said Matthew, "how carefully I am reguarded."

And again, when the guard was removed "for good and all," this impressible old man cried out,—

"Behold, I have been guarded, reguarded, and now I am disreguarded."

Once, while the sentinel was pacing up and down in front of his premises, the doctor persuaded him to go on an errand, and while he was absent, he shouldered the musket and kept guard over himself, much to the amusement of passers-by. He used to call the sentinel his observ-a-*tory.*

The early history of Boston is full of stories, of this odd, fun-loving parson. In early Boston poetry are found the following verses:

"Here's punning Byles provokes our smiles,
*   A man of stately parts,*
He visits folks to crack his jokes,
*   Which never mend their hearts.*

"With strutting gait and wig so great
*   He walks along the streets,*
And throws out wit, or what's like it,
*   To every one he meets."*

PROVOST CUNNINGHAM

Among the "last things" of the Revolution that the colonists loved to tell, were these two stories of Provost Cunningham of the British troops.

In Murray Street, New York city, stood a little tavern called "Day's Tavern." Day had raised above his building the new American flag.

Cunningham, hardly yet ready to surrender his command, seeing this flag, marched up to the tavern door.

"Come, you cur!" he shouted to Mr. Day. "I give you two minutes to haul down that rag. I'll have no such striped rag as that flying in the face of his Majesty's forces!"

"There it is, and there it shall stay!" said Day, quietly but firmly.

Cunningham turned to his guard.

"Arrest that man!" he ordered. "And as for this thing here, I'll haul it down myself!" and seizing the halyards, he began to lower the flag.

The crowd broke into fierce murmurs, uncertain what to do. But in the midst of the tumult, the door of the tavern flew open, and forth sallied Mrs. Day, armed with her trusty broom.

"Hands off that flag, you villain, and drop my husband!" she cried; and before the astonished Cunningham could realize the situation, the broom came down thwack! thwack! upon his powdered wig.

How the powder flew from the stiff white wig, and how, amidst jeers and laughter, the defeated provost-marshal withdrew from the unequal conquest, and fled before the sweep of Mrs. Day's all-conquering broom!

Another incident is told of the same day. Sir Guy Carleton, commander-in-chief of all his Majesty's forces in the colonies, stood at the foot of the flagstaff on the northern bastion of Fort George.

Before him filed the departing troops of his king. As the commander-in-chief passed down to the boats, to the strains of martial music, the red cross of St. George, England's royal flag, came fluttering down from its high staff on the northern bastion and the last of the rear guard wheeled toward the ship.

But Cunningham, the provost-marshal, still angered by the scene at Day's tavern, declared roundly that no rebel flag should go up that staff in sight of King George's men.

"Come, lively now, you blue-jackets!" he shouted, turning to some of the sailors from the fleet. "Unreef the halyards, quick! Slush down the pole, knock off the stepping cleats. Then let them run

411

their flag up if they can!"

His orders were quickly obeyed, and the marshal left the city. In a few minutes, Colonel Jackson, halting before the flag-staff, ordered up the stars and A BRITISH GRENADIER stripes.

"The halyards are cut, colonel," reported the color-sergeant. "The cleats are gone and the pole is slashed."

"A mean trick indeed!" exclaimed the indignant colonel.

"Who will climb the staff and reef the halyards for the stars and stripes!"

"I want no money for the job," said a young sailor lad, as he tried it manfully once, twice, thrice, each time slipping down covered with slush and shame. "If ye'll but saw me up some cleats, I'll run that flag to the top, in spite of all the Tories from 'Sopus to Sandy Hook."

Tying the halyards round his waist, and filling his jacket pockets with cleats and nails, he worked his way up the flag-pole, nailing as he went.

And now he reached the top, now the halyards are reefed, and as the beautiful flag goes up the staff, a mighty cheer is heard, and a round of thirteen guns salutes the stars and stripes and the brave soldier lad who did the gallant deed.

AMERICA; OR MY COUNTRY, 'TIS OF THEE

AMERICA; OR, MY COUNTRY, 'TIS OF THEE. 153

S. F. SMITH.

1. My coun-try, 'tis of thee, Sweet land of
2. My na-tive coun-try, thee, Land of the
3. Let mu-sic swell the breeze, And ring from
4. Our fa-thers' God, to Thee, Au-thor of

Lib-er-ty, Of thee I sing; Land where my
no-ble, free, Thy name I love; I love thy
all the trees Sweet free-dom's song: Let mor-tal
Lib-er-ty, To Thee we sing; Long may our

fa-thers died, Land of the pil-grim's pride,
rocks and rills, Thy woods and tem-pled hills;
tongues a-wake; Let all that breathe par-take;
land be bright With free-dom's ho-ly light;

From ev-'ry moun-tain side Let free-dom ring.
My heart with rap-ture thrills Like that a-bove.
Let rocks their si-lence break, The sound pro-long.
Pro-tect us by Thy might, Great God, our King.

GENERAL JOSEPH WARREN'S ADDRESS

JUNE 17, 1775

Stand! the ground's your own, my braves!
Will ye give it up to slaves?
Will ye look for greener graves?
Hope ye mercy still?
What's the mercy despots feel?
Hear it in that battle peal!
Read it on yon bristling steel!
Ask it, ye who will.

Fear ye foes who kill for hire?
Will ye to your homes retire?
Look behind you! they're afire!
And, before you, see
Who have done it! From the vale
On they come!—and will ye quail?
Leaden rain and iron hail
Let their welcome be!

In the God of battles trust!
Die we may, and die we must;
But, oh, where can dust to dust
        Be consigned so well
As where heaven its dews shall shed
On the martyred patriot's bed,
And the rocks shall raise their head.
        Of his deeds to tell?

                                    -JOHN PIERPONT.

MY COUNTRY

I love my country's pine-clad hills,
Her thousand bright and gushing rills,
Her sunshine and her storms;
Her rough and rugged rocks that rear
Their hoary heads high in the air
In wild fantastic forms.

I love her rivers deep and wide,
Those mighty streams that seaward glide
To seek the ocean's breast;
Her smiling fields, her pleasant vales,
Her shady dells, her flowery dales,
The haunts of peaceful rest.

Her forests and her valleys fair,
Her flowers that scent the morning air,
Have all their charms for me;
But more I love my country's name,
Those words that echo deathless fame,—
"The land of liberty."

- Hesperian.

MY COUNTRY

I see the living tide roll on,
It crowns with fiery towers
The icy capes of Labrador,
The Spaniard's "land of flowers!"
It streams beyond the splintered ridge
That parts the northern showers,
From eastern rock to sunset wave,
The Continent is ours.

-O. W. HOLMES.

MEMORY GEMS

Land of the West—beneath the Heaven
    There's not a fairer, lovelier clime;
Nor one to which was ever given
    A destiny more high, sublime.

                                 -W. D. GALLAGHER

Our country!—'tis a glorious land!
    With broad arms stretched from shore to shore,
The broad Pacific chafes her strand,
    She hears the dark Atlantic roar;
And nurtured on her ample breast,
How many a goodly prospect lies
In nature's wildest, grandeur chest
    Enammell'd with the loveliest dyes.

                                 -W. J. PABODIE.

Then, too, sail on, O Ship of State!
Sail on, O Union, strong and great!
Humanity with all its fears,
With all its hopes of future wars,
Is hanging breathless on thy fate.
We know what Master laid thy keel.

Land of the forest and the rock,
Of dark blue lake and mighty river,
Of mountains reared on high to mock
The storm's career and lightning's shock,
My own green land forever!
Oh! never may a son of thine,
Where'er his wandering feet incline
Forget the sky that bent above
His childhood like a dream of love!

- W HITTIEH.

AMERICAN HISTORY STORIES, VOLUME III

THE CAPITOL, WASHINGTON.

THE NATION

In all the history of our people up to this time, you have heard always the terms *colonies* and *colonists*; but now, after the Revolution, these colonists re-organized themselves under a new government, with a President at the head. They now called the different colonies *States*, and spoke of themselves henceforth as the *American Nation*.

For a long time after the Revolution, the kind of government they should have was a question of great dispute. Some would have liked a government similar to that of England, with a king at the head; others declared they would have nothing like the English government, and were especially determined never again to be ruled by a king—not even a king of their own choosing.

Finally, in 1787, a convention of fifty of the leading men of the country met at Philadelphia to decide upon some form of government which should, as nearly as possible, suit all the colonies.

For four whole months they worked together, and at last presented to the people the "Constitution," as it was called, which to this day forms the basis of our government.

Of course, the constitution, wise as it was, could not suit everybody. Franklin himself, who was one of the fifty who wrote it, was not entirely satisfied with it; but, with each of the thirteen colonies wanting something different from every other, it was the best that they could do. On the whole, it gave very good satisfaction; ten of the colonies—States, I should say now—accepted it at once. Three States, however, held out against it for some time. But two of them gave way without much trouble. Rhode Island, the smallest State of all—so small that it is called Little Rhody—then stood alone, stoutly refusing for a year or more to come into the ranks. This shows, I suppose, that even the little Rhodys and little Johnnies may be as plucky as the larger ones, if only they believe they are in the right. Little Rhody, however, finally gave way, and entered the Union with the same good will to all, no doubt, that had been shown by the other States.

Now a flag—the United States Flag—with its thirteen stars and thirteen stripes—was unfurled to the breezes; and the colonies were indeed the "United States of America."

THE FIRST PRESIDENT

When, at last, the States had all agreed to accept the Constitution as the basis of government, the next thing to do was to elect a President, and so establish themselves as the American Nation at once.

As might be expected, Washington was the man chosen for this important office; and when we recall how generous, how brave, and how wise he had been during the Revolution, we cannot doubt for a moment that he was the very best choice for this new position.

It was decided to make New York City the capital of the United States; and thither Washington in his coach-and-four set forth from his beautiful home in Virginia to take his place as first President of the United States of America. It is said that his journey was one ovation from the time he left Mt. Vernon (his home) until he reached New York City. Crowds of gaily-dressed people, bearing baskets and wreaths of flowers, hailed his appearance at every village, with shouts and songs of joy.

STATUE OF WASHINGTON. UNITED STATES TREASURY BUILDING, NEW YORK CITY. ON THIS SITE IN FEDERAL HALL, APRIL 30, 1789, GEORGE WASHINGTON TOOK THE OATH AS THE FIRST PRESIDENT OF THE UNITED STATES OF AMERICA.

When he reached Trenton—the very place where, a few years before, so heartsick and discouraged he had crossed the Delaware on that wintry Christmas night to attack the drunken Hessians,—at this very place the road was strewn with roses, the young maidens held arches of flowers over him, and the air rang with songs of gratitude and welcome.

In New York City a grand ball was given. Never before had this little community seen so much elegance. Washington had left off his blue "soldier coat," and was now dressed in a handsome suit of black velvet, with white silk stockings, beautiful silver buckles, and satin waistcoat. He was very tall, and straight, and manly looking; and with his elegant dress, and his powdered hair, he must indeed have made a very distinguished appearance.

John Adams, the Vice-president, was there, and so was Hamilton, the Secretary of the Treasury. General Knox, too, with his beautiful wife—the most beautiful woman of her time, so it is said, was there. Jefferson, who had been in France some time, now came back to America to be present at this "Inauguration Ball." He took everybody by surprise by appearing dressed as were the French people at that time—in white broadcloth coat, scarlet waistcoat, and breeches, cocked hat, and white stockings. It was indeed a wonderful ball, and I am sure there were beauty, and elegance, and grace, such as any court in Europe might well have been proud of.

In all the large towns celebrations of all sorts were held. In the city of New York there was a grand procession, such as never before had been seen in America. This procession was headed by a man dressed to look like Columbus, the discoverer of the country. Behind him were long lines of men with axes, who represented the pioneers—that is, the men who first came here from Europe, and felled the trees and cleared the places for roads and cities; then came lines of men dressed to represent the farmers, with plows, and scythes, and reapers; then came carts, fitted up like work-shops to represent the different trades. One cart, which represented a bake-shop, had upon it a huge loaf of bread, ten feet high, on which were printed the names of all the states; the coopers were putting together a barrel with thirteen staves, and binding it with a strong iron band, which they called

"The New Constitution;" the butchers were roasting a whole ox, which, when the celebration was over, was to be eaten by the people in the procession.

In the procession there were thirteen boys, each thirteen years old, dressed in white, with ribbons and garlands of green.

On another cart was a printing press; and, as it passed along, the printers printed copies of patriotic verses, and flung them right and left to the people.

Greatest of all, was a big ship—the "Ship of State"—drawn by ten large milk-white horses. O, it was a grand day for New York! The people shouted and hurrahed till they were hoarse; and, at last, when the procession had been everywhere and had been seen by everybody, all went into a great tent, decorated with flags and banners, where the women of the city had prepared a feast for them; then they shouted and hurrahed more, listened to speeches, drank toasts to the "new Government" and to the "new President," and finally went to their different homes, prouder than ever, I've no doubt, of the new "American Nation."

We hear in these days a great deal of fault found over the manner in which our Presidents from time to time choose their aids. It is often said, perhaps unjustly, that they are chosen with very little regard to their fitness for the offices which they are to fill, but rather because they chance to be friends or relations, or to have some other claim upon the president.

Whether this is so or not, Washington certainly set for all his successors a glorious example in this one line.

During his administration as President of the United States, a gentleman, a friend of the President throughout the whole course of the Revolutionary war, applied for a certain office. The gentleman was at all times welcome to Washington's table. He had been, to a certain degree, necessary to the man who had for seven years fought the battles of his country. At all times and in all places Washington regarded his Revolutionary associate with an eye of partiality and confidence.

He was a jovial, pleasant, companion; and in applying for the office, his friends already cheered him in his prospect of success.

The opponent of this gentleman was known to be an enemy of Washington. He dared, however, to stand as a candidate for the office to which the friend and favorite of Washington aspired.

Every one considered the appointment of this man hopeless. No flattering testimonial of merit had he to present to the eye of Washington. He was known to be his political enemy. He was opposed by a favorite of the General; and yet with such fearful odds he dared to stand as a candidate. What was the result? The enemy of Washington was appointed to the office, and his table companion left destitute and rejected.

A mutual friend, who interested himself in the affair, ventured to remonstrate with the President for the injustice of his appointment. "My friend," said he, "I receive with a cordial welcome. He is welcome to my house and welcome to my heart. But, with all his good qualities, he is not a man of business. His opponent is, with all his political hostility to me, a man of business. My private feelings have nothing to do in this case. I am not George Washington, but President of the United States. As George Washington, I would do this man any kindness in my power; but as President of the United States I can do nothing."

WASHINGTON'S ADMINISTRATION

Ad-min-is-tra'-tion is a large word, perhaps you think. But, after all, it isn't very much larger than Revolution, or Constitution; and when you come to know what it means, and why we have to use it, you will find it just as easy as many words which are perhaps not quite so long.

While a President holds his office we speak of it as his administration; and those events which occur while a certain person is President, are always spoken of as the events of that President's administration.

Although it was no doubt a great honor to have been chosen first President of the United States, and although it must have been very pleasant to Washington to know that his people so loved and trusted him, still he knew there was hard, hard work ahead, and no little worriment; for, although the States had accepted the Constitution, still there were persons here and there who still clung to the idea of having each State rule itself without any President at all or any Congress; others there were, who had wanted a king and who would have much preferred to keep the government out of the hands of the common people. All these critics were of course watching every movement of the new President, ready to find fault, and say, "Just what we expected," if the least thing went wrongly. Then, too, there were other difficulties. The treasury was nearly empty, and no other nation was willing to lend money to this new government; the Indians were rioting, burning and plundering on the frontiers; pirates from the Barbary States were attacking American ships and putting American seamen into prison; Spain had refused to allow the Americans the use of the Mississippi River for their trade; England, too, would not make any treaty of commerce with the new country—and, worst of all, there was the empty treasury— no money with which to raise armies to fight the Indians; no money with which to send ships to attack the Barbary States; no money to offer Spain; no money even with which to pay the old debts of the Revolution. A perplexing place it was, indeed, for Washington and his cabinet. But they were equal to the occasion. Hamilton, the Secretary of the Treasury, managed the money affairs so successfully that he has ever since been held up as an example of wisdom to all succeeding Treasurers. He established a National Bank, and levied taxes in order to raise the money which the government so much needed.

I shall not attempt to tell you how all these things were brought about, for you could not understand it, and it would not be very interesting to you even if you could.

All I want you to remember just now is, that Washington and his Cabinet were very wise in their dealings with all these troubles—so wise that, when, eight years later, Washington retired from public life, the money troubles were greatly improved, the Indians had been held back, Spain had been made to allow the Americans the use of the Mississippi, and the Barbary States had given up the prisoners, and had promised not to interfere further with American vessels.

The country, you see, was in a far better condition than it had been when, eight years before, Washington was made President.

As the President's term is four years, Washington had, you will understand, served two terms. As the time for a third election drew near, Washington resigned his office, saying that he had tried to serve his country faithfully through its darkest hours, and that now, being sixty-five years old, he wished to retire to his home at Mt. Vernon and spend the rest of this life in rest and quiet.

There had been on all sides men who said, during Washington's administration, "Washington will be King yet. He means to be King. He will hold his office until he *is* King." But I wonder what these men said when, at the end of the second term, Washington so quietly and modestly retired to his own home, thus proving how little he cared for public life except when his country needed him.

Washington did not live very long after his return to his home. Not many months had passed when there came news of his sudden death.

Every possible honor was paid this brave, good man, the Father of his Country, as he was called. In England and France even, the highest honors were paid him. The English ships were ordered to wear their flags at half mast, and the French ruler ordered that the banners be draped with crape.

Wherever Washington's name was mentioned, it was always with tender reverence and love.

WASHINGTON'S GRAVE, MOUNT VERNON.

WASHINGTON'S THOUGHT FOR OTHERS

In no way, perhaps, do we show ourselves to be gentle-bred, more than in our consideration for others.

After Cornwallis had surrendered at Yorktown, he dined one day with Washington. Rochambeau, the French commander, was also present, and according to the custom, being asked for a toast, he said, "The United States."

Washington, in turn, gave "The King of France."

When Cornwallis's turn came he said, simply, "The King."

—"Of England," added Washington with a smile. "Keep him there and I'll drink him a full bumper!"—and so saying he filled his glass to overflowing.

THE WHISKEY INSURRECTION

In order to raise money during this trying time in the nation's history, a tax was put upon whiskey and other alcoholic liquors.

This movement met with much rebellion among the people; and in Pennsylvania there was an open outbreak known as "The Whiskey Insurrection."

During this outbreak, the leader, Bradford, gained great power over a certain wealthy farmer named John Mitchel, and in some underhand manner, drew him into the conspiracy. Mitchel was young and full of vigor, and believed he was doing right.

One night Bradford came to Mitchel and said, "I believe letters have been written, and are now on the way to the President, telling of our plans for insurrection here. Now, those letters someway must be seized. You are the man to do it. As the mail-wagon passes along this road, you are to stop it, get that mail-bag and destroy those letters."

Robbery of the mails was then an offence punishable by death; but Mitchel, convinced that he was risking his life to serve his country, joined by two other men, stopped the wagon on a lonely road, between Washington and Pittsburgh, and carried the mail-bag to Bradford's house. It was opened, the damaging letters taken out, and the rest returned to the post-office at Pittsburgh.

When the insurrection was over, all the leaders escaped excepting John Mitchel. He rode into camp, and, finding General Morgan, gave himself up.

"I have been a fool," he said. "I see that plainly. I am ready to bear the punishment of my folly."

General Morgan, who knew that he had been deceived by Bradford, was sorry that he had not made his escape with him. He believed Mitchel to be at heart an honest man; and, knowing that if he were brought to trial the punishment would be death, he determined to give him a chance to escape.

"You cannot be tried here," he said. "I will give you a pass to Philadelphia. Report yourself there."

"I am to have a guard?"

"No, none."

The General turned on his heel and walked away. He intended and expected Mitchel to fly as soon as he had reached the wilderness; but the young farmer's honor was a stricter guard than soldiers would have been, and it drove him without flinching to his death.

He bade farewell to his wife and child, and started alone on horseback to Philadelphia. It was a three weeks' journey, at any hour of which he could have escaped. He reported himself as a prisoner, was tried, convicted, and sentenced to be hanged.

When the news reached General Morgan, he sent a special messenger to the President, with an account of the facts in the case. Washington, it is said, was deeply touched, and at once sent a full pardon to Mitchel, giving him at the same time this fatherly advice: "Go home to your wife and child; and forevermore keep clear of conspirators. You could hardly expect to escape again, for we are very apt to be judged by the company we keep."

WASHINGTON AS A FIGHTER

When it was necessary, peace-loving as he was, Washington could fight. His clear sense of the thing that must not be done as well as the thing that must be done was what made him of such value both as General and as President.

This incident shows his strength, his firmness, and his quickness to act. At one time, Colonel Glover's Marblehead soldiers and Morgan's Virginia riflemen had fallen into a disgraceful quarrel. The Virginians had laughed at the somewhat peculiar dialect and the short round jackets of the fishermen soldiers; the Marbleheaders, on the other hand, had made fun of the hunting-shirts and leggings of the riflemen.

The two regiments had gone on from words to blows, until at last, as Washington rode up, they were in full riot.

In an instant Washington's practiced eye took in the situation. Leaping from his horse, and throwing the bridle to his servant Pompey, who stood near, he dashed into the midst of the fight, seized two of the biggest, brawniest of the riflemen by their throats, and holding them at arm's length, shook them, until with surprise and breathlessness they were glad to cry for quarter.

Then, quietly giving orders that the two men be taken to their camps and that there should be no more quarreling between the two regiments, he rode away, leaving all—officers and soldiers—blank with amazement at this sudden outburst from their commander-in-chief.

WASHINGTON'S AIDS

Washington was wise in his choice of men to help him carry on his work as President. He was as wise in his judgment of men, a friend once said of him, as he was in his judgment of horses. As he never trained for the saddle a colt that was fitted to the plow, so he never chose as an aid in government a man who was better fitted for other lines of work.

"In choosing Alexander Hamilton and Col. Meade for his aids," said Col. Meade himself, "Washington displayed his usual good judgment. For Hamilton was a vigorous writer and a strong thinker. I was only a fearless horseman. So you see Hamilton did the headwork and I did the riding."

At the close of the war, when Washington was taking leave of his aids, he said:—

"Hamilton, you ought to go to the bar. You might easily become a leading lawyer. And you, friend, Dick, should go to your plantation. You have it in you to make a noble, honest farmer—just such a one as our country needs. It is indeed such men as you that make a country."

Hamilton did become a leader of the New York Bar, and Meade became the famous plantation holder that Washington had hoped he might become.

Several years after this, Meade visited Washington at his home. Washington, gallant host that he was, rode out to meet him. They met at a pair of draw-bars—one on either side.

"Allow me to let down the bars," said Meade, "for my worthy General."

"Friend Dick," said Washington, "here, as your host, it is *my* privilege to take down the bars."

For an instant both stood, hats in hand, each courteously waiting to serve the other.

Then with the ready wit and hearty manner which belonged always to Meade, he said, "Very well, General, then allow me to be your *aid* still."

JOHN ADAMS.

JOHN ADAMS' ADMINISTRATION

During the eight years of Washington's administration, so many important matters had come up that the people, by taking sides in the different discussions, had come to form two political parties. They called themselves Federalists and Republicans just as the political parties to-day call themselves Democrats and Republicans. The Federalists were those who believed in having a Congress, and a President who should stand at the head of the government. The Republicans said that was too much like having a king, and they believe that some time the President would become the king. They wanted each State to govern itself separately, have its own officers, and make its own laws. It would be time enough for the States to unite under one leader, so the Republicans said, when there was war, or when some other such matter of general interest came up.

And so it came about that at the end of Washington's administration, when it became necessary to elect a new president, each party had a candidate of its own. It was agreed that the candidate receiving the largest number of votes should be President, and the other one should be Vice-president.

John Adams was selected as candidate by the Federalists, and Thomas Jefferson by the Republicans.

I hardly think it will pay in a little history like this to go into the particulars of the contest. All we need to know now is, that Adams became the next President, and Jefferson the Vice-president. These two men, although bitterly opposed to each other in their political ideas, were nevertheless strong personal friends. During the Revolution they had stood bravely side by side, and after their terms of office had ended, they again became firm friends. It seems quite remarkable that on the 4th of July, 1826, the day when the "Declaration of Independence" was just fifty years old, both of these men died.

The last words of John Adams were, "My friend, Thomas Jefferson, still lives." He did not know that Jefferson had died only a few hours before in his Virginia home.

The one thing that marks the administration of John Adams, was the passing of the "Alien and Sedition Laws," as they were called. By these laws, the President had a right to expel from the country any foreigner who seemed dangerous to the country, and to fine or imprison any American who *libelled* the Congress, the President, or the Government.

These laws excited much bitter feeling; for the Republicans at once declared that it was intended to take away their freedom of speech, and that it was but one step towards bringing them all upon their knees before a king. The Federalists, many of them, thought this new law rather too strong, and began to take sides with the Republicans. And so it came about that when Adams's term was out, the Republican party had become so strong that Jefferson was elected the next President.

During the administration of Adams, the country came very near having war with France. Charles Pinckney was sent to France to see what could be done. The French government hinted to Pinckney that if the United States would pay to France a certain amount of money they, the French, would agree to make no trouble for them.

One would suppose the French government would have known better than to make such an offer to a country that had just fought so bravely for her liberty, and had since struggled so hard to meet its honest debts, and make for itself a place among the nations of the world.

Pinckney was very indignant. "No," said he, "millions for defence, but not one cent for tribute," was his bold, manly reply.

What the result might have been we cannot tell, had the threatened war burst upon us; but it happened that matters in Europe took such a turn that France did not carry out its threat against us.

It was during Adams' administration that the capitol was changed from New York to a new city, just laid out on the banks of the Potomac, which had been named Washington.

Here the building for the future presidents of the United States was erected; and President Adams and his good wife went there to begin housekeeping.

Poor Mrs. President had rather a trying time of it. Rough indeed was this new capitol. Except a few public buildings, there was hardly a house in sight. Although wood was plenty, they could hardly find laborers to cut it, and, as Mrs. Adams once wrote to a friend, they were really afraid they could not keep warm enough to drive away the shivers. Such was the Capitol of our country at the beginning of this century.

Thomas Jefferson.

ADMINISTRATION OF THOMAS JEFFERSON

The country had all this time been growing richer and richer. The people were spreading out over the western country, towns were being built, and great tracts of land were being made into thrifty farms. Several new States had already been added to the Union— Vermont, Kentucky, and Tennessee;—and now Ohio even, which so short a time before had been but an Indian hunting ground, was added, a new star, to those already upon the Flag.

You remember that Spain had at one time refused the Americans the use of the Mississippi River. Spain owned the land from the mouth of the river up to the Falls of St. Anthony; and, although agreements had been made with Spain regarding the use of the river, still the United States much preferred to own the land bordering upon the river, and so be sure of their control of its navigation.

Spain had recently ceded all this country, then called Louisiana, to the French. Jefferson now offered $15,000,000 to France for this country, and, as France was greatly in need of money, the offer was accepted at once. When asked why he did it, Jefferson said, "There is no trouble threatened at present, I know; but I believe in having a good big country, with no troublesome neighbors at the back door, as there might have been had the Spaniards or the French held that country."

Meantime the pirates of the Barbary States were alive again. They began capturing our vessels, taking our men prisoners, and selling them as slaves.

It is wonderful how these pirates had frightened the European nations even, and had kept them in terror for years. Italy was as afraid of them as a mouse is of a cat; Holland and Sweden trembled at the very sound of their name; Denmark every year paid them a large sum of money to keep them at peace; even England preferred to keep out of their way rather than run the risk of meeting them on the ocean.

An unlucky ship, which found itself near the Atlantic coast of Africa, might see at any moment an odd-looking boat with long lateen sails, swooping down upon her from some sheltered inlet or harbor, where she had lain at watch for her prey. In a twinkling she would sail alongside the vessel, grapple her, drop her long sails over the vessel's side, and a host of swarthy Moors, with bare, sharp sabres held between their teeth, belts stuck thick with knives and pistols, would come swarming over, boarding their prizes from all sides at once.

Exasperated with these pirates, the United States sent a fleet to attack them. Decatur, a young officer, steered boldly into their harbor one night; burned one of their vessels, and, before the pirates could get themselves together, sailed coolly out, and was soon beyond their reach. Many other brilliant attacks were made upon them, until the pirates began to understand they had a new sort of foe to deal with. Peace was declared, and there was no more trouble with pirates for a time.

Another important event in Jefferson's administration was the duel between Alexander Hamilton and Aaron Burr, in which duel Hamilton was killed.

Hamilton, you remember, had been Secretary of the Treasury; Aaron Burr had been a brave soldier in the Revolutionary times, and was now Vice-president with Jefferson.

Washington had always been suspicious of Burr, even during the war; and Hamilton had always distrusted him fully. These two had been opposed to each other many times in political schemes, but never had quarreled outright.

Duel between Hamilton and Burr.

In those days duels were common. If a man felt that he had been insulted, he would challenge his enemy to meet him in fight. Then these two would stand face to face and shoot at each other.

Notwithstanding that duelling was fashionable among men at this time, the death of Alexander Hamilton, a man so well known, and so much respected, seemed to awaken the whole country to the horror of the deed. Burr was looked upon as no less than a murderer, and from that time he sank in public opinion.

Finding himself now looked upon with such contempt and anger, he left the State, and for a long time wandered about through the western part of the country.

All at once, like a bomb, came the report that Aaron Burr had been detected in a plot against the government. He had been secretly plotting to invade Louisiana, seize the city of New Orleans, stir up a rebellion in these Western States, and so break up the Union.

The country was wild with excitement. Burr was arrested and tried for treason, but nothing could really be proved against him.

The once brilliant Aaron Burr was from thenceforth a disgraced and ruined man; and his name ranked next to that of Benedict Arnold in the opinion of many people.

But the greatest event of these days was the invention of the steam-boat by Robert Fulton. For a long time it had been known that Fulton was trying to make a boat that would go without oars and without sails. Of course people would not believe such a thing could be done, and I am afraid the poor man, like more inventors, had to endure a great amount of ridicule.

At last the boat was ready. At a certain hour it was promised that it should start on its first trip up the Hudson River to Albany. The docks were crowded with people jeering and mocking, ready almost to mob the brave Fulton in case the boat proved a failure.

At last the signal was given. Imagine the anxiety in the heart of Fulton! I fancy his heart almost stopped its beating as he listened for the first thud of the machinery.

But see! the piston rises! now it falls! now a splashing of the water against the pier! and the boat is certainly moving away! On, on, she went, steadily though slowly, scaring all the other vessels from her track. The people on the dock stood with eyes and mouths wide open, staring at the moving boat. Not a jeer nor a laugh; they were too surprised even to speak.

Up the river it passed, sending forth its puffs of black smoke, and bringing the people down to the river-side as it passed along. When darkness had fallen, and the boat went puffing up the river, sending out its showers of sparks, the people who had heard nothing of this wonderful invention ran to their houses in fright. Some thought it a sign from heaven; others thought it surely must be the very Evil One himself.

THE CLERMONT, 1807.

JEFFERSON had been elected by the Republicans; that is, by the party who hated all form and ceremony, and who were determined to have no government that was at all like a kingdom.

Jefferson was a man after their own hearts. Although he had been brought up in wealth as Washington had been, his ideas were very different. In Washington's time there had been brilliant social gatherings at the capitol, and Washington himself always rode about in his elegant family coach.

Jefferson at once put a stop to all displays at the capitol, saying that the simple living there should be a lesson to the country. It is said that when he went to the capitol to be made President, he rode on horseback, dressed in his plain every-day clothes; that he leaped from his horse, hitched it near the entrance, and walked in unattended to the hall in which he was to take the President's oath and make his speech.

Of course such a man as this made strong friends and equally strong enemies. His friends could find no language strong enough to express their admiration of him, and even his enemies could not but respect him.

As I told you in the story of the administration of John Adams, Jefferson died on the Fourth of July, 1826. Just as he was passing away, he heard the clanging of the bells. Listening for a second, he said, "This is the Fourth of July." These were the last words of this brave, steadfast soul; this man who had stood so firmly by his country in just that way which had seemed to him right.

JEFFERSON AND RANDOLPH

Here is an anecdote of Jefferson and Randolph, told by an old Virginia senator.:

"When I was a boy of nine or ten I often dined with my father at Monticello. Jefferson was a lonely man, the beauty and purity of whose family relations have been only recently made known in his biography by his niece. He took great pride in Monticello. Wanting a Chinese gong for the clock tower, in order to certainly secure it, he sent by three different vessels going to China. As it happened, each vessel brought a gong, and one he sent to my father.

"I finally presented it to the Staunton fire department. When, in those troublous days, we were melting up bells into cannon, that was also sent, but was returned as too valuable a souvenir to be destroyed.

"I did not like John Randolph. He was the most spiteful of men. If he was witty, his wit always left a sting. When I was a young man I went down to Richmond. Randolph was then in the Assembly. Charles Fenton Russell, a fine, genial man, was just concluding an address, saying, 'I am sorry to have been obliged to consume so much of the time of my fellow-members.'

"'So am I,' squeaked out Randolph, in his high, shrill voice.

"But he did not always get the best of it. Daniel Sheffey was a little Dutch shoemaker in one of the western counties, who showed such ability that some influential person interested in him had him taught to read; he afterwards studied law and became one of the most brilliant and prominent men in the State. He and Randolph were in Congress together.

"Randolph was intensely aristocratic, and felt no small contempt for the Dutch shoemaker. One day in Congress, Sheffey made a fine speech, and one in which he had shown no small degree of humor.

"This was more than Randolph could bear. He got up and in the most elaborate manner began to compliment Sheffey on his convincing logic; but added, 'Let my honorable friend keep out of the field of humor, in which his powers have not fitted him to shine.'

"Quick as a flash Sheffey was on his feet. 'The honorable member is right,' he said; 'and since he never trenches on my province, I will hereafter never intrude on his.'"

"To know Sheffey's appearance is necessary to appreciate the force of his quick retort on the house, for he had a little head, an enormous paunch, little short legs, and resembled more than anything else a human frog."

JEFFERSON'S FIDDLE

Jefferson's fiddle was, I fancy, as dear to him as Robinson Crusoe's man Friday. At any rate it was well understood among the members of his household that any lack of care, any neglect or carelessness towards his precious fiddle could not easily be atoned for.

He used to often say, in joking with his wife, as he so enjoyed doing, "It was the fiddle that won the 'Widow Skelton.'"

The Widow Skelton was quite a belle in Virginia society, and had, as the stories say, "throngs of admirers."

One day, two of her suitors, bent on learning their fate from her own lips, met in the hall of her house.

The sound of music caused them to listen. The widow was playing on the harpsichord and singing a love-song, while Jefferson accompanied her with voice and violin.

Something in the song, and in the manner of her singing, showed them that they might as well go away. So quietly leaving the hall, they mounted their horses and rode away, sadder but wiser men. In a week or two, the engagement of Mrs. Martha Skelton to Thomas Jefferson was among the rumors of the day.

Jefferson was always fond of the violin. When his paternal home was burned he asked, "Are all the books destroyed?"

"Yes, massa, dey is, but we saved de fiddle," answered the old family servant, who knew his master's pet vanity.

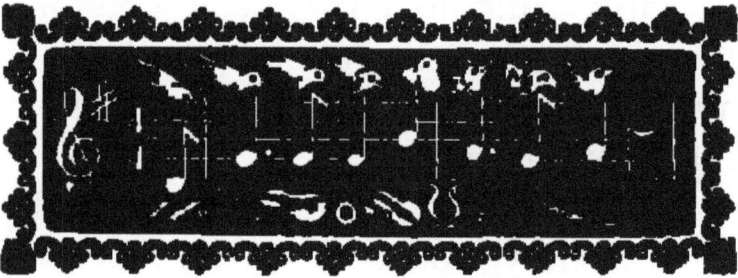

PRESIDENT MADISON.

THE ADMINISTRATION OF JAMES MADISON

The next President was James Madison. He, too, was chosen by the Republicans. He had been a near and dear friend of Jefferson, and in simplicity of manners and living was very like him. He was usually dressed in a plain suit of black broadcloth, and was always very quiet and gentlemanly in his bearing. The wearing of gay colors had very much gone out of fashion since the days of Washington and Adams, and so they were not very often worn, either at the capitol or elsewhere.

When Madison became president, affairs were very prosperous and quiet. There was a prospect of trouble ahead, however, both from the Indians and from the English.

The Indians had been very quiet since the time of Washington, when Anthony Wayne had attacked them so furiously; but now there had arisen among them a young chief, Tecumseh, who was wise enough to see that the Indians were being pushed farther and farther from their "happy hunting grounds," and that unless the white man could be driven away, they would some time have no hunting-grounds at all. And so when Harrison, the Governor of Indiana, bought from some of the chiefs a piece of land, and was about to take possession of it, this chief felt that the time had come to speak; and accordingly the Flying Tiger, as he was called, came to Harrison about it.

"I wish to talk with you," said Tecumseh.

"Very well," said Harrison, "will you come into my house?"

"No," said Tecumseh; "the air of the white man's wigwam stifles me. I will talk outside."

As Tecumseh and his warriors, and Harrison and his officers gathered, one of the officers said, "Tecumseh, sit down beside your father," pointing to Harrison.

"My father!" cried the chief, contemptuously. "the Sun is my Father!"

Tecumseh then went on to explain that the Indian was being driven every year farther west, that the broad lands of the country were theirs, and that no Indian had any right to sell, nor a white man any right to buy the land.

Governor Harrison tried to explain, but Tecumseh would not understand; and although he went away quietly enough, Harrison well knew that an outbreak might at any time be expected.

Tecumseh's great plan now, was to unite all the Indian tribes into one body, and so make a fearful attack upon the white men. And for this purpose he left his tribe in the care of his brother, "The Big Prophet," and travelled about from tribe to tribe, telling his story and urging them to fight against these "pale-faces," as he called the white men. If Tecumseh had succeeded in his plan, I fear it would have been a sad, sad day for those states bordering upon the Indian camps. But while Tecumseh was away, Harrison attacked the Indian camp on the Tippecanoe river, broke up their town, and drove the tribe into the forests beyond.

Tecumseh on his return, finding his own tribe broken up, and knowing that now his plan was hopeless, vowed vengeance on the Americans. Knowing that America was just on the verge of another war with England, he again journeyed from tribe to tribe, telling them what had been done during his absence, and urging them to join the English against the Americans.

Having inflamed all the Indians who would listen to him with his own desire for revenge, he hastened to the British officers and offered himself and his warriors to fight against the Americans.

Satisfied that revenge was sure, Tecumseh and his followers were quiet during the winter months—quiet, but not idle, as the Americans learned to their sorrow a few months later.

"DOLLY MADISON"

Mrs. Madison was one of the most popular women of the White House. It was well indeed that hers was a heart open to social life, and that she had that warmth of heart and that brilliancy and ready wit that made her so popular and gave such charm to the White House hospitality during that administration, for Madison was, though filling nobly his political position, cold, snarling, hardly courteous in his social life.

"Dolly" was of very common "extraction," as we say, her father being a simple Quaker.

Madison was forty-three years old when he carried the brilliant, simple-hearted Dolly to the White House.

In "Presidents of the United States," John Frost, L.L.D., gives the following account of this kind-hearted and much loved lady:

"At Richmond, I first saw Mrs. Madison, and the instant my eye fell on her I felt that I was looking on a *Queen*. A queen she was; one of nature's queens:—she looked the character; her person, carriage, manners, language, would have been in place in any of the most polished Courts of Europe. She was large and dignified, yet she moved with easy grace. Hers was a face that seemed to bid you welcome, and to ask, 'what can I do for you?' Having once seen her, I could credit what had frequently been told me, that her husband owed much of the success of his administration (so far as his popularity was concerned), to the influence of his wife. Her power over him was great, and all who sought favors of any kinds, addressed themselves, naturally, to her, as the readiest and surest channel of access to the President. Madison was cold and shy, and a timid suitor would often have met, not with repulse, but with a polite refusal; but Mrs. Madison anybody could approach, and if his request was reasonable he might count upon at least her good offices.

"Another beautiful trait of her character was her fondness for the young. No one could have seen her in company with young ladies, and fail to be struck with this peculiarity. It became the more remarkable as she advanced in years.—At an age when to most of those who reach it the liveliness and chatter of young people is a burden, she had still the same fondness for their company; nor was there a kinder lady to be found in introducing and encouraging bashful young girls just entering society. She gained their confidence at once, and in a large mixed company, you would always find a group of youthful faces around her, all whose pleasures seemed to be her own.

"In almost every picture of Mrs. Madison she is drawn with a turban; and very properly; for it was, I believe, her constant head dress.

However the fashions might change, and however, in other respects, she conformed to them, she still retained this peculiarity. It became her well, nor could she, probably, have laid it aside for anything that would have set off her features to better advantage. So much was the eye accustomed to see it that it became, in fact, a part of her figure. It was to her much what Frederick's three cornered hat was to him. The Prussian army would have been very much surprised to see their king without his hat; but no more so than would have been the people of those days to find Mrs. Madison without her turban.

THE WAR OF 1812

"Taxation without representation" was the cause of the American Revolution. A long phrase for little folks to remember, but easy enough after you understand what it means.

I shall have to ask you to remember a longer phrase, but I will try to explain it to you so that it will be as easy as that giving the cause of the Revolution.

The cause of this second war with England, was *"the impressments of American sailors and the capturing of our vessels."*

Now let us see if we can understand what *"impressments of American sailors"* means.

Of course, England did not feel very kindly towards the American colonies after the Revolution. Not only had she met with a most humiliating defeat from those whom she had laughed at and called barnyard soldiers, clod-hopper militia, and many other such contemptuous names, but she had also lost a very valuable colony, one that would have been a source of great wealth to her as it grew in numbers and in power.

Every since the Constitution had been formed, and the American Nation had seemed so full of success, England had been doing everything possible to injure American commerce. England had for a long, long time called herself the "Mistress of the Sea," and had prided herself on having the finest navy in the world.

The United States, dreading to go to war again, had borne many an insult both from England and from France. But when the English began *impressing* our sailors,—that was a little more than we could endure.

It had long been the custom in England to fill up their ship's crews by "impressment," as they called it. This is the way they went about it. When they could not find enough men who were willing to become sailors, a party of rough men, called the "press-gang," would go upon land, look about for hearty, strong-looking young men, and, when they had found one who seemed likely to make a good sailor, would seize upon him, bind him, and carry him off to a ship.

IMPRESSMENT OF AMERICAN SAILORS.

Sometimes they did not seize upon these men, but would invite one to drink with them; and then when they had made him drunk, would carry him off to their vessel, throw him into the hold and leave him there until he became sober. Many a poor lad has awakened from his stupor to find himself on shipboard, away from home and friends, bound on a voyage which was, perhaps, to last for years. If he refused to work, he was whipped until he cried for mercy. The "press-gang" was indeed the terror of all Europe.

You see now what *impressment of sailors* means; just simply this: stealing them and forcing them to become sailors on English ships.

And now, when I tell you that thousands of Americans had been seized in just this way by these English ships, do you wonder that again America declared war against England?

It was just at the close of Jefferson's Administration that an event occurred that aroused the Americans to act at once.

As the Chesapeake, one of our vessels, was crossing the ocean, it was ordered by the Leopard, an English vessel, to stop.

"I order you to stand and be searched," said the English officer.

"What do you expect to find?" asked Captain Barron.

"I search for English sailors," was the reply.

"We have no English sailors on board, and we shall not stop," answered our captain.

"You are all Englishmen, and in the name of the English government, I demand that you be searched." Immediately the English ship fired upon the Chesapeake, killing and wounding several of the crew. Three sailors were taken from the vessel and forced to serve as slaves. Such outrages as this were enough to stir the anger of any nation; and if ever war was right, it was right in such a time as this.

But in spite of all this the Federalists were opposed to war with England. They declared that if war with England was entered into, the United States would surely fall into the power of France, who was still at war with England.

It was just here that Henry Clay and John C. Calhoun, two of the greatest statesmen that America ever had, came into notice. Henry Clay was the leader of the Federalists, and was opposed to the war; John C. Calhoun was the leader of the Republicans, and was in favor of war.

Thus matters stood, when, in June, 1812, Congress declared war with England.

Great was the joy in the hearts of these impressed sailors on the English ships. Many of them at once refused to pull another rope on board a ship belonging to a nation at war with their own country.

"Will you do your duty on this ship?" asked one captain of an American who was suffering under the lash for refusal to work the ship. "Yes sir," answered the man, with his back bleeding at every pore. "It is my duty to blow up this ship, an enemy to my country, and if I get a chance, I'll do it."

The captain looked round in astonishment. "I think this man must be an American," he said. "No English sailor would talk like that. He is probably crazy, and you may untie him and let him go."

Over twenty-five hundred Americans who had been impressed and who thus refused to serve, were sent to prison in England, where they were kept in the most wretched imprisonment until the war closed.

Many of the men were flogged—some of them till they dropped dead—but they showed the same brave spirit that they had shown years before in the Revolution. One would suppose that after being so completely defeated by the American *colonies* England would hardly have cared to go to war with the American *States*.

HULL'S SURRENDER OF DETROIT

"What!" cried the Federalists; "fight with the English on the *sea!* Expect this new weak navy of ours to fight with the great ships of England! It is madness!"

"Just wait," said the Republicans. "Just wait," said the seamen, who were burning to avenge the wrongs of their fellow sailors. They did wait, and they did see.

"We shall soon conquer them this time," said the English. "The Indians will keep up an attack on them on the western border, and we, with our great fleets, will attack them along the Atlantic, along the gulf, and along the lakes on the north. Very likely we shall gain back all that we lost in the Revolution," said they.

And so the fighting began on the Canada border. Gen. Hull was in command of a fort there. And although he had a small garrison, still there is not doubt he might have defended the fort and have saved it from the English.

Brock, the English commander, approached the fort and demanded that it be surrendered at once. "If you don't surrender," said he, "I'll let the Indians loose upon you, and you know what Indian warfare is."

Unfortunately, Hull *did* know too well what Indian warfare was, and his fear of the tomahawk evidently overcame his fear of disgrace; for, without consulting his officers, he hung out the white flag of surrender, and the fort with all its provisions fell into the hands of the enemy.

His soldiers and his officers, who were ready and eager to fight, were angry and mortified that they had been sold so meanly. One man, it is said, broke his sword in pieces, and tearing his gilt lace from his coat, trampled them under foot, saying, "We have been made to disgrace our uniform by surrendering in this cowardly fashion, without one blow."

Hull was tried for treason; but no proof could be brought against him, and he was acquitted of that charge. He was, however, sentenced to death for cowardice.

He claimed to have surrendered the fort to save his men from the horrors of Indian slaughter. Perhaps it was so; but most people believed that he could very easily have kept back both Indians and English had he tried. Hull was pardoned by the President, and lived ever after in the quiet of his home.

THE AMERICAN ARMY OF TWO

During the war of 1812, there lived in a little seaport town of Massachusetts a child named Rebecca Bates. Rebecca's father was the lighthouse-keeper, and he with his family lived in a little white cottage on a point of land jutting out into the bay. This little cottage, which stood just behind the tall lighthouse, had been Rebecca's home ever since she was born.

One day Rebecca and a little girl friend of hers were sitting on the point looking off across the sunny water, when they noticed afar off, a ship apparently making in for the harbor. There was something about this ship which, though so far away, struck terror to these girls' hearts; for these were very trying days—these days of 1812—when the British war ships could be seen bearing down upon the little sea-ports, and unloading their British soldiers to march upon the people.

For an hour or two this ship tacked, and stood off to sea, and tacked again, and finally anchored at the mouth of the harbor. The people watching from the shore could see the boats being lowered, and the soldiers preparing to land.

Rebecca and her friend had hastened up into the tower of the light-house, and eagerly watched the movements of the soldiers in their glittering armor and gay red coats.

"O, if I were only a man!" cried Rebecca, as she thought that before night her little home might lie in ashes, burned by these cruel British soldiers.

"What would you do?" asked her friend; "see how many soldiers there are, and how many guns they have."

"I don't care," cried the hot-headed Rebecca. "I'd fight 'em—I'd use father's old gun—I'd—"

"I wonder if there will be a fight?" broke in Sarah.

"I don't know—the men in the village will do all they can."

"But see how quiet it is! Not a man to be seen on the shore!"

"O, but they are hiding till the soldiers get close to land, then we shall hear the shot and the drum! O, but the drum! the drum! it's here in the light-house. Father brought it here only yesterday to be mended!"

"O, dear! what shall we do?" cried the excited Rebecca. "And see! they have reached that little sloop and are going to burn her! O, how mean! It's a shame! Where's that drum? I have a mind to go and beat it!"

"What good would that do?"

"It might scare them if nothing more."

"They would see it is only two girls, and would go on burning just the same."

"No; we could hide behind the sand-hills and bushes. Come let's go!"

"O, look! look! the sloop's on fire!"

"There! I won't stay one minute longer and see those cowardly British burn our boats! The cowards! why don't they go up into the village and fight like men? Come, let's get the drum. It will do no harm at any rate."

"All right," said Sarah, now thoroughly aroused. "There's the fife too! I'll get that."

And away the two girls ran down to the cottage for the fife and the drum; and away they scrambled among the rocks, behind the bushes and the sand hills, out towards the end of the point.

"Drum! drum! drum! Squeak! squeak! squeak!"

The soldiers out at the harbor mouth stopped their unloading, and listened.

"Drum! drum! drum! Squeak! squeak! squeak!"

"What does that mean?" asked a British soldier.

"Troops! troops!" cried another. "Troops are formed and are marching down to hem us in from the point. Hark! isn't the drumming advancing?"

"Drum! drum! drum! Squeak! squeak! squeak!"

"They're coming to the point surely!"

"We'd better get outside the point before we are hemmed in completely," cried another. And then the commanding officer gave the order to regain the ship.

Scrabble, scrabble! Up over the sides of the vessel like frightened rats went the red-coated soldiers, who a minute before had stepped forth so bravely into the boats intent upon subduing the simple village folk.

It took very little time for the ship to be turned about; and by the time the "American Army of Two" had reached the point, the great ship was speeding away, looking for all the world as if it had but one idea—that of getting away as soon as possible.

Rebecca and Sarah had all the time kept one eye out towards the ship, and when they saw the effect of their drum, drum, drum, and their squeak, squeak, squeak had upon the mighty enemy, they could scarcely keep their time, so convulsed they were with laughter.

The people in the village meantime had been as much filled with surprise as had the British soldiers.

"What can it be?" said one.

"It must be troops from Boston," said another.

"And just in time to save us," said a third.

Then after the ship had sailed away, down rushed the villagers to the point to see the Boston troops.

Imagine their surprise to see, sitting comfortably on the rocks, their drum and fife by their side, these two girls, Rebecca and Sarah.

You perhaps can imagine what the villagers said and what the girls said; how the story of this "American Army of Two," as they were ever after called, spread through the villages and towns, and how these two girls were honored and looked upon as the preservers of their little town by the village folk.

Sarah and Rebecca grew up to be good, noble women, and when, only a few years ago, Rebecca died, her story was told all over again by the newspapers of our country, and in many a school and church honorable notice was given the good old lady, who as a child had done so much for her little town on the sea-coast of Massachusetts.

THE CONSTITUTION AND THE GUERRIERE

About a fortnight before the unfortunate surrender of General Hull, his nephew, Captain Isaac Hull, set sail from Boston Harbor, in a vessel called the Constitution. This little vessel, which afterward became so famous, carried fifty-four guns, and was manned by as brave a body of men as we have ever read about in the history of our country.

They sailed up to the Gulf of St. Lawrence, where they cruised about for several days, watching for English vessels. One evening, at about six o'clock, the English frigate Guerriere was seen not far away, making signs to the American vessel to come and fight.

"We are quite as ready to come as they are to have us," said Captain Hull; and he at once ordered his men to put on full sail, and go to meet the Guerriere.

"I wonder what vessel that is," said the English Captain; "It can not be an American ship, I am sure."

"I am sure she shows the American flag," answered an officer, who was watching her through a glass.

"It can't be," said the captain; "no American vessel would dare approach us so boldly. See! she is coming as fast as she can—under full sail."

In a few minutes, however, all doubts were settled. The Constitution drew nearer, until the stars and stripes were plainly to be seen.

"What daring!" cried the English crew; and at once the Guerriere opened upon the approaching vessel a terrible volley.

Not a gun was discharged from the American vessel.

Another broadside from the Guerriere! Hull's officers began to mutter among themselves. "Why may we not return the fire?" asked they.

"Not yet," answered Hull firmly. "But one man has already been killed by the British fire," said one of the crew. "Is it not time to fire, then?" said another.

"Not quite yet," returned Hull, watching the British boat, and pacing up and down the deck in great excitement.

Nearer and nearer drew the vessels, until they stood almost side by side.

"Now! fire!" commanded Hull. Bang! bang! bang! went the guns, sending such a deadly storm of fire that the Guerriere was nearly swept clear of officers and men. Rivers of blood poured over the deck in the track of the terrible fire.

Never was battle more terrible! Both ships seemed wrapped in flame and smoke; and when the smoke had cleared away, there lay the Guerriere, her masts broken, her sided torn with balls—a mere useless hulk, already sinking into the sea.

The "Constitution" now drew near, cut down the English flag, unfurled the stars and stripes in its place, took prisoner the few remaining officers and crew, and then set fire to the wreck.

Such was the battle between the Constitution and the Guerriere! a brave, daring attack on the part of Hull and his men, we know— and a brave resistance on the part of the English ship. But what can compensate for such a bloody ghastly contest!

OLD IRONSIDES

[The following lines were called forth by a rumor that the frigate Constitution was about to be broken up as unfit for service.]

Ay, tear her tattered ensign down!
    Long has it waved on high,
And many an eye has danced to see
    That banner in the sky:
Beneath it rung the battle-shout,
    And burst the cannon's roar;
The meteor of the ocean-air
    Shall sweep the clouds no more.

Her deck, once red with heroes' blood,
    Where knelt the vanquished foe,
When winds were hurrying o'er the flood,
    And waves were white below,
No more shall feel the victor's tread,
    Or know the conquered knee;
The harpies of the shore shall pluck
    The eagle of the sea.

Oh, better that her shattered hulk
Should sink beneath the wave;
Her thunders shook the mighty deep,
And there should be her grave.
Nail to the mast her holy flag,
Set every threadbare sail,
And give her to the god of storms—
The lightning and the gale.

—O. W. HOLMES.

THE WASP AND THE FROLIC

Between ships with such lively names as these, we might well expect a lively battle.

One Sunday morning, just after sunrise, an American vessel, the Wasp fell in with the Frolic, a vessel which was guarding some merchant vessels on their way from the West Indies.

The Wasp began at once to get herself ready for a real wasp fight. The Frolic did the same; but as she had only just weathered a severe storm, I fear she did not feel in a very frolicsome mood.

It was a rough morning. The sea rolled, the waves piled up and broke over the vessels' sides, making even the oldest sea-dogs stagger about, as they prepared for battle.

At last the signal was given, and bang! bang! bang! bang! bang! bang! went the guns from both the Wasp and the Frolic. For a time it was uncertain which would stand the storm of fire.

At the very first volley the Wasp lost mast and rigging and pitched wildly about on the foaming sea, tossing her men in every direction over the slippery deck.

But, swinging round, she quickly brought her side over against the bows of the Frolic, and let fire a volley which raked the other vessel from stem to stern, carrying death to nearly every soul on deck.

And now, so close were they, that the crew of the Wasp, with yells and howls, swarmed over the sides of their vessel, boarding the Frolic with wild cheers of triumph.

Two other naval battles took place during this year of 1812, in both of which the Americans were victorious.

The English were struck dumb with amazement; and I suspect the Americans themselves were hardly less surprised. The English newspapers growled and snarled. "What!" said they; "shall an English man-of-war, which has not been beaten since the days of Queen Elizabeth, be beaten now by a parcel of American-built ships, manned by raw sailors! Shall our Britannia, which so long has ruled the sea, be beaten by this upstart nation!"

But notwithstanding all that *had been*, it *now was* that the American nation had proved itself as brave on sea as on land; and the great English navy was forced to acknowledge a rival.

THE LOST WAR-SLOOP

("THE WASP," 1814)

O, the pride of Portsmouth water,
Toast of every brimming beaker,—
Eighteen hundred and fourteen on land and sea—
Was the "Wasp," the gallant war-sloop,
Built of oaks Kearsarge had guarded,
Pines of Maine to lift her colors high and free!
Every timber scorning cowards:
Every port alert for foemen
From the masthead seen on weather-side or lee;—
With eleven guns to starboard,
And eleven guns to larboard,
All for glory on a morn of May sailed she.

British ships were in the offing;
Swift and light she sped between them,—
Well her daring crew knew shoal and wind and tide;
They had come from Portsmouth river,
Sea-girt Marblehead and Salem,
Bays and islands where the fisher-folk abide;
Come for love of home and country,
Come with wrongs that cried for vengeance,—
Every man among them brave and true and tried.
"Hearts of oak" are British seamen?
Hearts of fire were these their kindred,

THE LOST WAR-SLOOP

Flaming till the haughty foe should be descried!
From the mountains, from the prairies
Blew the west winds glad to waft her;—
Ah, what goodly ships before her guns went down!
Ships with wealth of London laden,
Ships with treasures of the Indies,
Till her name brought fear to British wharf and town;
Till the war-sloops "Reindeer," "Avon,"
To her valor struck their colors,
Making coast and ocean ring with her renown;
While her captain cried exultant,
"Britain, to the bold Republic,
Of the empire of the seas shall yield the crown!"

Oh, the woeful, woeful ending
Of the pride of Portsmouth's water!
Never more to harbor or to shore came she?
Springs returned but brought no tidings;
Mothers, maidens broken-hearted
Wept the gallant lads that sailed away in glee.
Did the bolts of heaven blast her?
Did the hurricanes o'erwhelm her
With her starry banner and her tall masts three?
Was a pirate fleet her captor?
Did she drift to polar oceans?
Who shall tell the awful secret of the sea?

Who shall tell? yet many a sailor
In his watch at dawn or midnight,
When the wind is wildest and the black waves moan,
Sees a staunch three-master looming;
Hears the hurried calls to quarters,
The drum's quick beat and the bugle fiercely blown;—
Then the cannon's direful thunder
Echoes far along the billows;
Then the victor's shout for the foe overthrown;—
And the watcher knows the phantom
Is the "Wasp," the gallant war-sloop,
Still a rover of the seas and glory's own!

—EDNA DEAN PROCTOR.

"DON'T GIVE UP THE SHIP"

This has come to be so much a watchword among our people, that it would never do for us to pass on without learning what it means. You have already learned the meaning of "Taxation without Representation," "Millions for defense, but not one cent for tribute." You will recall, too, that battle in the Revolution where "Molly Stark" was the watchword; then there was the attack by Ethan Allen on the fort—when he cried, "In the name of the Great Jehovah and the Continental Congress I command you to surrender."

All these sayings uttered at one time or another by some loyal son of America, have been passed down in our history, until they have come to be *immortal*, that is, never-dying sayings.

And now let us see how it was that "Don't give up the Ship!" came to be another of these "immortal sayings."

There was in our navy, a ship called the *Hornet*—a twin, perhaps to the fiery *Wasp* that you have just heard about. This *Hornet*, with Captain Lawrence as its commander, was buzzing about in pretty nearly the same part of the ocean in which we found the Wasp—on the lookout for some unlucky English vessel into which to fix its stings. Soon up came the English Peacock,—strutting along, I imagine, under full sail, feeling as vain and sure of success as a real peacock might have felt when about to attack so small a thing as a hornet. But size isn't everything; as we have already found in many a battle of the history of our country.

The *Peacock* gave the signal for battle. Instantly the furious little *Hornet* flew at the *Peacock*, and an angrier little hornet, with hotter stings, you never saw.

Boom! boom! boom! buzz! buzz! buzz! hiss! hiss! hiss! went the fire from both Peacock and Hornet. So fast and so thick flew the balls, so hot and so terrible was the battle, that in fifteen minutes the proud Peacock had lost all her glory and her pride, all her beauty and her courage, and lay upon the waters a complete wreck.

Her hold was now half full of water; and, knowing that she must sink, her commander surrendered to Lawrence, the crew were taken prisoners and transferred to the Hornet.

The generous way in which Lawrence treated his prisoners won the hearts of the British even; and his bravery carried delight to the hearts of his countrymen.

When he came into Boston harbor with the Hornet, he was greeted with shouts and hurrahs; and another vessel was given him, while the Hornet was set aside for repairs.

Now, this new vessel which was given into the charge of Captain Lawrence, had been, from its very beginning, an unlucky vessel. So much so, indeed, that the sailors were afraid to board her, believing that she was fated, and must surely bring only sorrow to her crew.

But brave Captain Lawrence willingly took command of her; feeling confident and secure after his recent victory.

No sooner was he ready to sail forth from Boston Harbor, than he met in battle the

Shannon, an English vessel. I wish I could tell you that the gallant Lawrence again came out victorious. But, instead, I shall have to tell you that after a hot, fierce battle of only fifteen minutes—a battle as fierce, and hot, and terrible as had been that between the Wasp and the Frolic, or between the Hornet and the Peacock—the unlucky vessel was reduced to a mere wreck. At the very beginning of the fight, Lawrence himself, who always stood in the very thickest of the fire, fell mortally wounded.

FIGHT BETWEEN THE *CHESAPEAKE* AND THE *SHANNON*.

Thus folded in his country's flag, Lawrence was carried by the British to Halifax, where he was buried with the respect and honor which he so richly deserved.

Very carefully did his officers carry below their much loved commander; and Lawrence, not forgetting his charge even in dying, whispered almost with his last breath, "Don't give up the ship!"

The British, wild with delight, that at last, after so many defeats, victory was once more on their side, swarmed upon the deck of the American vessel, singing and shouting with joy.

But when they found the brave Lawrence lying dead, they did not forget how nobly and how kindly he had dealt with the English prisoners at his victory over the English Peacock. And so, seizing the American flag, which they had torn from the mast with such yells of delight, they carefully lifted the unfortunate commander, and wrapped around him this banner which he had so loved, and for which he had so bravely fought.

THE FRIENDLY FOES

Just before the "Wasp" set out on her cruise an American commodore, named Rogers, put to sea with a number of ships. One of these named the "United States" and in charge of the famous Captain Stephen Decatur, started off alone across the Atlantic to the southeast.

The "United States" was beautifully fitted up, and captain and lieutenant had spared no pains in training her crew, that she might be the most strongly manned of any vessel in the United States service.

As the vessel drew near Maderia report came of a strange vessel sighted to the southward.

"If it is an English frigate, we know what that means for us," said the crew, filled with excitement.

How intently the approaching vessel was watched! It comes nearer now—almost, almost,—yes,—now her banners can be seen. Yes, it is an English vessel. A little nearer and her name! M-a-c-e-d-o-n-i-a-n!

"The 'Macedonian'!" cried the commander. "Do you say it is the 'Macedonian'? Are you sure it is the 'Macedonian'?"

"Aye, aye, sir," replied the mate; "and a fine frigate she is said to be—as fine a one as sails the English waters."

"The 'Macedonian,'" said the commander, a troubled look creeping into his eyes. "I would rather it had been any English vessel than that," said he, half to himself, looking sadly out across the water at the approaching vessel.

Now it had happened that in times of peace, Decatur, our American commander, cruising around in his frigate, had often come across this frigate "Macedonian," and the two captains had grown to be warm friends. Often they had said, "What should we do if some time our frigates should meet as foes?" And as always Decatur had said, "Let us not think of such a ting; for it is sure to go hard with any English foe my frigate might encounter; for I would fight, fight to the last man. No enemy should haul down her colors as long as I had left a hulk to raise them from!"

And now here were these two warm friends face to face in deadly battle. American and England were at war.

"Be ready, every man at his gun!" sternly commanded Decatur.

Nearer and nearer drew the "Macedonian." Now she is in range. The command is given; and out blaze the guns. Such a volley! The United States frigate was wrapped in smoke. The English frigate was raked from stem to stern.

"She is on fire! She is on fire!" shouted the British crew.

But she was not on fire. Another volley—another—another!

Down went one mast. "That volley made a brig of her!" said Decatur. "Another, boys, and she'll be a sloop!"

How the "Macedonian" creaked and rolled! Down came her great mizzen mast—and then the "Macedonian" surrendered. Poor "Macedonian"! Masts all broken, her sides full of holes—what else was there for the brave vessel to do?

Now all was quiet. The firing ceased. The smoke cleared away—there lay the brave "Macedonian," a poor, broken wreck.

Captain Carden, the commander, the friend of Decatur came on board the United States frigate, and, as is the custom, stood before Decatur, surrendering his sword.

It was a hard, bitter moment for both men. Little joy was there to Decatur in a victory that defeated and ruined his friend.

"I cannot take your sword," said he to Carden. "I will take your hand instead."

Then the two friendly foes clasped hands. The contest, the victory, and the defeat made a strange experience to them. England said, "Another frigate lost!" America said, "Hurrah! Hurrah! another victory over the British!"

A YOUNG HERO

On board the "United States," and during the battle you have just read about, was a boy only ten years of age, Jack Creamer by name.

In those days very many young boys were employed on shipboard, but their names were not entered upon the muster roll of the ship until they had reached a certain age, or served a certain time.

When Jack, our young hero, saw the "Macedonian" bearing down upon the American frigate, he looked troubled, "Ho! ho! Jack," cried his comrades, "you are afraid!"

"I'm not!" cried Jack, indignantly; and he hurried away to find the captain.

"Well Jack, what's wanting now?" said the captain, as the bashful boy sidled up to him, evidently wishing, yet dreading, to make some request.

"Please, Commodore, will you put my name upon the muster roll before the battle begins?"

"Why, what for, my lad?" asked Decatur, surprised.

"So that I can draw my share of the prize money when we capture the British vessel," replied the boy, bravely.

"All right;" laughed the captain: "since you are so sure we shall have the prize money to divide."

"I am sure we shall," answered Jack, simply.

The battle came on; a quick, hot battle, as you have read. Jack was stationed on the main deck—in the thickest of the fight—as powder boy. Close to one of the great guns he stood; and to keep powder ready for this gun was his duty. Back and forth between the powder magazine and the gun he hurried, the cartridges closely hidden beneath his jacket so that no spark might reach them. Overhead, among the rigging, all about him on every side, whizzed the deadly leaden balls; but Jack took little heed. To keep his gun busy, to take the British ship, was all he thought or knew.

"Well, Jack," said the captain, when the battle was over, "we *did* capture the Britisher!"

"Yes, sir; yes, sir," answered Jack, his smoky, sooty face radiant with joy. "I knew we would."

"And now," continued the captain, "if we succeed in getting the old hulk safe into port, there'll be the prize money. Would you mind telling me what you propose to do with the two hundred dollars that will be your share?"

"O sir," answered Jack. "Half of it I shall send to my mother. The other half—with that I will get me a bit of schooling."

Decatur's kind heart was touched. You may be sure the brave boy got his "bit of schooling" and that he had ever after a warm friend in the good captain.

For many years the lad served under his friend in the navy, and in his service won many honors both through Decatur's friendly interest in him and through his own unfailing courage and his strong, ready, honest bravery.

A LUCKY SHOT

It was a beautiful Sabbath morning in July 1812, that the "Oneida," an American vessel, lay in Sacketts' Harbor. The vessel had just come into port after a long, busy season of active warfare, and the crew, tired out, were planning for a day of real rest.

But, in the early morning, just as the light began to dawn, report came, "The enemy are approaching—they have entered the harbor—they are upon us!"

At once the alarm was spread through the little town; and down to the shore rushed the people. There at the entrance of the harbor lay five men-of-war.

"What will they do?" asked the frightened people. "What can *we* avail against such a foe in this little close harbor of ours!"

Just then a little boat was lowered from the leader of the fleet.

"See, a messenger comes!" called one from the "Oneida," who was watching from his high place.

Swiftly the little boat advanced. The captain of the "Oneida" waited anxiously, but so quietly that every man around him took courage.

The little boat came alongside. "The captain of the 'Oneida?' " asked the man in the boat.

"I am he," answered the captain.

"This message from the captain of the fleet now stationed at the entrance to the harbor: 'Let the 'Oneida' surrender or the town will be destroyed.'"

But Commodore Woolsey, the brave officer who commanded the "Oneida," knew no such word as surrender. But what could he do? He could not escape, for there lay the enemy just outside the entrance.

"We do not know the word surrender," said the Commodore. At once he began giving orders for action.

The villagers threw up rough breastworks along the shore, dragged down their own great gun and set up on either side a cannon which, at some time, the plucky villagers had pulled up from the sunken hulk of an old British vessel. Commodore Woolsey, meantime, ordered his vessel to the entrance of the harbor. Then he placed her in such a way that her broadside of nine guns faced the enemy.

At eight o'clock the British man-of-war came up within range. Out pealed the great gun from the shore; but alas, it sent its volley only into the water and the enemy were by no means harmed.

"Hooray! Hooray! Hooray for the Yankee gun!" shouted the British, who had a way in this war as in the Revolution, of having their laugh in the early part of the contest—perhaps, because they so rarely had it on their side in the end.

For two hours the firing went on from the shore, from the "Oneida" and from the English vessels. In all that time no one was harmed, neither side had gained one point.

"This is child's play," said a villager, impatiently, as he loaded the great gun at which the British had shouted in scorn.

But just then a whizz-z-z, then a thud, and a great cannon ball from the British fleet rolled at the villager's feet.

"We've been playing ball with the red-coats now long enough," cried he, lifting the ball. "Now let's see if they can catch back again!"

And so saying he rammed the ball down the muzzle of the long gun. "Now then, old gun!" said he, as he sent the ball whizzing out across the water.

A boom, a whiz, a crack, and the Royal George was raked from stem to stern, and fourteen men lay wounded upon the deck.

A silence followed. There was hurrying to and fro along the vessel's decks—then—what do think? —the squadron put about, and sped out of the harbor as fast as ever it could, leaving the villagers so dumb with consternation that minutes passed before it occurred to them to rejoice in their victory.

"Hooray! Hooray! Hooray!" cried they, as the British sped away. "Hooray for the Yankee gun!"

AN ADVENTURE OF THE SHIP PRESIDENT

The "President," a Yankee frigate under Commodore Rogers, sailing into the Irish Channel, took up its position just where it could worry the British vessels going in and out and prey upon the British commerce.

"This must be stopped," said the British authorities. "That one little frigate is doing more harm and making more trouble than a whole squadron. We will send a squadron out to meet this vessel. It is weak, foolish, absurd for the English government to allow the vessel to cruise about our channels in this manner. Has the English navy no power, no authority, no dignity?"

And a squadron was sent out to meet this vessel. But no sooner did it set forth than Commodore Rogers, who someway seemed never to be caught napping, heard of its approach and put out to sea.

"We will go home," said Commodore Rogers, cheerily, "I think the British will remember us even if we do stay no longer in their waters."

It was a brisk September morning—so clear and bright. Gaily the little frigate sped before the breeze, her white canvas gleaming, her cordage creaking merrily, her prow cutting the dancing waves.

All was well. But towards evening a sail was seen. "It is a British vessel," said Rogers, scanning it closely. "I think they are following us—yes—I am sure they are."

"Quick, quick, my men," said Rogers. "Up with our British banners—on with your British uniforms, and remember *now* we are the British 'Sea Horse!'"

"Aye, aye, sir," answered the crew, ready enough to deceive the pursuing vessel—for 'all things,' you know they say, 'are fair in love and war.'"

On came the British vessel, nearer and nearer, till at last its banner could be seen. "Welcome the 'High flyer,' be ready, my men," shouted Rogers, "H. M. S.—the Highflyer."

Nearer and nearer came the vessel—now she is alongside. "Now, my good British lieutenant," said Rogers to one of his men, "you will go on board the 'Highflyer' with this message from the commodore of this, the English 'Sea Horse' to the commodore of the English 'Highflyer.'"

With great dignity and mock gravity, the lieutenant received his orders and went on board the "Highflyer."

"I am," said he to the "Highflyer," "the bearer of this message from the commodore of the British vessel, the 'Sea Horse,' it is requested that the ship books of the 'Highflyer' be sent on board the 'Sea Horse' for comparison and, if need be, for revision.

The commodore of the "Highflyer" received the lieutenant and his message with that courtesy always observed between officers either in the army or in the navy, and on his return to his own vessel accompanied him.

"Ah, this is a fine vessel," said the commodore of the "Highflyer" as he examined the "Sea Horse." "Indeed, you do not find such a ship as this in any outside the English navy. Ah, England is the mistress of the sea! Now those little American crafts—I boarded one once—paugh! such a vessel! And by the way, have you seen anything of that little frigate, the 'President!' We are to overtake her— she's made trouble enough for one frigate so we think. They say she put out to sea this morning. Probably knew we were after her, so ran away, coward that she is." And the commodore laughed loudly at what he considered a huge joke.

It was a joke, no doubt; for the commodore and the officers of the "Sea Horse" laughed— yes, roared with laughter; and the commodore of the "Highflyer" strutted and puffed up and down the deck, filled with pride and satisfaction at his own wit.

"By-the-by, what sort of a fish is that Rogers, the commodore of the 'President,'" asked Rogers, a twinkle in his eye.

"A mighty odd fish, I am told," answered the commodore of the "Highflyer." "At any rate he proves a hard fish to catch. But he shall be my prisoner yet," growled the commodore—and little mercy will he get from me. No sir! Americans—the miserable, cowardly——"

"Hold sir! do you know on whose vessel you stand—do you know to whom you speak?" interrupted Rogers, his eyes flashing fire at the word *cowardly*, as applied to his nation. "You are this minute on board the 'President,' I am Commodore Rogers and you are my prisoner.

"Hoist the American flag—down with the British banner!" called Rogers to his crew.

The commodore of the "Highflyer" stared, turned pale, actually gasped. But there was nothing to be said- —nothing to be done. The "Highflyer" was surrendered, and away sailed Rogers, a harder fish to catch than ever—at least so thought the "Highflyer" and its bragging, busting commodore.

A STORY OF SACKETT'S HARBOR

"It is useless," said the British officers stationed in Canada, "to attempt to march across the frontier to attack the Americans. But there are the lakes—their waters are open to us as well as to them. We will sail down upon them if we cannot march down upon them."

But you may be sure the Yankees' eyes were open—Yankees are not often caught napping, especially in war time. "The lakes must be fortified," said they. "The British will be sailing down upon us if we leave the great water course free to them."

But it was no easy thing to reach these frontiers in these early days. There were no railroads, not even roads through this section of the country. The same wildness, the same density of forests that prevented the march of the British down upon the American towns, made it a discouraging if not an impossible task to carry to the lakes the necessary guns and ammunition. More than that, the sailors themselves looked with scorn upon the ship life on land, as they called it. "We, who have sailed the Atlantic, do not propose to end our lives in those fish ponds," said they.

But after much hard work on the part of the government, much arguing and explaining, together with promise of larger pay to those seamen, who for their dear country's sake would thus martyr themselves, sailors were gathered together for the lake expeditions. They were a jolly crew, these sailors—a reckless, noisy crew. Sledges dashing up through the Maine, New Hampshire and Vermont woods, filled with these noisy, rollicking fellows, decked out in their red, white and blue, filling the woods with their shouts and songs were common sights in those days.

It was May, 1814, and the new frigate "Superior" lay in her dock at Sackett's Harbor. She was a trim little vessel; her builders were proud of her; her captain loved her; and the crew, ever the crew, eager to see her sail out over the sparkling waters of the lake.

But her stores, her cannon, her guns, her cordage—all these were to be brought from

Oswego Falls some fifty miles away. Now it would be easy enough to bring them up the Oswego River, but there were English vessels blockading the harbor—and to run an English blockade was not an easy thing to do, you may be sure.

But the stores must be brought. That was a fact. That it would be no easy matter was another fact equally plain.

But Yankees can always find a way if there is a way to be found; so finally, a captain, one who had grown up and grown old on and about the lakes, and so knew every inch of the way, was found who agreed to do the best he could, though even he hardly dared hope to reach the "Superior."

He set out with the stores and cannon. By dint of sailing the clear waters by night, and lying hidden up the creeks by day, the wise and wary old captain succeeded in getting within sixteen miles of Sackett's Harbor, where the English vessels lay in blockade.

But the hardest was not to come. How were those cannon, the stores, most of all, that enormous cable weighing ninety-six hundred pounds, to be taken across the country to the dock at Sackett's Harbor? Anyone but a "Yankee" would have given up in despair. But not so the brave captain and his faithful men. "The cannon we will load on to carts. They may sink in the marshes; they may break down in the forests; but we'll load them, we'll load them, my boys," said the captain.

"Aye, aye, sir!" replied the hearty sailors.

"But the cable; ninety-six hundred pounds of cable!" and the captain shook his wise old head ruefully.

The sailors looked at it too, and shook their heads. There it lay, a great heap of coiled rope. No cart could bear its weight; it could not be dragged; it could not be lifted; it could not be cut.

"If it would be divided among us—cut in pieces—there are two hundred of us—we—"

"Divide it! divide it! that's just the way!" shouted one great strong sailor. "'Rah for Teddy! 'Rah for Teddy! You shall have double rations for a week for that, my lad! Come on, boys, come on!"

And seizing one end of the cable, he tugged away at it, lifted it upon his shoulder, and facing Sackett's Harbor, broke into a hearty sailor song. "Come on, boys," said he. "Put your shoulder to the cable, every man of you.

Come now! Single file. Forward, march, to Sackett's Harbor!"

The two hundred jolly tars fell in at once with the plan and in this way the great cable reached its destination. What fun they had! How they laughed and shouted! How the forest rang with their sailor songs!

O, but it was heavy! Their backs ached; their shoulders grew raw and bleeding; and towards the end of the journey they were a weary, lame, exhausted file of men, indeed. But they reached the town, nevertheless, and were received with shouts of praise from the people. The shouts rang out over the harbor; the rockets blazed up above the house-tops; bands played; men shouted; the town was in a blaze of excitement; the sailors were feted and feasted, praised and honored till their very heads were turned. They were the heroes of the hour.

"What can have happened?" wondered the English squadron outside the harbor, as the shouts came out across the water, and the sky lighted up with the glare of the rockets.

"O, some Yankee victory," said one officer, bitterly.

"Those Yankees are a plucky set," answered his companion, shaking his head and scowling.

A STORY OF STONINGTON

It was one warm beautiful morning in August, 1814, that the people of Stonington, looking out across the water saw approaching, under full sail, a British vessel.

"She is coming straight into our little bay," said the frightened people, watching from their house-tops. "Yes, she is weighing anchor. She lowers a boat—she sends us a message—maybe a challenge.

But it was no challenge—only a message; and, still a message which the good people knew only too well, polite and civil and mild as it seemed, had all the force of a command. "We wish no harm to the people of Stonington. We only ask that they leave their town that we may occupy it."

"Leave our town! our homes! our fields! our houses!" exclaimed the people, indignant, frightened, sorrow-stricken.

"The militia! call together the militia! Let us decide and decide quickly—shall we leave our town or defend it?"

"Defend it!" shouted the militia, "and if need be, perish with it." And word was sent to the commodore—"the people of Stonington will defend their town to the last man."

Then such a hurrying to and fro as there was. Guns were dragged forward. Every man, woman and child set to work. Soon the British opened fire. Boom, boom, boom! went the cannons. It was a sharp, hot fight. How the women and children hurried hither and thither beating out the fires that every where about the village broke forth. How the men tugged and worked at the guns. Cannon ball after cannon ball came crashing into the village—still no one is killed, no home has been destroyed.

But see! the British have ceased firing! "It was not worth the lead," said the commodore, scornfully—and away he sailed out of the harbor. "Those Americans are strangely plucky," thought he to himself.

"Fifteen tons of lead!" exclaimed the Stonington people the next day, as they set to work to clear away their streets and repair their scorched buildings. "Fifteen tons of lead poured into our village and not one man killed!"

"Probably the Britisher wanted to lighten her cargo," said one old sailor, slyly.

"Write us a poem," said the people to their village rhymster. And here is what he wrote:

They killed a goose, they killed a hen,
Three hogs they wounded in a pen,
They dashed away, and pray, what then?
That was not taking Stonington.

The shells were thrown, the rockets flew,
But not a shell of all they threw,
Though every house was full in view,
Could burn a house in Stonington.

Not very classical poetry, is it? But it served to amuse the Stonington people for many a long day; and even now it stands in the old records of the town, a valued, treasured bit of history in rhyme.

COMMODORE PERRY

There was in the navy another brave young captain—Oliver Perry—who had been busy building a fleet of nine vessels to attack the British vessels which had taken possession of Lake Erie.

When these were finished, he named the one which he himself was to command, the *Lawrence*, in honor of our dead hero.

After the vessels were finished, it was a long time before men could be found to man them. General Harrison—you haven't forgotten General Harrison and the Indian chief, I hope—sent one hundred riflemen from Kentucky, who, dressed in their hunting suits and deer-skin leggings, made a very funny looking crew; and a little later, the New England States collected from their coasts another hundred men. These men were real sailors.

They had been in service on the Atlantic,—
some of them for long, long years.

When these sailors, some of them gray-
headed old seadogs, as they called themselves, were gathered together, it was found
their sea-legs, of which they were so proud,
and in which the country was putting so
much confidence, were entirely unfitted for
marching on land. They rolled around like
barrels, and had so little idea of military orders and marching, that their commander
declared he could do nothing with them.

Much fun did these "jolly tars" have over
their attempts to behave like soldiers; and I
fancy they were not very sorry when it was
decided to send them to Lake Erie in stage-
coaches.

So twelve great coaches were fitted out;
and with a band on top, flags and streamers
flying, these merry sailors started off across
the country, singing and shouting, the band
playing *Yankee Doodle, Hail Columbia*, and all
the other national airs, as they rattled
through the villages.

And now that the vessels were manned,
Captain Perry had only to wait for the appearance of the English fleet. Day after day he

waited; at last, one bright morning, the cry of "Sail, ho!" was heard from the mast-head. The English were really approaching! Word spread from vessel to vessel, and every officer and every sailor was on the alert.

Perry watched their approach through his glass, and found that there were only six ships, while he had nine; but as they drew nearer, he found that each vessel carried sixty-three guns, while his carried only fifty-four. This convinced him that if his vessels could get close upon the English, the advantage would be upon the American side; but if he allowed an engagement to take place at a distance, the sixty-three guns could do the deadlier work.

Explaining this to his men, it was agreed to advance quickly, and save their fire till they were close upon the English fleet. Then, bringing forth a simple banner, on which were inscribed "Don't give up the ship!" Perry said, "Boys, these were the dying words of the brave Lawrence. Shall we hoist this banner upon our vessel?"

Of course the men understood his meaning at once; and "Aye, aye, sir!" rang forth over the waters, followed by cheer on cheer, until it reached the very shores, and came re-sounding back, awaking in the hearts of the English crew a dread of what was about to happen.

Then followed a terrible scene of death and bloodshed. For three hours the battle raged. The decks ran blood; the air was filled with fire and smoke; and amid the deafening thunder of the guns, were heard the agoniz-ing cries of the wounded. The men fought as never men fought before, refusing to leave their guns, in spite of wounds upon wounds. At last, the Lawrence lay a battered hulk, at the mercy of the enemy. But Perry was not dismayed. Finding his own ship now helpless, only eighteen of his hundred brave men still standing, he ordered a boat to be lowered.

"To the Niagara! to the Niagara!" cried he; and wrapping himself in the flag, he leaped into the boat, and was rowed across to the Niagara.

Above him, below him, and on either side whizzed the English balls! Reaching the ves-sel, he hastily climbed her sides and again the terrible battle was renewed.

Bang! bang! went the Niagara's guns; and in fifteen minutes the battle was over. The English ships struck their colors, and the white flag of surrender was hoisted.

Two of the English ships turned to escape, but two of the American vessels gave chase, and soon they were brought back, prisoners.

The English officers, one by one, tendered their swords to Perry; but he generously refused to take them, and treated the prisoners throughout with such kindness that the English captain himself said, "Perry's kindness alone has earned him the name of hero."

"REMEMBER THE RIVER RAISIN"

But during this time of success on water, terrible things were happening on land. Tecumseh, the Indian chief who had sworn to have his revenge on the pale-faces, had leagued himself and his men with Proctor, a British general, and most brutal Indian slaughters had followed.

No British commander was ever more hated by the American people than this Gen. Proctor. He had taken the Indians as his allies, and had encouraged and spurred them on in their bloody work. He offered presents to the Indians for bringing to him American scalps, allowed the Indians to brutally murder Americans after a battle, even when they had surrendered and had begged for mercy.

But of all his brutal deeds, none were more brutal than the slaughter at Frenchtown, a little town upon the River Raisin.

The villagers, having heard of Gen. Hull's surrender, and knowing that now all that part of the country was in danger, had asked that Gen. Harrison, the hero of Tippecanoe, should send troops to protect them. He had, accordingly, sent a small body of soldiers, and these were now guarding the town. Gen. Winchester, too, was marching towards the town with more troops, when he was met by Proctor himself. With threats of Indian massacre with all its horrors, Proctor forced Winchester to write an order to the troops within the town, telling them to surrender to Proctor.

The troops, when Proctor appeared, bearing with him this order to surrender, very unwillingly yielded. They more than half doubted that Proctor had ever been given any such orders; but as there seemed little else to do, they at last threw down their arms, but only on condition that if they yielded themselves up thus, their wounded men in the town should be well cared for.

Proctor promised that everything should be as they wished, and then went away, taking with him the surrendered troops; but in less than twenty-four hours the yelling, war-painted savages rushed into the village, brandishing their tomahawks, driving the people from their homes, scalping and murdering their victims with the cruelty of demons.

When at last these savages had done their worst, had butchered all,—men, women and children,—except perhaps for a few who may have escaped into the forests, then they wound up their inhuman performance by piling up the dead and wounded in their homes where they had been slain, and, setting fire to the houses, danced, and drank, and howled the night away, around these terrible funeral pyres.

Proctor declared he had known nothing of the horrible intentions of the Indians, and so was not responsible for what they had done. Perhaps this may have been true; but these very scalps torn from the heads of the murdered villagers were carried into Proctor's camp; and, since the English general received them, and the Indians went on with the same terrible slaughter whenever opportunity came, we can but think that General Proctor was not very much displeased with the behavior of the savages.

The anger of the people all over the country was aroused and hundreds of men hastened to join Harrison's army, eager to march against the hated Proctor and his Indians.

Now, at the time of Perry's battle, General Harrison with eight thousand men were encamped on the shore awaiting the result. No sooner had the news of the defeat of this English fleet, which was on its way to join Proctor, reached the eager army, than Harrison marched his men on to Detroit, where Proctor and his Indians held the city.

Proctor, too, had heard of the defeat of the English; and when he learned that Harrison, with his eight thousand, was marching upon him, he set fire to the stores of powder and arms and fled up the river.

On reaching the deserted city, Harrison was joined by a thousand mounted soldiers; and without stopping to rest, all together they pushed on up the river in pursuit.

They overtook the army on the Thames river—eighty miles from the city. A more hungry, tired army never was, than this of Harrison's, after their long march; but throughout the march, when it seemed as if some *must* fall exhausted by the wayside, the cry of "Remember the River Raisin!" had always urged them on.

After a good night's rest, in which the army slept like children, they arose refreshed and ready for battle. The mounted Kentuckians, with the war cry of "Remember the River Raisin!" made the first onset.

A hot and terrible charge they made, spurred on by the thought that their dead at Frenchtown were thus avenged.

Proctor took to flight when he saw the battle turn against him. Tecumseh, burning with rage, and the desire to avenge his tribe, fought on, face to face, amid the balls which rained about him, wounded though he was time and time again, until, exhausted, he fell dead upon the field.

Then his warriors, finding their leader killed, with great yells and howls of grief, fled wildly into the forests. And thus ended the battle of the *Thames*—a complete though terrible victory for the American side.

OUR CAPITAL TAKEN BY THE ENGLISH

For some time the British ships had been blockading our coasts, and the name of their commander had come to be a word of terror in every home along the Atlantic shore. Here, there, and everywhere, his fleet had drawn up, and landed soldiers who would march up into the quiet, harmless little villages, set them on fire, and then march coolly away.

There was in England at this time a great general, the Duke of Wellington. He had just defeated the wonderful Napoleon Bonaparte in a great battle; and, as this Napoleon had been looked upon as a most wonderful being, never to be overcome by any army living, you can imagine with what respect and awe Wellington and his army were now looked upon. A general who had conquered Napoleon Bonaparte! Why, Franklin conquering the lightning was nothing compared with it!

And now it was reported that Wellington's army had joined the British fleet and was planning to lay waste the whole Atlantic coast. Indeed, the ships were already sailing up the Potomac. Think of it! the army that had defeated Napoleon! now marching straight to attack the capitol at Washington!

There were forty-five hundred men in all; but before they had reached the city, report said there were six, then seven, even eight thousand of them. Gen. Winder hastily got together a force of seven thousand men and some cavalry. They took their station outside the city and awaited the approach of this dreaded foe.

Three days later, the English marched up, tired and hot, ready to drop from the intensity of the heat. O, if the Americans could only have known this, if they could have known, too, that their own number was nearly twice that of the advancing foe!

But they knew only what report had told them; and so entered into the battle with little courage or hope of success.

The English army came up to them, drawn up in line just above a bridge, over which ran the road to the Capital. One charge from these Wellington troops across the bridge, and back they fell before the volley poured forth from the American lines! Another charge, quicker, fiercer, more determined! but this time the English won the bridge.

Another and another charge, and in less than four hours, the American lines were broken, and the men fled into the forests to escape the pursuit of the enemy. By evening, the English had entered our national capital. President Madison had been all day upon the battlefield; and when he saw that the defeat of the American army was sure, he rushed back to the city to warn the people of the advancing enemy. Mrs. Madison had already gathered together all that could be easily carried away, and was herself ready to leave the city.

At night, the army came into the deserted city. I suppose they expected to find much wealth and grandeur in this capital of the nation; but when you think that only fourteen years before the city had been but dense forests, you can easily understand that the seizing of this city wasn't, after all, so very great a gain to the English, nor yet so very great a loss to the country.

When the English officers entered the White House, it is said that they found the tables spread for a dinner, just as it had been prepared for the president and his party. These Englishmen sat down with a very good appetite, probably, after their hard day's work, and ate heartily. It is said that men are apt to be much better natured after having eaten a good dinner; but I am afraid it made very little difference with these officers, for they went at once to their soldiers, and ordered them to set fire to the city; then, fearing lest the Americans might return in numbers too strong for them, they marched back to their ships and sailed away.

Their next move was to attack Baltimore; but by the time they had reached that city, the people had learned how small a number they had, and so had lost their fear for them. They received here a strong repulse, and retired quite crestfallen.

There is a little incident connected with this attack upon Baltimore that is of interest to you all. While the soldiers were attacking the city, the English vessels lying in the bay were bombarding Fort McHenry. Just before the firing began, Francis Scott Key, an American soldier, had gone on board an English vessel to ask the commander to release certain prisoners that had been taken at Washington.

Key was kept on board during the entire bombardment. At midnight the firing ceased. What does the silence mean?

Have the forts surrendered, or are the English driven back? Hour after hour the brave soldier peered through the darkness, longing to catch one glimpse of the stars and stripes, which the day before had floated so proudly over the fort. Of course, if the English had taken the fort, they would at once have torn down the flag. It was during this night of anxious watching that he composed the good old song which very likely you and your schoolmates can sing. It is not so common perhaps as "Yankee Doodle," but it has become one of our national songs; and sometime when you hear the bands playing it on our national holidays, you will be glad to remember how it came to be written.

"Oh say, can you see, by the dawns' early light,
What so proudly we hailed at the twilight's last gleaming,
Whose broad stripes and bright stars, through the perilous
*   fight,*
O'er the ramparts we watched, were so gallantly streaming;—
And the rockets' red glare, the bombs bursting in air,
Gave proof through the night that our flag was still there.
CHORUS
Oh, say, does the star spangled banner yet wave
O'er the land of the free, and the home of the brave?"

THE END OF THE WAR

There were other battles upon the land and other battles upon the water in this War of 1812; but as battles are all the same old story of murder and bloodshed over and over again, no matter how just or how unjust the cause, I think you will by this time be glad enough to come out of this cloud of fire and smoke, and breathe once more under the clear quiet skies of peace.

The war ended finally with the battle of New Orleans. The commander of the American forces in this battle was General Andrew Jackson; the same Andrew Jackson who, in the Revolutionary times, had been knocked down for refusing to clean the boots of an English officer who had taken him prisoner. What he had seen and what he had suffered in those old days had filled him with a lifelong hatred of the English; and so there were

few generals in the American army better fitted to fight the English than this fiery Andrew
Jackson.

On reaching New Orleans, he went to work
with a will. He formed regiments of black
men—a thing unheard of in those days; and
when at last the enemy approached, he and
his men, both black and white, worked like
ants, piling up cotton bales, sugar barrels—
anything they could lay their hands on; until
they had about them a wall which Wellington
himself might well have dreaded to climb.

The battle which followed ended successfully for the Americans, and with it closed the
war. There was great joy throughout the
country. Messengers were sent, as at the
close of the Revolution, with all the speed
their horses could make, from State to State;
and everywhere the bells were rung, bonfires
were built, bands played and processions
marched, anything and everything was done
in celebration of another victory over the
English, and of another time of peace.

THE ATTACK ON NEW ORLEANS.

PRESIDENT MONROE.

THE ERA OF GOOD FEELING

Let us see. We have read of how many presidents now? Washington, John Adams, Jefferson, and Madison. And now, after the war had closed, when the country was at peace again, and both Democrats and Republicans were so glad over having conquered the English again, that they were almost willing to be good friends with each other, there came another president—James Monroe. Because of the quiet, peaceful times, during which Monroe was president, the years of his administration have been called the "era of good feeling."

One of the pleasantest things during his administration was the visit of Lafayette to America. Lafayette was a young Frenchman who, in the war of the Revolution, had come over to our assistance in a most brave and noble way. He was much loved by Washington, and by all indeed who had known him in those trying days. And now, an old man of more than sixty years, he came again to see the country for which he had fought so long ago.

Everybody was glad to see him. There were the old men and women who had been in the Revolution with him, happy indeed to sit down and talk over old times with him. The younger people, too, were hardly less glad; and so hi journey from city to city, and from town to town, was one long holiday. The people of every town turned out on parades, much as did they when Washington traveled from Mt. Vernon to New York to be made president.

Everywhere he went, he was met with honor and bursts of welcome. And it was well that it should be so. If American had in her years of success forgotten the brave Lafayette, who left his country to come to her aid when she was poor and in trouble, it would have been a disgrace to us all.

When Lafayette returned home, the United States fitted out a ship to carry him. This ship they named from a certain battle of the Revolution in which Lafayette had been wounded.

I wish I could tell you that this "era of good feeling" lasted a long, long time; but, alas! I am afraid it was, as people say, only the calm before the storm; for even before Monroe's administration was quite over, there began to be serious disputes and contests upon the "slavery question."

You see the Southern people had always kept slaves, ever since that time way back in the early days of the Colonies when slaves had been brought over in the Dutch trading vessels, and had been sold to the planters. Help was needed so much in those days that colonists eagerly bought these black men from Africa to work their farms. To be sure, those Dutch traders had no more right to steal these black men and sell them than they had to steal Englishmen or Frenchmen, neither had the colonists any more right to buy them; but the colonists reasoned like this:

"They are such wild, ignorant creatures, they are really little better than my cattle. And after a little while they will be far better off here on my plantation, with plenty to eat and drink and a warm cabin to sleep in, then they were wandering about in the wilds of Africa."

This sounded reasonable, and no doubt the Southern people were honest enough and kind enough in it all, but they forgot that these black men, low and ignorant as they were, were nevertheless human beings, — and that is reason enough why no man had any right to buy and sell them. What would you think now, children, to hear of men and women and little children being bought and sold?

As there were no State laws against slavery in those days, and even in later days, there began to be slaves here and there in all the colonies, in the North as well as in the South; but it was not very long before the States, one by one, began to make laws forbidding this selling of men and women who chanced to be black instead of white; until at last no States but the Southern now held slaves. The Southern States held that they *must* have these black people to do their work for them, because they were so big and strong, and were used to the hot climate of the tropics.

And so this had been going on all these years; but in the time of Monroe there began to be a strong feeling that this was wrong, and that something ought to be done to put a stop to it.

And something *was* done—a most terrible something, as very likely your grandpapas and gramdmammas can tell you; but I will not tell you just here about it. I want you first to hurry on with me over a few more administrations, and then I will tell you all about the "something" that was done, which, in the end, freed these black men and women and their little black boys and girls.

When John Quincy Adams took his seat as president, the United States were twenty-four in number. Quite a growth, you see, since the days of the thirteen little States that made Washington their President.

It was during this administration that John Adams and Thomas Jefferson dies. I have already told you that these two men, these life-long friends, died upon the same day.

It is said that a Fourth of July celebration was being held in the village where Mr. Adams lived; and he had sent to it a toast: "Independence forever." As he lay dying, at sunset time, those who watched by his bed could hear the distant shouting at the village, when the people heard the old man's last message.

J 2. Adams

One more event in this administration we must speak of, and then we will pass on to the administration of the plucky General Jackson, the man who made it so hot for the English at New Orleans during the war of 1812. The first railroad was laid during this administration—a little road only three miles long, leading from the granite quarries at Quincy, Mass., to the wharves. These cars were drawn by horses, and I fancy it was a funny enough looking train of cars. It was not until two years later that an engine was used. On the previous page is a picture of the first train of cars drawn by a real engine.

THE FIRST TRAIN OF CARS.

EVILS OF EARLY RISING

I am sure you will be glad to hear that there was one "great man" who enjoyed a morning nap as much as you and I do; and that he enjoyed a good joke at the expense of a certain other "great man" who was as fond of "rising with the lark" as the first man was of sleeping soundly.

John Quincy Adams was an enthusiastic advocate of early rising. He practiced it from boyhood, and attributed to it his good health, and physical vigor in old age. Judge Story, who was an intimate friend, loved dearly a good morning nap, and their opposite opinions often gave rise to sharp and witty discussions.

On one occasion, the judge invited the ex-President to talk to the students of his Law School, and Mr. Adams made interesting remarks, touching, among other topics, on his favorite theme of early rising. The Judge then delivered his usual lecture.

The afternoon was hot, and the lecture-room close. Towards the close of the lecture, he noticed that the class were nodding to each other and smiling. Looking first on his right hand and then on his left, he discovered the secret of their merriment. The distinguished visitor was asleep and nodding! He could not resist the temptation to add a post-script to his lecture. "Young gentlemen, I call your attention to the visible proof of the evils of early rising."

The loud laugh that followed awoke the gentleman, but he did not understand the joke that caused it.

ANDREW JACKSON

And now we come upon the next President,—a President who has been more widely popular than any other President since Washington.

We have already heard enough of this man to be able to form some idea of what his character was. Fiery, determined, as he was, hating England with all his heart, he was almost a dangerous man to put in power—except for one quality which offset all the rest; and that was that he loved his country more, far more, than he loved his own interests, and so was sure to be true to her, let come what would.

The greatest event of this administration, which as far as wars or home troubles are concerned was very uneventful, was the introduction of the first steam-engine for railroad traveling.

Ever since the success with the steam-boat, thoughtful men had been trying to invent some way of traveling on the land by steam. There was the same kind of hooting and sneering and joke-cracking over this that there had been so short a time before over the steam-boat. Strange, isn't it, children, that we do not learn from past experiences like these not to sneer and scoff at every new thing that comes up from time to time.

Jackson had opportunity before his term was over to display the force of his iron will in a way that will make him forever to be remembered. First, he made an attack upon the money system of the country. I shall not try to explain it to you; but when I tell you that he so upset the whole system that hundreds of wealthy bond-holders failed in their business, you can imagine that it was no slight disturbance. He actually forbade the putting of any more money into the National Bank, and dismissed the Secretary of the Treasury because he dared not obey his order. It was a fearful time for the country; but Jackson carried the day, and the Democrats were delighted.

PRESIDENT JACKSON.

Then came up trouble over the "tariff" question. The South said, "We want free trade, and we're going to have it. If Massachusetts wants "protection," let her have it. But WE are going to have "free trade."

But Congress said, "No; we can't make a law for one part of the United States which is not for the whole United States. Either *all* must have free trade, or *all* must have protection."

Then the South waxed hotter and hotter. They held public meetings, and these States, especially South Carolina, declared the tariff laws were "null and void" by that they meant they were useless and powerless, and that they would pay no attention to them. These Southern people were therefore called "Nulli-fiers." As the conflict went on, they went so far as to say they would withdraw from the *Union*, and have a government of their own, and to do what they pleased in their own states. They even began to raise an army with which to carry on the quarrel.

When news of this reached Andrew Jackson's ears you may be sure there was a blaze of wrath. "What! break up the Union!" said he. "Never! Haman's gallows were not high enough to hang the man upon who would raise his finger to pull down our Union." You may be sure it was not many hours before a proclamation was sent to those "Nullifiers," ordering them back into place. An army was raised; ships were sent to guard the harbors; the forts were ordered to be on the lookout for the first sign of disobedience—in short,

Jackson was ready, if that little State of South Carolina had dared make one show of rebellion, to crush her before she should have time to strike one blow. It is hardly necessary to say that under such determined action as this, the Nullifiers settled down; their public meetings were stopped; their army broke up and went quietly about its business—and there was peace again.

In the Senate, this matter was of course discussed. And just here, there came into notice three most remarkable men—men whom you must try to remember as long as you live. They were Daniel Webster, who stood staunch and firm for the Union, John C. Calhoun, who represented the Southern States and was, therefore, a hot "Nullifier," and Henry Clay, who, because he seemed always to find a way to settle the fiery disputes between these two, came to be called the "peace-maker."

After these troubles had been somewhat quieted, Jackson, or "Old Hickory," as his followers used to like to call him, was glad enough, when his second term was out, to go to his home and rest. He was getting old and was tired of office, he used to say; and when we recall what a life he had had, we can well believe that he did long for quiet in his remaining years. He was very anxious that Van Buren, his colleague in office, should be the next president; and he worked hard to secure his election. A word or two in the next chapter about "Old Hickory," and then we shall leave him, and hurry on to other Presidents.

HENRY CLAY.

ANDREW JACKSON'S NICK-NAME

They say that the way General Jackson came to be nick-named "Old Hickory" is as follows:—During the Creek War he had taken a severe cold, and his soldiers had made a shelter for him of hickory bark.

The next morning a tipsy soldier, not knowing what he was about, kicked at the bark shelter and over it went.

Jackson, speechless with rage, sprang out of the hickory heap and rushed towards the drunken offender.

"Why I didn't know you were in there, Old Hickory!' shouted the soldier.

For an instant a shout of laughter broke from the camp; but one soldier, quicker-witted than the others, called "Three cheers for Old Hickory."

The drunken soldier was saved a punishment, Jackson's temper was quieted, his dignity maintained—and he received a new name.

JACKSON'S OBSTINACY

That Jackson was very stubborn, even his closest friends admit. His stubborness, very likely, may not have added to his agreeableness as a friend and companion. But it is one of the things we Americans need to learn— that with the personal, home disposition of our public men we have nothing to do. Their public service is all that in any way concerns us or belongs to us.

That Jackson was stubborn there is no doubt, but his stubbornness certainly rendered this country good service during his administration.

This strong, self-educated, self-respecting man had certain peculiarities of pronunciation, which he had acquired in childhood. The word *development*, for example, he would pronounce as though it were written devil-*ope*-ment.

One day, during his Presidency, he was conversing with a foreign minister. The gentleman, though not an Englishman, had been educated in England, and prided himself upon his correct pronunciation of it. "Devil-*ope*-ment," said General Jackson, thereby causing the minister to raise his eyebrows, and to pronounce the word correctly. The President, apparently not noticing the impolite correction, again said, "devil-*ope*-ment."

Again the minister repeated the word with its proper accent, saying with emphasis, "de-*vel*-opment."

"Excuse me, Mr. Dash. You may call it de-*vel*-opment if you please; but I say devil-*ope*-ment, and will say devil-*ope*-ment, as long as I revere the memory of good old Dr. Waddell!" referring to a former respected teacher.

The anecdote is a graphic illustration of two traits which marked General Jackson. He feared the face of no man, and he allowed no one to *push* him from a position he had taken. Few men so imperfectly educated as was General Jackson would have had the courage to adhere to a false pronunciation in the face of a scholar who corrected him.

Of course, an obstinate, wrong-headed man is liable to make serious blunders. But that risk is compensated for by this fact: no man accomplishes much who has not stubborn resolution, and having a high standard does not stubbornly endeavor to attain it.

GENERAL JACKSON'S PORTRAIT

If President Jackson had been allowed to have his own way we should have no picture of him to grace our historic galleries; for if there was any one thing that this obstinate man disliked, it was "picture painting."

"Never! never!" thundered he, "shall my face be set up here and there and everywhere."

"My face shall be my own," shouted he, as a fellow-politician begged him to allow his likeness to be painted. "My country has a right to my likeness, do you say?" cried he rising in fury. "I say they have *not*. My years and my service are theirs; but my face! Never!"

Few dared brave the thunder of this man, much as his likeness was desirable.

At one time the King of France sent to Andrew Jackson an artist, with the request that the French court be favored with a portrait of

America's President. He found the ex-President sitting erect in his chair, surrounded by pillows, and his courteous presentation of his request and his credentials were received, with flashing eyes.

"You can't paint my portrait, sir!" roared the general. "The King of France or any other man cannot have my picture!"

"But," said Mr. Healy, "I have come many thousands of miles, at great labor and expense, upon a commission from a reigning monarch who greatly admires you. Pray reconsider your refusal."

"No, sir," said Jackson, "you can't paint my portrait! You are welcome to stay at the Hermitage the rest of your days if you like, but you can't have my portrait."

The shrewd artist seized his opportunity; he remained at the Hermitage, and at last, with the assistance of the general's family, induced the obstinate old gentleman to give him short sittings.

CALHOUN AT HOME

Although Calhoun and Webster were always bitterly opposed in political life, they did not fail to appreciate each other's talent and real honest worth. We aren't all of us always so fair as the little boy who said of a rival classmate, "I hate Jimmie Waters 'cause he gets ahead of me; but just the same I know he's a heap smarter than I am."

To hold a fair, honest judgment of an enemy, to judge him without petty personal prejudice, is a thing that many a grown-up boy and girl fails to do.

Webster was big and broad enough to do this. While hating Calhoun as a politician and an enemy, no one more thoroughly appreciated his talent and respected his manhood than he did. On Calhoun's death it was Webster who pronounced his eulogy and gloried in the opportunity to do the dead man justice.

Webster's famous eulogy was a noble compliment; but nobler still was the love and reverence of Calhoun's own household. To remain a hero for a lifetime in one's own family, to be still respected and reverenced by those who have for years known one's daily life, is a greater proof of real nobility than any public eulogy can ever be.

The great man's family loved him even more than they admired him; and yet they exulted in his career. "Come soon again," said a younger brother to the eldest son, as he was leaving the homestead for his home in Alabama. "Come soon again and see us, for do you not see that father is growing old? and he is the dearest and best old man in the world!"

His own daughter in speaking of him, to a gentleman with whom she was conversing, said, "I wish you had known my father;" "You would have loved him. People admired him, but those who knew him in his family reverenced him. We all worshipped him."

She often went with her father to Washington during the Congressional session. Great and self-reliant as was the statesman, he took pleasure in talking with his gifted child, and often made her his confidant in perplexing cases.

"Of course," she said, referring to the high compliment he paid her, "I do not understand as he does, for I am comparatively a stranger to the world; yet he likes my opinion, and I frankly tell him my views on any subject about which he inquires of me."

His tenderness and consideration for his children was remarkable in so busy and per-plexed a life as his.

A younger daughter, being an invalid, found her favorite occupation in reading. She was allowed to go to the letter-bag when it came from the office, and select the papers she wished to read. Once, two papers concerning news of importance which her father was anxious to see, were taken by her to her own room. But he would allow no one to disturb her until she had finished reading them.

Our public men are often tempted to sacri-fice their families to official life. If Mr. Calhoun was thus tempted, he never yielded to it. His cheerful home was more attractive to him than the Senate Chamber.

DANIEL WEBSTER.

THE HOME OF WEBSTER

Daniel Webster loved nothing better than to get away from the noise and hurry of his political life and shut himself away in the quiet little village of Marshfield, where he could hunt and fish and farm to his heart's content.

He used sometimes to say, "I doubt if the applause of the Senate gives me half such real pleasure as my good broad acres, with all the rest they bring me."

We can usually judge a man's character by his house and lands. Some seem satisfied with a plain, staring, square box of a house, hedged in by street and block; others choose broad grand prospects, or beautiful hilly bits of woodland.

Webster's home, as we might suppose, was broad and grand; it had the hill, the plain, the woods, and the ocean.

A writer who saw it some years ago, before the house was burned in 1878, describes it as follows:

A long, stone wall, painted white, runs in front of the farm. Within, one sees a large meadow and an old, scattering orchard. It is a broad domain. Leaving the road and entering the winding drive-way, one passes under beautiful shade-trees, till at length he reaches a large, ancient-looking white house.

Near it stood a little white building, scarcely more than ten feet square. Here the famous orator spent many days in hard thought and study.

A very interesting spot is the resting-place of Webster. We pass by the house and the large barn and little lakes and ornamental trees, and walk on through field, and meadow, and orchard.

Now we come out upon a little open plateau of land covering two or three acres. There is not a tree or shrub upon it. It is native soil, unturned by any plow.

To the north, a vast marsh stretches away for several miles. To the west, more marsh, and then higher land, with timber. To the south, a level half mile of open field;—

Webster's field, and then hills and woods. To the east, low, marshy land and the sound of the surf-beating ocean two miles away. There is no house near. Only the quiet or rugged aspects of nature; of broad-handed, far-reaching nature.

It is here that the gifted senator and his family rest. On the southern slope of this elevation of land a space is fenced off by an iron railing, some eight feet high.

In this inclosure lies buried the Webster family. Within this iron fence lies the wife whom Webster tenderly loved. Also Major Edward, his son, who died in the Mexican War, and Col. Fletcher, who died in 1862-3, from wounds received in his country's service. The Websters were a race of brave men.

Webster's grave is situated at the north end of the plot in this little jut of land. A mound of earth is thrown up, some four feet high, and overgrown with grass; at the head of this is a simple, pure white marble slab, some fifteen by ten inches, bearing this inscription,— "Daniel Webster."

In this obscure place reposes this man whose eloquence charmed a nation; upon whose lips ten thousand hung delighted; who

walked among crowds of noble men, "the observed of all observers."

DANIEL WEBSTER'S FISHING

This great man, as we please to call him, could enjoy a quiet day of hunting and fishing, and could, moreover, appreciate fun as well as any boy you know. A friend of his, relating anecdotes of this great man, once told the following:

"As I was quite an expert in trouting and shooting, Webster used always to send for me to dance attendance on him, while he was here to enjoy himself and relieve his mind from the toil and trouble of Congress.

"One day he came for me to go to Marshpee River, on a two day's trouting trip. We arrived there at night; and in the morning we were at the brook or river at eight o'clock, and pulling on his long rubber boots (he always took them when he went fishing: they were very long, and kept in position by a kind of suspenders) "we stepped into the brook and waded down stream, fishing with live bait (mummy chubs); he went ahead and caught all the large ones.

"I followed behind and caught what escaped his hook. I also carried a net. We had been fishing for a couple of hours with good success, when I heard him call,—

"'George, George, come here quick! I have got a mighty fellow hooked!'

"I hurried down to him, and saw his line leading under the bank. I riled up the water with mud above so that the trout could not see me, then run my net under the bank and scooped out the trout; he was a noble fellow, weighing at least three and a half pounds.

"'Ah! ah!' exclaimed Webster, 'we have him! Look at him, George; did you ever see such a big fellow?'

"'Yes,' said I, 'I have caught as big a trout as that.'

"'Confine yourself to the question,' said Mr. Webster; 'did you ever see so big a trout, George?'

"'Seen as big a one?'

"'Yes.'

"'Yes, I have seen and caught as big a trout as that.'

"Mr. Webster surveyed me as I stood there deep in the water, and said: 'Ah, George! I fear I shall never make anything of you! You are an amphibious creature. You *lie* in the water, and you *lie* out of the water. Come let's start home.'"

PRESIDENT VAN BUREN.

VAN BUREN

There is very little of interest to little folks in this administration. You will find Van Buren very severely criticised by some; but when we think what a hard position he had to fill just after Jackson's hot-headed career, we shall wonder that he did as well as he did. All these bank changes which Jackson had made, had caused much trouble among business men. And this, together with other money affairs, had thrown the country into a panic. Rich men failed, and poor men were without work; provisions came to be very high, and there was no money to buy with. These were "hard times," indeed; and because everybody blamed the government, they seemed to think Van Buren was to be blamed too, though I'm sure I don't see why he was to blame for what had been brought about by the previous administration, or for the ill luck of speculators and other business men.

"TIPPECANOE AND TYLER TOO"

When Van Buren's term was nearly out, his party nominated him for President again; but the other party set up Harrison, the hero of Tippecanoe, with John Tyler for Vice-President, in opposition, and made the land so ring with their song "Tippecanoe and Tyler too," that they carried the country by storm.

It is said that this was one of the most exciting times our country ever saw. The Republicans had now taken on the name Democrats, and the Federalists now called themselves Whigs, in remembrance of the Whigs of Revolutionary times. Party feeling was now hot again and the campaign was a lively one.

General Harrison had been living very quietly in a log-cabin out in the western part of the country ever since the war of 1812; and so when he was nominated for president by the Whigs, the Democrats said, "Pshaw! give Harrison a cabin and a barrel of hard cider, and he'd never care whether he became president or not." At this the Whigs raised the cry of "Cabins and hard cider for us!" and from that, the campaign has ever since been called the "log cabin and hard cider campaign." It was a hot contest; but there was much fun mixed up with it. The newspapers had pictures of log cabins at their heads, there was "log-cabin calico," and "log-cabin wall-paper." The women used to meet together and make "log-cabin quilts," and the men and boys used to roll barrels of cider through the streets.

It ended in "Tippecanoe and Tyler too" as President and Vice-President. There can be no doubt, judging from the bravery and wisdom of General Harrison in all that we have heard of him, that he would have made a good president; but in only one month from the time he took his chair he died,—worn out, it was said, by the excitement and hard work of his election.

Tyler, the Vice-President, now took the chair. The great event of his time was the invention of the telegraph system. We have read of the invention of the steam-boat and of the railroad, and now comes the telegraph. Of course there were plenty of people who pooh-poohed at the idea of "talking through a wire," but the invention succeeded nevertheless in spite of their scoffs.

PRESIDENT TYLER.

At the same time Samuel Morse was busy inventing his telegraph here in America, another man in England, and another in

Germany were busy with the same kind of work.

By and by, when Morse's telegraph had been tried between Baltimore and Washington, and had been found successful, he went to Europe to try to get it accepted there. There the three inventors, the American, the Englishman, and the German met. Of course each presented his own invention, and hoped his might be the one to be accepted By the country; and just here you must know what a brave unselfish thing the German did. Much as he wished his own invention to be accepted, he carefully examined the machine that Morse had brought, and seeing that Morse's was really the better, he generously said, "Gentlemen, I willingly withdraw from the field; Mr. Morse's invention is better than mine."

Wasn't this big-hearted in the German—to give up so nobly his life-work and his chance at being remembered for ages as the inventor of this wonderful machine, and to turn and frankly take the hand of his rival and wish him all success? Captain Lawrence and Oliver Perry, and all the other naval and military heroes were indeed brave men, and we admire them for their courage; but it takes a bigger, grander soul, boys, to frankly and generously acknowledge the inferiority of one's self, than to face the cannon's roar.

A SMALL-TAIL MOVEMENT

In no campaign, perhaps, has there been so much rollicking "good time," so much extravagant parade and noise, so much ridiculous story-telling as in this campaign of "1840."

It is said that in a certain village of Western Virginia, while a speaker was setting forth in glowing colors the wonderful generalship of Harrison, a tall, angular farmer rose and called out,

"Mister! Mister! I want to ax a question!"

"I shall be happy to answer any question, if I can," replied the orator.

"We are told, fellow-citizens," said the quaint man, addressing the crowd, "that Gineral Harrison is a mighty great gineral; but I say he's one of the meanest sort of ginerals. We are told that he defended himself bravely at Fort Meigs; but I tell you that on that occasion he was guilty of the *Small-Tail Movement,* and I challenge the speaker to deny it!"

"I don't know, my friend," replied the orator, "what you mean by the 'Small-Tail Movement.'"

"I'll tell you," said the quaint man. "I've got it here in black and white. Here is 'Quinshaw's History of the United States'"—holding up the book—"and I'll read what it says: 'At this critical moment, General Harrison executed a *novel* movement!' Does the gentleman deny this statement?"

"No; go on."

"Well, he executed 'a *novel* movement.' Now here's Johnson's Dictionary,"—taking a small book out of his pocket, "and it says, 'Novel—*a small tale!'* This was the kind of movement Gineral Harrison was guilty of. Now, I'm no soger, and don't know much of milentary tic-tacks,—but this I do say: a man who, in the face of an enemy, is guilty of a *Small-Tail Movement,* is not fit to be the President of the United States, and he shan't have my vote."

JAMES K. POLK

THE next President was James K. Polk. His administration is marked by the Mexican War—and a terrible war it was indeed. We do not hear so much about this war, and do not realize how fierce a fight it was, because the battles were all fought away off in the Mexican neighborhood, and we did not therefore *see* the battles fought as we did in the other wars.

Away back in those times when the different European nations were all sending men over here to find lands and gold, the Spaniards had taken possession of that part of the country called Mexico.

Some time I want you to read about the wonderful people the Spaniards found living there. They had cities and elegant palaces and gardens; they had a king, and a brave king he was, too, and lived on the whole, in quite as civilized a way as did the Spaniards themselves. It seems strange that these people should have been so civilized when all the other Indians throughout the country were so wild and savage. It is a great mystery where these people came from and who they were; but as they had no written history, it doesn't seem very likely that we shall ever find out. It is all very wonderful; and when, down in this Mexican country, and out through our Western States, we dig up here and there axes, chisels, knives, beads, bracelets, even bits of cloth and pieces of vases which we know must be hundreds and hundreds of years old, it makes us think that this Earth of ours has rolled on and on for many, many more years than we have any idea of.

But you will think I have forgotten all about the Mexican war. Mexico, as I said before, was in the possession of the Spaniards. Spain had never been very successful with her American possessions, some way. She had had, from time to time, to give up a part of her land, once to France, and again to the United States. Then, too, from the very beginning, the Spanish rulers had been very cruel and overbearing in the treatment of the people whom they had found in Mexico. It is no wonder, then, that after a time the Mexicans rose in arms, and declared they would no longer be ruled by Spain. Many a hot battle they had; but at last Spain gave up her claim upon them, and they were independent.

There were, in that part of Mexico called Texas, many Americans who had gone there to farm and raise cattle. These Americans took part in the uprising of the Mexicans against Spain, and helped them to throw off the Spanish rule.

As time went on, and cattle-raising came to be a very paying business, Texas began very rapidly to fill up with these shrewd Yankees, anxious to grow rich as soon as possible.

The Mexicans at last began to grow afraid and jealous of these thrifty Yankees. "They will get our land away from us," they said. And so, when the American colony in Texas sent Stephen Austin to the Mexican government to ask that Texas should be allowed to join the Mexican Union, instead of giving him a ready answer, and sending him back to his people, they kept him for a long time in uncertainty. Austin was angry enough at this needless delay, and he wrote a letter to the

Texas people telling them to rise in arms and declare themselves independent of Mexican rule. This letter fell into the hands of the Mexicans, and Austin was put in prison.

This kindled the anger of the Texans, and they rose indeed. There was much sharp fighting, and in the end Texas declared herself independent, made a government of her own and chose a governor of her own.

Very soon, she asked the United States to allow her to join *their* Union, and so be under the protection of some government greater than her own. For a long time congress talked and talked about the matter. The Northern States said, "No, Texas is a slave-state, and we have too many slave-states already; besides we shall be sure to get into a war with Mexico, if we have anything to do in this matter." The Southern States argued in just the opposite way; but at last the State was accepted, and as the Northern States had predicted, war did follow.

I shall make no attempt to tell you much about this war—it was like all other wars a series of terrible battles in which thousands of men were killed, and thousands of homes made desolate. It ended at last in the victory of the Americans over the Mexicans, and Texas now belonged to the United States—a far dearer purchase, I think, than that of Lousiana away back in Jefferson's time.

There are a few names and incidents connected with this war which you need to know, even if you don't quite yet learn the names and stories of the battle. Certainly you must know about "Old Zack," as his men used to call him. He was a sturdy old soldier who had fought like a "Trojan," as people say, in the battle of 1812. He was very much such a man as "Old Put" had been in the Revolutionary times, and "Old Hickory" whom you heard of in that famous battle at New Orleans. And for this reason, his men had given him the pet name of "Old Zach." He did some lively work in the Mexican war, lived through it all and came out of it hale and hearty, and so much respected by the nation, that they made him President by and by.

There are several little stories told of General Taylor in this war. At one time Santa Anna, the Mexican general, sent a messenger to General Taylor. On reaching there the messenger found Taylor sitting idly on his horse, with one leg thrown over the pummel of the saddle.

"What are you waiting for?" asked the messenger, amazed at such coolness in battle.

"I am waiting for Santa Anna to surrender," replied he calmly.

At another time, some one of Taylor's officers suggested that his pet horse, "Whitney" could be too easily singled out by the enemy's shot and urged him to take another and send "Whitney" away. "Not a step," said General Taylor, "the old fellow missed the fun at the other battle but she's going to have her share in this one."

Then there was General Kearney, who had a way of marching straight into the little mud-built villages, demanding the governor of the town to present himself, and then, having surrounded him with American officers, compelled him to swear faithfulness to the United States. He would then unfurl the stars and stripes over the house of the governor, and march coolly on.

There was Captain Fremont, a noble young officer, who fully deserved his promotion to *captainship*. He had crossed the Rocky mountains at one time, had climbed one of its very highest peaks, and had there unfurled the stars and stripes. That peak, which when you come to study geography, you will be very likely to hear about, is now called *Mt. Fremont* or *Fremont's Peak*. Soon after this young officer was made captain, he started off to Oregon, passing through Mexican territory on his march. I wish I could tell you about his guide, Kit Carson, who had lived for years among these wild mountain regions. Kit Carson was a wonderful story-teller; he could tell you bear stories and Indian stories of the most exciting kind. There were hundreds of these—all out of his own life—and terrible enough some of them, to make your hair stand on end.

Toward the end of the war General Scott, who was as great a general in this war as General Taylor, was preparing to storm a place know as Grass-hopper Hill. It was a fearful place to attack, situated as it was on a rocky height, a hundred and fifty feet above the plain. A stone-wall surrounded it at the top, and within this was a military school of a hundred boys from ten to twenty years of age.

Two columns of soldiers advanced to attack the fort from either side. Slowly they toiled up the rocky steep, up to the very cannon's mouths. Pillow, the leader of one column, when half way up, fell, terribly wounded by a Mexican shell. "Carry me up with you, boys," he begged, "that I may be there to see the victory." His soldiers carried him up amid the fire rained down upon them from the fort; and he did see a victory.

CAPTAIN FREMONT.

Reaching the top, quick as a flash the ladders are thrown against the walls, the men scramble over, pell-mell, helter-skelter, in order and out of order, and met the Mexicans hand-to-hand. In the midst of the blood-shed, fighting as hotly as the oldest warriors, were the hundred lion-hearted boys.

GENERAL WINFIELD SCOTT.

"They were pretty little fellows, and they fought like little soldiers, as they were," said an American officer in speaking of them after the war.

It was a cruel battle; but I am glad to say it was the last of the war. The next morning,

General Scott rode into the city square and took possession. The Mexicans were glad enough to accept almost any terms of peace, after the battles in which they had been so terribly beaten.

It is said that after one of these terrible battles, the Mexican women gathered upon the bloody field, working through the long, dark night, comforting and aiding the wounded and dying, both American and Mexican. Brave, tender-hearted Mexic women! Many a dying soldier that night had reason to thank the women of a nation he had tried so hard that day to crush.

War may seem to you a very grand thing, my boys, when you see the soldiers marching along your street, dressed in their gold and silver bands and with their plumes waving so gaily in the breeze; but when you think of the heartache, the pain, the agony, the death that follows in every battle, no matter how grand and victorious your generals may have been—then war loses its brightness and its flash; and we have only the dark, black cloud of death to look upon.

THE ANGELS OF BUENA VISTA

Speak and tell us, our Ximena, looking northward far away,
O'er the camp of the invaders, o'er the Mexican array,
Who is losing? who is winning? are they far or come they near?
Look abroad, and tell us, sister, whither rolls the storm we
*   hear.*

"Down the hills of Angostura still the storm of battle rolls;
Blood is flowing, men are dying; God have mercy on their
*   souls!"*
Who is losing? who is winning?—"Over hill and over plain,
I see but smoke of cannon clouding through the mountain
*   rain."*

Nearer came the storm and nearer, rolling fast and frightful
*   on!*
Speak, Ximena, speak and tell us, who has lost and who has
*   won!*
"Alas! alas! I know not; friend and foe together fall;
O'er the dying rush the living: pray, my sisters, for them all!

Dry thy tears, my poor Ximena; lay thy dear one down to rest;
Let his hands be meekly folded, lay the cross upon his breast;
Let his dirge be sung hereafter, and his funeral masses said:
To-day, thou poor bereaved one, the living ask thy aid.

Close beside her, faintly moaning, fair and young, a soldier lay,
Torn with shot and pierced with lances, bleeding slow his life
    away;
But, as tenderly before him the lorn Ximena knelt,
She saw the Northern eagle shining on his pistol-belt.

With a stifled cry of horror straight she turned away her head;
With a sad and bitter feeling looked she back upon her dead;
But she heard the youth's low moaning, and his struggled
    breath of pain,
And she raised the cooling water to his parching lips again.

Look forth once more, Ximena!" "Like a cloud before the wind
Rolls the battle down the mountains, leaving blood and death
    behind;
Ah! they plead in vain for mercy; in the dust the wounded
    strive;
Hide your faces, holy angels! Oh, thou Christ of God, forgive!"

Sink, O Night, among thy mountains; let thy cool, gray shadows
    fall;
Dying brothers, fighting demons—drop they curtain over all!
Through the quickening winter twilight, wide apart the battle
    rolled;
In his sheath the sabre rested, and the cannon's lips grew cold.

But the holy Mexic women still their holy task pursued,
Through that long, dark night of sorrow, worn and faint, and
    lacking food;
Over the weak and suffering brothers with a tender care they
    hung,
And they dying foeman blessed them in a strange and North-
    ern tongue.

Not wholly lost, O Father, is this evil world of ours;
Upward through its blood and ashes spring afresh the Eden
   flowers.

THE MARTYR OF MONTEREY

The strife was stern at Monterey,
*   When those high towers were lost, and won;*
And, pealing through that mortal fray,
*   Flash'd the strong batteries vengeful gun;*
Yet, heedless of its deadly rain,
*   She stood, in toil and danger first,*
To bind the bleeding soldier's vein,
*   And slake the dying soldier's thirst.*

She found a pale and stricken foe,
*   Sinking in nature's last eclipse,*
And on the red earth kneeling low,
*   She wet his parch'd and fever'd lips;*
When thick as winter's driving sleet,
*   The booming shot and flaming shell*
Swept with wild rage that gory street,
*   And she—the good and gentle—fell!*

They laid her in her narrow bed—
*   The foemen of her land and race;*
And sighs were breathed and tears were shed
*   Above her lowly resting-place.*
Ay! glory's crimson worshippers
*   Wept over her unkindly fall,*
For deeds of mercy such as hers
*   Subdue the heart and eyes of all.*

To sound her worth were guilt and shame
*   In us, who love but gold and ease;*
They heed alike our praise or blame,
*   Who live and die in works like these,*
Far greater than the wise or brave,
*   Far happier than the fair or gay,*
Was she who found a martyr's grave
*   On that red field of Monterey.*

—REV. J. G. LYONS.

ZACHARY TAYLOR

ZACHARY TAYLOR

The Whigs were now beginning to want a hand in the government. They had been out of power so long, that they thought it worth while to try to find a man as their candidate who would be likely to catch the vote of the people.

They settled upon "Old Zach," or as he had come to be called during the late war, "Old Rough and Ready." This wasn't as exciting a time as that campaign when Log Cabins and Hard Cider had been the campaign watchwords; but it was somewhat like it. Now everything was "Rough and Ready,"—there were "Rough and Ready" hats and "Rough and Ready" boots; —and at the end, the Whigs, to their great delight, succeeded in electing their "Rough and Ready" president. President Taylor died before his term of office was ended, and his Vice-President, Millard Filmore,

served the remainder of the term. After Filmore came Franklin Pierce, and after Pierce,
James Buchanan.

The administrations of these presidents are
so swallowed up in the great question of
"slavery," that I shall not try to keep them
separate in this little history. You have heard
already of the slavery question, but you did

not know, I think, how in all this time the excitement regarding it had been increasing. The political parties which in Washington's time were divided on the form of government, and later, on the war with England, and later still, on "State Rights," were now divided on the one great question of slavery. For some time, whenever a new territory wanted to join the Union, there had been a hot fight in Congress over it. The question would be, not whether there were people enough in the territory, or whether they would be likely to be of service to the Union, but, "Will this new State be a slave-state?" If it seemed likely that it would be a slave-state, then the North would fight against its admission. They wanted no more slave-states. On the other hand, if it was not to be a slave-state, the South would fight just as hotly against it.

Away back when South Carolina had made an attempt to leave the Union, and "Old Hickory" had brought it so quickly to terms, he had said then—wise, far seeing old man that he was:

"This disturbance about the tariff is only a make believe; the real object in trying to withdraw from the Union is to secure the right to hold slaves. Slavery, or the Negro Question, will be the next trouble this country will have to face."

And surely enough his prophecy was coming true. Henry Clay and Daniel Webster worked harder than ever in these days; for the South again had threatened to leave the Union—this time making no pretence to keep back their real object, the slave question.

THE ABOLITIONISTS

Another long word, children; but as very likely your own grandfather was an abolitionist himself in those days, you will want to know what the word means.

We are now close upon the terrible war which was brought about by this disagreement between the North and the South, The Abolitionists—that is, the people who believed in doing away with slavery—had come to be quite large in number. The North had all these years believed that slavery was not right; and while they had done away with it in their own States, they had not pushed very hard in the matter against the South. But now the Abolitionists had come. They not only *believed* that slavery was wrong, but they were determined it should be abolished.

The Southerners hated and feared these Abolitionists. "What if they should come here among our slaves and teach them about liberty and freedom!" said they.

The first Abolitionist of the times was Benjamin Lunday, one of the good old Pennsylvania Quakers. He began talking up this matter with everybody he met, till at last his name and his sayings began to be talked about in the newspapers; other newspapers took it up, and others, and others,—some praising the good Quaker, others condemning him. But whether they praised or condemned, they set people all over the country to thinking, and many a one who had never given it a thought before, began now to wonder in their own minds if the Quaker wasn't right, after all.

Benjamin Lunday came to Boston at length; and there he found William Lloyd Garrison, who was as full of the desire to see the slaves free as he was himself.

And such talk and such excitement as these two men did stir up in good old Boston! There had been nothing like it since the old Revolutionary times. Garrison went to work and published a newspaper called the "Liberator," in which he set forth freely his opinions on the slavery question. The whole country was set boiling by this paper. His very life was in danger. In one State, five thousand dollars were offered for his head.

The people of Boston itself threatened to tar and feather him if he did not hold his peace. "I am right, and I will speak!" was his answer. At last he was seized by a mob, and dragged about the streets by a rope. I don't know what would have become of him had not the mayor of the city come to his rescue. He was put in jail that he might be safe from the mob.

Out in Illinois, another newspaper editor was doing the same sort of work. He, too, was mobbed, his presses destroyed, and he himself killed in the fray.

All this time the little party of men and women who called themselves Abolitionists were growing stronger and stronger. And now when the news of this murder reached the ears of the Boston Abolitionists, a meeting was called in the old "Cradle of Liberty."

And it was at this meeting that Wendell Phillips, the silver-tongued orator, first came into notice. He was young, and rich, and educated, belonging to the very best families in Massachusetts, having everything in his favor whereby to make for himself a high place in the world. But all this he threw aside, and came and joined the little band of despised Abolitionists, joining with William Lloyd Garrison as a leader in the cause of freedom for the negroes.

At the same time, our dear old Quaker poet, as he is called now, joined the ranks. He was young then, and was just beginning to come into notice among the people of the land, He, too, had a life of ease and glory before him if only he had not taken up the slavery question; but when he began to plead for the poor negro of the South through his beautiful verses, just as Wendell Phillips was pleading for them from the platform, then the people turned against him as they had turned against Wendell Phillips; and for thirty years this poet whom now we all love so much, and regard with such tender reverence, was looked upon with contempt, and was insulted and scoffed at by the people. Dear, tender-hearted Whittier! Are not you glad, children, that he has lived to see the day when his countrymen do love him as he deserved? What do you suppose the people in those Abolition days would have said if some one had told them that in less than thirty years John G. Whittier's verses would be in all our books, and better still, in all our hearts; and that the children all over the country would be celebrating this self-same Whittier's birthdays in their school-rooms, reading and speaking and singing of the "gentle Quaker poet?"

JOHN G. WHITTIER.

THE FUGITIVE SLAVE LAW

Sometimes these slaves used to run away. If they could get into the Northern States, that is, into the free states, they themselves were free. Of course this did not please the slave owners; and so Henry Clay, who as we have heard before, was always presenting some sort of a bill in Congress that served to keep the North and South from an actual quarrel, brought before the Senate a law which was called "The Fugitive Slave Law." Fugitive means runaway—and by means of this new law, a slave holder was given the right to pursue a runaway slave into any State, and bring him back. This law seemed all right at first, and no doubt Henry Clay meant that it should be all right. At any rate, he brought it before the Senate at a time when the South would, but for this law, have broken out in open rebellion.

This proved to be a very cruel law, however, for some of the slave holders would pursue their runaway slaves just as they would have pursued runaway cattle, and would drive them home with the lash. Of course, some of the slaves had very kind masters, but many slaves so dreaded to go back, that when they found their masters were coming for them, they would kill themselves rather than be taken. Sometimes mothers would kill their little children rather than they should grow up slaves.

JOHN BROWN

I wonder if you have any idea, when you sing that old song about "John Brown's body," what it all means. I'm sure I didn't know when I was a child, and I can remember just how I used to enjoy singing it at the top of my voice! Let me see—it goes something like this, doesn't it?

John Brown's body lies a'mouldering in the grave,
John Brown's body lies a'mouldering in the grave,
John Brown's body lies a'mouldering in the grave,
But his soul goes marching on.
Glory, glory, hallelujah, etc.

There was a great struggle going on in Kansas between the people in it who believed in slavery and the people in it who did not believe in slavery.

Soldiers had even been sent to Kansas from the South to try to subdue the Free-State people. Four or five hundred of these soldiers came to Ossawatomie, where John Brown lived, for the purpose of attacking the town. John Brown had only thirty men to meet his force with, and so could not expect to be victorious; but so skillfully did he manage his thirty, that he led them to a safe retreat with the loss of only five or six, while the enemy lost thirty-one and had more than twice that number wounded, beside having had a close, hard fight.

Several months later there came into Virginia a white-haired old man with some younger men who were said to be his sons. These men hired a farm near Harper's Ferry, and set to work upon it. They received a great many boxes and packages by rail, which they said were their farming tools.

At Harper's Ferry was an arsenal, stored with guns and powder, and all the munitions of war. One night, as the three watchmen were guarding the gates, up marched a company of twenty-two men. In a twinkling the three watchmen were seized, and bound hand and foot; then the twenty-two marched in and took possession of the arsenal.

Now you have guessed who this white-haired farmer with his sons is! John Brown, of course; but what is he going to do? Simply this: he is going to prepare for war against slavery. It seems at first absurd that a little band of twenty-two should set themselves up against a nation; but they were stronger than they seemed. Already his allies outside had cut down the telegraph wires, and had torn up railroads, so that news of their deed could not spread over the country.

Out into the town John Brown and his men marched, taking prisoner every citizen they met.

"What does this mean?" the astonished prisoners would say.

"It means we are going to free the slaves!" answered John Brown.

"In whose name do you do this?"

"Not in the name of Congress, but in the name of Almighty God."

John Brown had made arrangements with, and was expecting a band of a hundred slaves to join him as soon as they should know that the arsenal was taken. For some unknown reason, these slaves did not appear. He waited for them until too late. By noon, a company of militia marched to the arsenal, and now all hope of escape was cut off. By evening, fifteen hundred soldiers had arrived, and a bloody contest followed. John Brown's men knew, of course, that their doom was sealed, but they fought like tigers to the very last.

At night the party in the arsenal numbered only seven, and three of those were sorely wounded. All night long John Brown sat upon the floor between his two sons, one dead, the other slowly dying. At daybreak the door was broken in, and the soldiers were in the presence of this old hero, John Brown.

And so ended "John Brown's Raid," as it was called. He was tried by the Virginia court, and sentenced to be hanged. He was very brave during the time he lay in prison, and when the day on which he was to be hanged came, he was calm and full of courage.

He felt that he had done only what was right. "I have broken the laws of the State," said he; "but I have kept the laws of God; and the laws of God are greater than any laws of State."

As he walked forth from his jail on this last morning of his life, there stood at the gateway a slave woman with her baby in her arms. As he passed her he stooped and kissed the baby, and then went on sadly, but quietly.

On the scaffold he was blindfolded and led out upon the drop. For ten minutes he was kept standing there, expecting every second to hear the death signal. There seemed little need of this last stroke of cruelty; and even the mob about the scaffold began at last to cry, "Shame! Shame!" Then the drop fell, and John Brown was dead.

TRAMP! TRAMP! TRAMP!

In the prison-cell I sit, thinking, mother dear, of you,
*   And our bright and happy home so far away,*
And the tears they fill my eyes, spite of all that I can do,
*   Though I try to cheer my comrades and be gay.*

CHORUS

Tramp, tramp, tramp, the boys are marching,
*   Cheer up, comrades, they will come;*
And beneath the starry flag we shall breathe the air again
*   Of the freeland in our beloved home.*

In the battle-front we stood when their fiercest charge they
*   made,*
*   And they swept us off a hundred men or more;*
But before we reached their lines they were beaten back dis-
*   mayed,*
*   And we heard the cry of vict'ry o'er and o'er.*

So within the prison-cell we are waiting for the day
*   That shall some to open wide the iron door;*
And the hollow eye grows bright, and the poor heart almost
*   gay,*
*   As we think of seeing home and friends once more.*

—GEORGE F. ROOT

AMERICAN HISTORY STORIES, VOLUME IV

ABRAHAM LINCOLN

ABRAHAM LINCOLN

ABRAHAM LINCOLN was the President during this dark time in our nation's history,—the Civil War.

He was not a handsome man, not an educated man, not a society-mannered man; but a more honest, more loyal-hearted, more grand-souled man than Abraham Lincoln, never stood at the head of our government. He was as honest as George Washington, as sturdy as Andrew Jackson, as brave as the bravest General, and, in the end, as noble as the noblest martyr.

He had had a hard life as a boy. He had been brought up on a Kentucky farm, where he had learned to hoe and to plant, to drive oxen, to build log-houses, to split rails, to fell trees;— everything that a farmer boy away out in a new country would have to do, this boy had done. Indeed, when he was named for President by the Republican party, the opposing parties sneered at him, calling him a "vulgar rail-splitter," "an ignorant boor, unfit for the society of gentlemen."

But for all his hoeing and his rail-splitting, for all his poverty and his hard labor, for all his rough home and his common companions, Abraham Lincoln soon proved that he had a something in his head and in his heart that any gentleman might well have been proud to own—a something that a world of fine houses and fine clothes could not buy—something which, by and by, prompted him to set all the poor black men and women free.

Although Abraham Lincoln did live in the backwoods, and did not go to school, nevertheless, he was all this time in the best of society. Fortunately for him, his mother was a real lady in heart, and tried always to keep her boy from growing up a coarse, ignorant "rail-splitter," as his party opponents called him. She taught him always to keep his eyes open, and his thoughts awake to the beauties about him in nature. She taught him that it was a noble heart that could see God in the beautiful flowers, in the birds, in the fields, in the forests, and in the waters; that it was the artist's soul that loved to watch the beautiful sunset lights and the deepening shadows; she taught him to read the few books that she owned, and helped him to earn a few more; she encouraged his love for reading, and was careful that his reading was always of the best kind.

LINCOLN'S FIRST HOUSE IN ILLINOIS

The result was, that when Abraham Lincoln came to be President, and had to write letters and make speeches, he always had the very best style of English at his command. When he said a thing, it was so simply and so correctly said, that every one knew just what he meant. And behind his words, too, there was always his big, honest, truthful heart. Is it any wonder, then, when, by and by, this good man died—shot down by an enemy of our Union—that all the country mourned for him, and felt for a time as if no one could be found to fill this good, great man's place.

Here is what a good woman says of him: "When Abraham Lincoln wrote a thing, you read what he meant. The meaning was not covered up under a heap of useless words. One thing was apparent in him from boyhood. This was his straightforward truthfulness and sincerity of purpose. No political experience ever twisted him; he ended life as he began it, an honest, sincere, trustworthy man. One of the great outcries against him by his opponents after he was elected was, 'He is an uncouth, rough backwoodsman. He is *no gentleman.*' It is true that he was very uncouth in face and figure; never handsome to look at, although the soul of the man sometimes shone through the plain features in a way that transfigured them, and his deep gray eyes were full of a great sadness, that seemed almost to prophesy his tragic fate. He had not the manners of a court, but he did deeds from the promptings of a simple, manly heart that a king might have been proud to own, and if he was not a true gentleman, God does not make many now-a-days."

When the Republicans chose Abraham Lincoln, the South was furious—not because they had chosen Lincoln, because they had chosen any one at all. "If a Republican President is elected," said these Southern States, "we will go out of the Union."

Now, it is said that the Southerners really were in hopes that a Republican President would be elected, so that they might have an excuse for leaving the Union. "We will go off by ourselves," said one of the Southern leaders, "and build up a government of our own; and we will have slavery for its very corner stone." They were very angry, these Southern slave-holders; for one reason, because they were now made by the United States Government to pay such high prices for slaves. One slave-dealer said, he wasn't going to pay a thousand dollars for a slave in Virginia, when he could go to Africa and buy better ones for fifty dollars a head! What do you think of a business that employed agents to catch colored men and women as you would catch animals, bring them into market, and sell them at a price, according to their size, or weight, or age, or strength for work!

JEFFERSON DAVIS

We ought all to be glad that the United States Government at last came to its senses, and made all the States give up this wicked traffic.

Lincoln was in due time elected President, and the Southern States, as they had threatened, declared themselves no longer members of the Union. They made for themselves a new government, put Jefferson Davis at its head as President, and called themselves "The Confederate States of America."

These Southerners believed that, although the States had all at one time banded together under one government, still each State had a right to step out and set up a government of its own if it chose. This is what John C. Calhoun said in his speeches before Congress, and without doubt he believed what he said was true. This was the same old question of "State rights" of which you heard away back as far as when Washington was President. Don't you remember how jealous of each other the political parties were even in those early times? How afraid one party was that too much power would be given to the central government, that is, to the President and Congress? And how equally afraid the other party was that the power would be too much scattered around among the different States? And do you remember in Jackson's administration, that some of these same Southern States declared the central government "null and void," and said they had a right to leave the Union if they wanted to? They even went so far as to form a league, and would really have made trouble enough had not Jackson rushed down upon them before they had time to do any mischief.

Here was this same old question up again, in a new dress to be sure, but it was the same old question.

The Northern people had no idea how much this matter meant to the Southern people. Even when South Carolina really "seceded" from the Union—even then the Northerners thought it was only a threat.

But lest we should be too severe in our judgment on these Southerners, let us stop and see why it was they cared so little about that "Union," which, to a Northerner, is so dear. This is the reason: the Southerner had been brought up from his babyhood to love his *State*, his *State flag*, his *State Government*. To him, his *State* was everything. He had been brought up to say, "I am a Virginian!" or "I am a South Carolinian!" It was his *State* flag that he had seen raised on festal days; it was the *State* flag that waved over the public buildings, and over their forts. Everything to him was State! State! State! He loved his State, he was proud of her, and he was ready to die for her.

Now let us see how the Northerner had been brought up. He, I am inclined to think, hardly knew what his State flag was—he never heard anything about it, never saw it. It was always the "Stars and Stripes" that floated before him in these Northern States. "The Star Spangled Banner," "My Country, 'tis of Thee," "God Bless Our Union," were the songs he had always sung. He never said, "I am a New Yorker!" or "I am a Rhode Islander!" but always, *"I am an American!"* Everything to him was Union! Union! Union! He loved the Union, he was proud of her, he was ready to die for her. So you see, these two parties could not understand each other. The Northerner could not believe that the Southerner would do such an *awful* thing as to break up the sacred Union, and the Southerner, on the other side, could not see that there was anything awful at all in breaking up the Union, which to him was not sacred at all.

LINCOLN IS MADE PRESIDENT

While this quarrel was boiling and bub-
bling, the day was drawing near when Lincoln
was to take his place at the head of the nation.

He started from his simple home full of
hope for his country, even in so threatening a
time as this; full of honest intention to serve
her faithfully, and with no wish to wage war
upon any State or States. Innocent in his own
heart, free from all malice, he could not believe it when he was told that a plot had been
laid to murder him as he passed through the
city of Baltimore. It was too true, however;
and the friends of the new President found it
necessary to have him pass through this city
at night, under the cover of darkness.

On reaching the capital, he made his inau-
gural address, as all the Presidents have done
since the time when Washington made his

from the balcony to the people on the green below.

This address was honest and manly, as everything that Lincoln said was sure to be. He told the South that he had no wish to make any trouble for those States, no wish to interfere with their rights; he only desired that they should abide by the laws of the country. He said, however, that they had no right to withdraw from the Union, no right to take into their own hands the forts or any other property belonging to the Union; if they did these things, it was his duty, as the chief officer of the Government, to demand that they return to the Union, and give up any property they had taken.

Now, as both these things had already been done in the South, that party at once said, "Lincoln has no right to say we *shall* stay in the Union; we will *not* give up the forts that are on our own coasts; we will fight for them; we will not be ruled by any Union Government." And now the war was close at hand.

Fort Sumter

"FORT SUMTER"

During the last months of Buchanan's administration, Major Robert Anderson, who held command over the forts in Charleston harbor, had asked over and over again for men and provisions for these forts. He had shown the President plainly that he could not much longer hold them against the "seceding" States, unless help were given; but still no help had come. When Lincoln became President, Anderson asked again. Lincoln replied that help should at once be sent. The leaders of the "Confederates" or "Seceders"—you must remember both these names, for they both mean the Southern people—the leaders of these Southerners, hearing of this, went to Major Anderson and ordered him to surrender the fort to them it once.

Anderson, of course, refused. He knew only too well that he had no men, guns or powder with which to hold the fort, if the Confederates saw fit to fire upon it; still, loyal Unionist that he was, he determined to hold out to the very last. "It shall not be said that the Stars and Stripes are hauled down without a struggle," said he.

He had only eighty men, but he thought he could hold out as long as the provisions lasted, and so this little band prepared for action.

There were three more forts in the harbor, all in Confederate hands, and beside this, they had built two great rafts upon which they had fixed cannons. These they floated round in front of the fort, and on *Friday, April 12, 1861,* the Confederates opened fire from these five points, all upon the one little fort with its eighty men. The "Civil War" had begun.

Major Anderson

Down came the rain of shot and shell, around the fort, across the fort, into the fort. The wooden barracks inside took fire again and again; and on the second day, they were burned to the ground. It was a hot time for the brave little garrison. The air was so hot, and the smoke was so choking and so blinding, that they could work only with their faces covered with wet cloths. Every hour the fort grew to look more and more like a great ruin.

FORT SUMTER AFTER THE FIRING

It was plain enough that Major Anderson must surrender. All this time, however, the Stars and Stripes had been kept flying from above the fort. Even when they had been torn down by the flying balls from the enemy, some man had always been ready to nail them up again. But now the white flag of surrender had to be shown. The firing ceased, and the Confederates came over to the fort in boats to make terms with Major Anderson. It was agreed, after long discussion, that Anderson and his men should be allowed to march out with flying colors, should be allowed to salute the dear old flag with fifty guns, and then should march away in peace.

This was done; and as soon as they had gone, General Beauregard, the Confederate leader, marched into the ruined fort, tore down the "Stars and Stripes," and ran up the South Carolina State flag in its place.

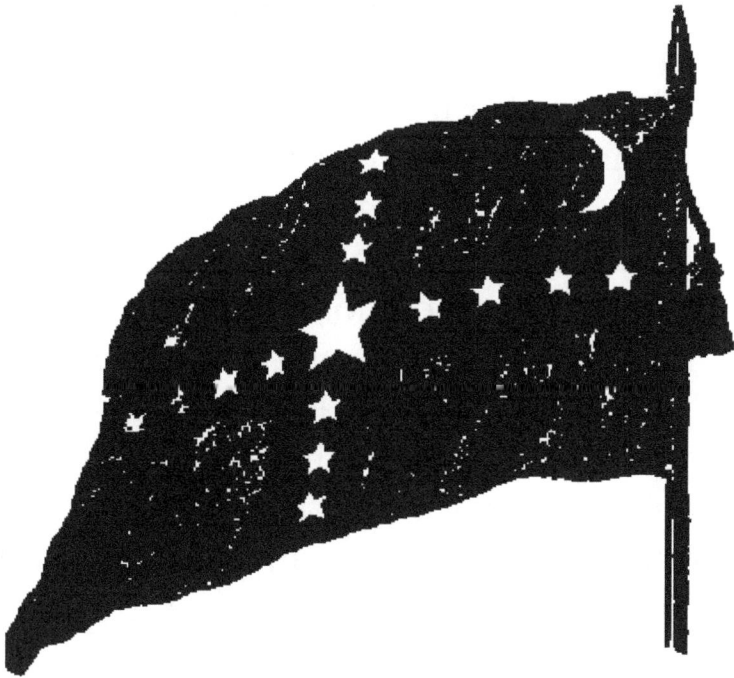

THE SOUTH CAROLINA FLAG

This is a brief story of the bombarding of "Fort Sumter." Not a single life was lost on either side; but if millions upon millions of lives had been lost, there could not have been greater excitement throughout the country. Ask your fathers and your mothers, or your grandfathers and your grandmothers, to tell you about it. It was less than thirty years ago, and anywhere you can find men and women who remember those early times of the Civil War.

They were exciting days indeed! The different political parties of the North, forgetting all differences, all ill feelings, all quarrels, now joined hands and hearts in this terrible time. There was but one cry in the hearts of all— "Save the Union! Save the Union!" Nothing more was to be heard about Democrats or Republicans, tariff or no tariff,—Unionists or Confederates were the words now on every lip. No longer was it Republicans against Democrats, but the North against the South, the South against the North.

And now, President Lincoln sent forth a call for help—for men to go against the South. Seventy-five thousand men, he asked for, to help him "to preserve the Union." From every city, and town, and village, answers came. It seemed as if every man in the country was ready. Rich men and poor men marched away together side by side; willing to bear all the hardships of the soldiers' lot.

The women, too, were as alive as the men. It seemed as if the Revolutionary spirit had revived again in them. No woman was too rich or too poor, too high or too low, too strong or too weak, not to do something for the Union soldier. Little children, too, caught the spirit of the times. When they saw their fathers and their big brothers march away, their little hearts were full of tears, I fear, but they were all the readier to work for the soldiers because their own dear ones had gone away with them.

In the South the same feeling of loyalty to what they believed was right was shown among the men and women there. Remember they loved their States as truly as the Northerners loved the Union.

When the news that Fort Sumter had fallen into their hands was heard throughout the South, men and women were wild with joy. Songs were sung, verses were written, public meetings were held, and the South was boiling over with excitement.

Such was the excitement in the North and in the South after the taking of Fort Sumter by the Confederates. Let us see now what next was done.

THE FIRST BLOODSHED

Do you remember what happened in the Revolution on one 19th of April?

And now we have another 19th of April to learn about—19th of April, 1861.

In answer to Lincoln's call for seventy-five thousand men, many a small company from the different States had been got together, and were training for service. One of these companies, the "Sixth Massachusetts Regiment," reached Baltimore, on its way to Washington, on this morning of the 19th of April, 1861. When the cars which brought them reached the city, it was met by a crowd of angry people armed with sticks, and clubs, and guns—a blacker, angrier mob was never seen.

These cars were drawn through the city from one depot to another, the soldiers inside. The mob followed, throwing stones and brick-bats into the windows from every side.

Passing Through Baltimore

At last, unable to endure it any longer, the officer, ordered the soldiers to form into ranks, and march in a solid column to the depot.

On they marched, the brick-bats and balls whizzing about their ears. Just as they reached the depot, the command was given, "Fire!"

Then the troops turned their guns into the crowd; and many a man fell before the fire of these soldiers whom they had attacked. For a moment there was a lull! The mob itself stood still before its awful work! But only for a moment; then with yells of rage and threats of revenge, they fell upon the troops, surrounded the cars, filling the air with howls and curses. Amid this terrible scene the cars rolled out of the depot. Three of the soldiers had been killed, and there were eighteen wounded.

FEDERAL HILL

During all this time the Confederates had been threatening to attack Washington, and tear down the Union flag from the Capitol. They had even said they would yet have their own flag waving over Faneuil Hall in Boston. Think of it, imagine anything but the "Stars and Stripes" waving over that old "Cradle of Liberty."

Even then the Northerners did not realize how full of hate the Southerners were. Washington was indeed poorly guarded, but the idea of attacking the Nation's Capitol! It didn't seem possible. But now there came a cry, "Washington is in danger! Help, help for Washington!" And help came. The Seventh Regiment of New York, a regiment of young men, kept up to this time only for parades, never expecting to be called into real war, came forward and *volunteered*, that is, offered to go to protect the capital.

How the people shrank from accepting this noble sacrifice! This pet regiment of the State! made up of the very "flower of volunteer troops," as it was said then, to go into battle to be shot down, very likely, like dogs! But they were ready; the country needed them, and so, one morning in April, this regiment marched down Broadway, the main street of New York city, to the cars that should carry them to Washington.

That was a great day in New York city! Crowds and crowds of men and women filled the squares and the sidewalks, and cheers upon cheers rent the air as these boys marched down the street. Theodore Winthrop, one of the young men in this noble regiment, in writing of this day, says:

"It was worth a life, that march. Only one who passed as we did through that tempest of cheers, two miles long, can know the terrible enthusiasm of the day. We knew now, if we had not known before, that our great city was with us as one man, united in the cause we were marching to sustain."

This regiment was joined by the Eighth Massachusetts Regiment, with General Benjamin F. Butler as one of its volunteer generals. It was supposed that General Butler had always had much sympathy with the South, and had been always in favor of allowing the South all the freedom to carry out their own ideas that could possibly be given them without real harm to the Government. But, when the South set out to break up the Union, no one rose quicker in its defence than did General Butler. When one of his Southern friends told him what the South was planning to do, Butler said:

"If you do that, I trust you are ready for war."

"Pooh! the North will not fight," said the Southerner.

"The North *will* fight," replied Butler. "You touch the Union flag and you'll find that the

North will rise in a solid body against you; and if war *does* come, down will go your Confederacy, slavery and all."

But the South did not believe it, although they had good reason to know that General Butler had a "long head," as we often say when we mean that a person understands what he is talking about. Imagine their surprise then, when they found that even Butler himself was against them, when it came to be a real question with him whether to stand by the South, or to stand by the Union. Alas! it took the Southerners a long time to understand what the *Union* meant to a Northerner. And, alas, it took the Northerners a long time to understand what the *State* meant to the Southerner. It proved a bitter, bitter lesson to them both.

These regiments, the Seventh New York and the Eighth Massachusetts, arrived safely at Washington, and the capital was safe. But on account of the Secessionists in Baltimore, these troops had been obliged to get to Washington in a very roundabout way, to avoid being attacked as the Massachusetts Sixth had been.

"Now," said Butler, when he had fairly got his regiment in order after their march, "the city of Baltimore must be taken. The city is made up of Union men and women, but they are kept down by the few "Secessionists" there. That city must be freed. We can't bother to take our troops around through the woods and up the rivers every time we want to bring them to Washington, when there is a railroad straight through that city. No, Baltimore must be taken; and I will go and take it!"

Accordingly, he marched to Baltimore; and one night, when the sky was black and the rain was pouring, the wind howling, the lightning flashing and the thunder mumbling and rolling on every side, up he marched with his men and his cannon to the top of Federal Hill. There he was when the morning dawned, his flags flying, his guns ready, his great black cannons looking down upon the city as much as to say, "Make one move against the Union, lift one finger against our troops, and our black throats are ready to pour out fire and death upon you."

The Secessionists understood the language of the cannons, and from that time the Union soldiers marched in peace through the city of Baltimore.

THE CONFEDERATE STATES

The States that first withdrew from the Union were States farthest removed from the North. These States supposed that all the other slave States would at once join with them in their Confederacy. Those States which were farther north, nearer the Northern States, had more of the neighborly feeling than the first seceding States had ever dreamed of. In those States, Unionists and Confederates dwelt side by side, and in their legislatures, Unionists and Confederates voted side by side. So you see it was not so easy after all to pass "Secession" laws in these States.

Virginia was the first State to join the seven that had banded together to form their Confederacy. "Hurrah! hurrah!" cried the Confederates, "Virginia, Old Virginia, Virginia the mother of the Presidents, the home of George Washington, has joined us!"

But the Confederate joy was dampened a little when the western part of Virginia rose in rebellion, and said she would not belong to a secession State. This western Virginia held meetings, withdrew from the State, appealed to Congress, and, as a reward for her loyalty to the Union, was set off a State by herself, known ever after as "West Virginia."

THE CONFEDERATE FLAG

Soon Arkansas joined the Confederacy; then followed North Carolina, then Tennessee. It is believed that Tennessee would not have seceded, had the Unionists not been threatened with "bullets and cold steel" if they dared say one word against the South, in the convention which was to be held in that State.

Kentucky and Missouri wished to have nothing to do with either side. They would stand by the Union, but they would not fight the South. Maryland, awed by the prompt action of Butler, was kept in the Union. Delaware, loyal little State that she was, and cautious too, preferred to stay where she was in comfort, rather than to join so uncertain a movement as this surely seemed to be.

The Confederacy then stood as follows:

These were the States that had left the Union and were ready to fight for their State rights, as they believed them to be. These were the States that had hauled down the "Stars and Stripes," and had hoisted in its place the Secession flag.

SEVEN ORIGINAL SECESSION STATES.

SOUTH CAROLINA.
ALABAMA.
GEORGIA.
MISSISSIPPI.
FLORIDA.
LOUISIANA.
TEXAS.

THE LATER STATES.

OLD VIRGINIA.
TENNESSEE.
NORTH CAROLINA.
ARKANSAS.

THE SOUTHERN CONFEDERACY.

SOUTH CAROLINA.
OLD VIRGINIA.
GEORGIA.
TENNESSEE.
ALABAMA.
ARKANSAS.
LOUISIANA.
FLORIDA.
NORTH CAROLINA.
MISSISSIPPI.
TEXAS.

President of the Confederacy
JEFFERSON DAVIS

YOUNG COLONEL ELLSWORTH

There was a great deal of threatening all this time against the Union troops if they should *dare* set foot upon the "sacred soil of Old Virginia" as the Southerners called it. But for all that, the Government saw fit very early in 1861 to send troops into that very State.

The "New York Zouaves," led by Colonel Ellsworth, were the first to enter. The young colonel was handsome, and brave, and daring; and his troops, dressed in brilliant uniforms of red and yellow and blue, were the pride and delight of the army.

Ellsworth's troops entered the town of Alexandria, beyond the Potomac in Virginia, full of life and hope, and full of faith in their gay young colonel. On they marched, their colors flying, the drums beating, straight up to a hotel from whose top was seen a secession flag.

A Zouave

"Halt!" came the command as they reached the hotel entrance. Rushing into the building, up the stair-case, he pulled down the secession flag, and marched with it down the stairs again. But at the foot of the stairway, stood the tavern-keeper, ready to resent this insult to his flag. Bang went his gun, and young Ellsworth fell dead. Bang! went another gun, and down by Ellsworth's side dropped the tavern-keeper, shot dead by one of Ellsworth's men.

I cannot tell you what excitement the death of this young colonel caused throughout the North. Every honor was paid him; every school-boy was told of the martyred Ellsworth; little babies were named for him; little boys were dressed in Zouave suits in imitation of him, and everywhere the name of Ellsworth was a household word

CONTRABANDS

There were many forts up and down the coast that had been taken by the Confederates; and there were others, still held by the United States Government, which the Confederates were equally anxious to get into their power.

To one of these, Fortress Monroe, Butler had been sent with troops. As soon as he had settled in his new quarters, Butler began to make short marches here and there about the country, that, by and by, when the people round about should rise against him, he might have some sort of an idea what kind of a place he was in,—where the roads were, where they led to, where the villages were, and how many people were in the villages.

Everywhere he went, he was met by negroes, who, when they saw his Union soldiers, would come up to them singing the funniest old songs, all about freedom, bondage, and the year of jubilee. Negroes, you know, are always a jolly class among themselves, always dancing, and singing their strange old tunes. These negroes, too, in spite of all their years of slavery, were still full of noise and music. Some of their songs are very funny, both in words and tune; others are so sad and weary; they speak to you of those dark, dark days when these poor men and women worked like cattle through the long hot days, were whipped and driven like cattle, and were bought and sold like cattle in the market place.

It began to be a serious question what to do with these negroes. The object of the war was not to free the slaves, but to preserve the Union. Many a soldier, many an officer in the Union ranks, believed yet in the right of the South to keep slaves if she wanted to. They were fighting only to save the Union. Others there were, who declared slavery a wicked sin; and these men claimed the right to save these slaves and free them.

But now the slaves themselves began to ask, "Are

you coming to free us, or are you not?" And no one was quite ready to say.

The negroes supposed they were to be freed; and frequently slaves came into the Union camp, begging to be carried away somewhere, anywhere, only to be free. What to do with them was getting every day to be a puzzle.

Again General Butler came forward. "What shall we do with these negroes!" said he; "why, it's plain enough. The Southerners have always said these slaves are their property just as their horses and their cows, their to-bacco and their cotton are their property. Very well! then we are to treat them just as we would treat the cows and the horses, the tobacco and the cotton—that is, we will take them for our own use. That is the rule in war, that on entering an enemy's country, the army shall take everything it needs for its own use. Those things which the enemy takes are called "contraband goods." Therefore, since the negro is the property of the Confederate, we may take him just as we would take a Confederate Barrel of flour. He is, like the flour, contraband goods."

Nobody could find any fault with this, certainly. It was true enough. And after that the negro was called the "Contraband."

THE CONTRABAND OF PORT ROYAL

THE CONTRABAND OF PORT ROYAL

1. Oh, praise an' tanks! de Lord He come To set de peo-ple free; An' mas-sa tink it day of doom, An' we ob ju-bi-lee. De Lord dat heap de Red Sea waves, He jus' as 'trong as den; He

2. Ole mas-sa on he trab-bles gone, He leab de land be-hind: De Lord's breff blow him fur-der on, Like corn-shuck in de wind. We own de hoe, We own de plow, We own de hands dat hold; We

3. We pray de Lord: he gib us signs Dat some day we be free; De Norf-wind tell it to de pines, De wild-duck to de sea. We tink it when de church bell ring, We dream it in de dream; De

4. We know de prom-ise neb-ber fail, An' neb-ber lie de word. So like de 'pos-tles in de jail, We wait-ed for de Lord: 'An now he o-pen eb-ery door, An' trow a-way de key; He

677

say de word: we las' night slaves: To-day, de Lord's freemen.
sell de pig, we sell de cow, But neb-ber chile be sold.
rice-bird mean it when he sing, De ca - gle when he scream.
tink we lub him so be - fore, We lub him bet - ter free.

CHORUS.

De yam will grow, de cot - ton blow, We'll
hab. de rice an' corn: Oh, neb-ber you fear, if
neb-ber you hear De driv - er blow his horn.

SILVER BELL.

A NEGRO'S ANSWER

While the Union soldiers were in the slave States, the negroes, although most of them were at heart with the Union cause, had to be very careful what they said.

The answers, these negroes would make when asked which side they were on, were often very laughable. You see, there were so many spies around, that the poor negro never could be sure whether it was a Unionist or a Confederate that was talking with him. And he knew well enough that if he should make a mistake, and tell a Confederate he was a Unionist or if he should tell a Unionist he was a Confederate, he might be shot down.

One day, a gray-haired negro was seen perched on the top of a rail fence watching the soldiers with great interest. One soldier, thinking to have some fun, called out to him:

"Well, uncle, are you for the Confederates or the Yankees?"

A smile lit up his weather-beaten face, as he replied:

"Why, you see, massa, 'taint for an old nigger like me to know anything 'bout politics."

The soldier said rather sternly: "Well, sir, let me know which side you are on, any way."

The old man kept up his smile for a moment, and then putting on a grave look, which was, quite laughable, answered:

"I'm on de Lord's side, massa, and he'll work out his salvation; bress de Lord."

"BIG BETHEL" AND "LITTLE BETHEL."

With Butler at Fortress Munroe, was young Theodore Winthrop, who, when his regiment was no longer needed at Washington, had offered to join Butler's regiment and go to Fortress Munroe.

From one of these Contrabands, Winthrop had learned that about two thousand Confederates had encamped at two churches called "Little Bethel" and "Big Bethel."

Butler and Winthrop at once began to plan an attack upon these Confederates. Their plan was this; the troops were to be divided into two bodies and fall upon the Rebels at Little Bethel, close around them, and prevent their getting to their companions at Big Bethel.

The two lines marched out quietly in the darkness, and came upon Little Bethel as they had planned. But here a terrible mistake took place. Just as these two lines met near the church they fired into each other's ranks, each thinking the other line the enemy. A scene of confusion followed and before orders could be given, the soldiers at Little Bethel had fled to those at Big Bethel, and together they were ready to rain down their hot fire upon the Union ranks. A quick hard fight, followed; and Winthrop himself, while mounted on a log to cheer his men, was shot dead.

Again there was mourning throughout the North that so promising a young officer should have fallen. The names of Ellsworth and Winthrop have always been held in respect; and for many a day were household words; until the time came when officers and men fell so thick and fast they could hardly be named or numbered, and their losses were known only in the hearts of their own friends, and in their own homes.

BETHEL

We mustered at midnight, in darkness we formed,
And the whisper went round of a fort to be stormed;
But no drum-beat had called us, no trumpet we heard,
And no voice of command but our colonel's low word,—
        "Column! Forward!"

And out, through the mist and the murk of the moon,
From the beaches of Hampton our barges were borne;
And we heard not a sound save a sweep of the oar,
Till the word of our colonel came up from the shore,—
        "Column! Forward!"

Through green-tasseled cornfields our columns were thrown,
And like corn by the red scythe of fire we were mown;
While the cannon's fierce ploughings new-furrowed the plain.
That our blood might be planted for Liberty's grain,—
        "Column! Forward!"

Oh! the fields of fair June have no lack of sweet flowers,
But their rarest and best breathe no fragrance like ours;
And the sunshine of June sprinkling gold on the corn,
Hath no harvest that ripeneth like Bethel's red morn,—
        "Column! Forward!"

When our heroes, like bridegrooms, with lips and with breath
Drank the first kiss of Danger, and clasped her in death;
And the heart of brave Winthrop[1] grew mute with his lyre,
When the plumes of his genius lay moulting in fire,—
    "Column! Forward!"

Where he fell shall be sunshine as bright as his flame,
And the grass where he slept shall be green as his fame;
For the gold of the Pen and the steel of the Sword
Write his deeds—in his blood—on the land he adored,—
    "Column! Forward!"

And the soul of our comrade shall sweeten the air,
And the flowers and the grass-blades his memory upbear;
While the breath of his genius, like music in leaves,
With the corn-tassels whisper, and sings in the sheaves'—
    "Column! Forward!"

—A. J. H. Duganne.

---

[1] Major Theodore Winthrop fell while cheering on his men and was left on the battle-field. Lieutenant Greble was also killed in this battle.

DIXIE'S LAND AND JOHN BROWN'S BODY

In any war, each side has always some one piece of music which its armies delight to march by. An English Army, I presume, would march to "God Save the Queen;" a French army to the "Marseilles Hymn;" a German army to "The Watch on the Rhine."

And so in this war, each side had its own music. The Confederate army's especial favorite was "Dixie's Land;" while the Union soldiers delighted in "John Brown's Body lies a moulderin' in the Ground," or "Rally 'round the Flag, Boys."

I think you boys and girls ought to know these songs as well as to know the battles of the war; anything that helps to give us an idea of the thought of the people at a time, is a part of the history of that time. For this reason, I hope your teacher will find time to let you sing these songs now and then.

THE BATTLE CRY OF FREEDOM

1. Yes, we'll ral-ly round the flag, boys, we'll ral-ly once a - gain,
2. We are springing to the call of our brothers gone be - fore,

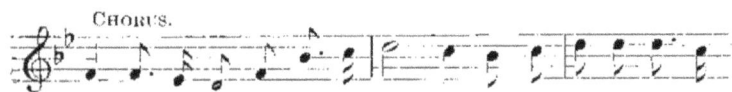

Chorus.

Shouting the bat-tle cry of Free-dom, We will ral-ly from the
Shouting the bat-tle cry of Free-dom, And we'll fill the va - cant

Chorus.

hill-side, we'll gath-er from the plain Shouting the bat-tle cry of
ranks with a mil-lion freemen more Shouting the bat-tle cry of

Fortissimo.

Free-dom. The Un-ion for-ev-er, Hur-rah boys, hur-rah!

Down with the trait-or, Up with the star, While we ral-ly round the

flag, boys, ral-ly once again, Shouting the bat-tle cry of Freedom.

BATTLE OF BULL RUN

The Confederates had camped at a railroad junction in Virginia, where the railroads running west and those running south met. It was, as you see, important that such a place as that should be kept out of the hands of the Confederates, lest all means of railroad travel for the Unionists be cut off. The railroad leading direct to Richmond, the city which the Confederates had made the capital of their Confederacy, led from this junction. Because of this, the Confederates were carefully guarding this junction.

General Beauregard, the same Confederate who had ordered the attack upon Fort Sumter, was in command here, He was an odd looking little man, with snapping black eyes; and snow white hair. He hated "Yankees" as he hated rats; and used often to say, "We'll whip 'em, boys, if we have nothing but pitch-forks to do it with."

The Confederate army was camped by the side of a stream called "Bull Run." With Beauregard was another general of whom you need to know, General Johnston.

General McDowell was coming with the Union army to meet this foe. At nine o'clock one Sunday morning, the armies met, and a terrible battle followed. The Confederates began breaking up and giving way. It seemed as if victory was to be on the Union side. But General Jackson turned the tide—Jackson, the cool-headed, iron-hearted, immovable Confederate General.

"Boys, there stands Jackson cool and firm as a stonewall!" said a soldier, as he saw him in the midst of this fearful slaughter, sitting as quietly upon his horse, giving his orders as coolly, as if he were in the quiet fields of his own plantation.

"Jackson like a stone-wall," flew along the lines, from mouth to mouth, and ever after this grim old general was called "Stonewall Jackson."

At noon time, fresh Confederate forces came up, and the already exhausted Unionists rallied to fight again. Back and forth the lines surged against each other. Guns were taken and retaken over and over. No one could tell which side was winning.

All this time, the Confederate leaders had been watching for new troops which were expected every hour from the Shenandoah valley.

"STONEWALL" JACKSON

The Shenandoah troops arrived! Woe, woe to the Union lines! the first knowledge they had of their new foe, was the yell that arose from every side, "The enemy are upon us! the enemy are upon us!"

Now followed a terrible fright. The Union soldiers, frightened and confused, dropped guns, knapsacks, everything and fled;—fled like wild animals with no reason and no order.

On, on they ran towards Washington, frightening the villagers as they passed along, calling to them to run for their lives from the foe behind. It was one of the most disgraceful flights ever known in history; and when it became really known what had been done, the North was indeed filled with shame and despair.

Here are two little stories connected with this battle of Bull Run, which although not what some people would call "real history," will help you to remember the battle.

Several dwelling-houses stood within the limits of the place where the fight was hottest, among them the house of Mrs. Judith Henry. Not suspecting that it was to be the scene of a battle, the family remained in the house until it was too late to escape. The noise of the battle came nearer and nearer, and soon cannon-shot began to plow up the ground around the house. Mrs. Henry, who was an invalid, was carried by her son and daughter to a gully, or kind of hollow washed out by running water, and there the three lay in safety until the army had passed by. Thinking themselves safe, the children bore their aged mother to the house again; but the Union troops were driven back, and the fight again raged so hotly around them that it was impossible to leave. The old lady lay there amid all the remaining terrors of the day; the house was riddled with balls, and when the tide of battle had rolled on, she was found so badly wounded that she died soon after.

EDDY, THE DRUMMER BOY

One of the saddest stories of the war is the story of Little Eddy, the Drummer Boy.

His father, a Union man of East Tennessee, had been killed, and his mother had gone to St. Louis with Eddy, then about twelve years old, in hope of finding a sister who lived there. Failing in this, and getting out of money, she applied to the captain of one of the companies in the Iowa First to get Eddy a position as drummer boy. The regiment had only six weeks longer to serve, and she hoped that during that time she might get work for herself and find her sister. The captain was about to say that he could not take so small a boy, when Eddy spoke out, "Don't be afraid, captain, I can drum."

Upon this, the captain replied, with a smile, "Well, well, sergeant, bring the drum, and order the fifer to come forward."

The fifer, a lank, round-shouldered fellow, more than six feet high, came forward, and bending down with his hands on his knees, asked, "My little man, can you drum?"

"Yes, sir," said Eddie, "I drummed for Captain Hill in Tennessee."

The fifer straightened himself up and played one of the most difficult tunes to follow with the drum; but Eddy kept pace with him through all the hardest parts and showed that he was a master of the drum.

"Madam, I will take your boy," said the captain. "What is his name?"

"Edward Lee," she replied, wiping a tear from her eye. "Oh! captain, if he is not killed, you will bring him back with you, won't you?"

"Yes, we'll be sure to bring him back. We shall be discharged in six weeks."

Eddy became a great favorite with the soldiers; and the tall, lank fifer used often to carry him "pick-a-back" over the hard roads and muddy places.

After the battle of Wilson's Creek, little Eddy could not be found. By and by the corporal, who had been searching for him, heard the sound of his drum not far away.

The company was to march away in a very few minutes, but not liking to leave the little fellow, the corporal went to find him.

He found him sitting up against a tree, looking deadly pale.

"O corporal, I am so glad you came! Do give me a drink of water! You don't think I'll die, do you? That man lying there said the doctor would cure my feet."

Poor little Eddy! both feet had been shot off by a cannon ball. Looking around, the corporal found a Confederate soldier lying dead not far from Eddy. He, poor soldier, although he was himself dying, had crept up to Eddy and tried to bandage the little boy's feet.

While Eddy was telling the story, a Confederate officer came up and took the corporal and his little friend prisoners.

Very tenderly the officer lifted Eddy upon the horse before him, and started for the camp; but before they reached it, the little drummer boy was dead.

TENTING ON THE OLD CAMP GROUND

TENTING ON THE OLD CAMP GROUND

1. We're tent-ing to-night on the old Camp ground, Give us a song to
2. We've been tenting to-night on the old Camp ground, Thinking of days gone
3. We are tired of war on the old Camp ground, Many are dead and
4. We've been fighting to-day on the old Camp ground, Many are ly-ing

cheer. Our wea-ry hearts, a song of home, And
by, Of the lov'd ones at home that gave us the hand, And the
gone, Of the brave and true who've left their homes, Oth -
near; Some are dead, and some are dy - ing, Ma-

CHORUS.

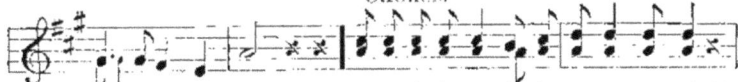

friends we love so dear. Many are the hearts that are weary to-night,
tear that said "good-bye!"
ers been wounded long.
ny are in tears.

Wishing for the war to cease, Many are the hearts, looking for the right, To

see the dawn of peace. Tent-ing to-night, tent-ing to-night,

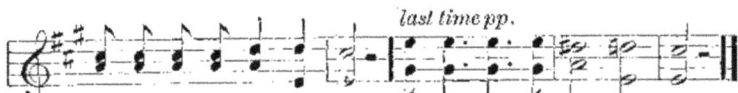

last time pp.

Tent-ing on the old Camp ground, Dying on the old Camp ground.

697

THE SEA-ISLAND COTTON PLANTATIONS

After this defeat of the Union forces, the South was in high spirits. They thought the war was as good as ended in this one battle; but they did not know, as well as they did later, what the Northerners were made of, if they imagined one defeat would make them give up the "Union."

These soldiers, who had enlisted only for three months, were now, many of them going home; but other troops were pouring in from every town and village of the North. The North was indeed awake now. Now a great army was raised, and put under the charge of General McClellan, one of the finest military officers of the war. He very soon got his army into such fine order that they moved about as if they had been brought up, every one, from babyhood, in battle lines. This army was called the "Army of the Potomac." The only fault that was ever found with this army was that all this long fall and winter the army lay idle, except for two or three little battles of no great importance.

GEN. G. B. MCCLELLAN

Every evening, as the Northerner sat down to read his evening paper, he read, "All quiet along the Potomac." This was well enough for a time; but as week after week passed, the North began to complain. Still, all remained "quiet along, the Potomac"—until at last the very sound of the sentence came to excite indignation and anger among the waiting Northerners.

THE PICKET GUARD

"All quiet along the Potomac," they say,
*   "Except now and then a stray picket*
Is shot, as he walks on his beat to and fro,
By a rifleman hid in the thicket.
'Tis nothing; a private or two now and then
*   Will not count in the news of the battle;*
Not an officer lost—only one of the men,
*   Moaning; out all alone the death-rattle."*

All quiet along the Potomac to-night,
*   Where the soldiers lie peacefully dreaming;*
Their tents in the rays of the clear autumn moon
*   Or the light of the watch-fires are gleaming.*
A tremulous sigh, as the gentle night-wind,
*   Thro' the forest leaves softly is creeping;*
While stars up above, with their glittering eyes,
*   Keep guard—for the army is sleeping.*

There's only the sound of the lone sentry's tread
*   As he tramps from the rock to the fountain,*
And he thinks of the two in the lone trundle bed,
*   Far away in the cot in the mountain.*
His musket falls slack; his face dark and grim,
*   Grows gentle with memories tender,*
As he mutters a prayer for the children asleep,
*   For their mother—may heaven defend her!*

He passes the fountain, the blasted pine-tree—
The footstep is lagging and weary;
Yet onward he goes through the broad belt of light
Toward the shades of the forest so dreary.
Hark! was it the night wind that rustled the leaves?
Was it moonlight so wondrously flashing?
It looks like a rifle! "Ha, Mary, good-by!"
And the life-blood is ebbing and plashing.

All quiet along the Potomac to-night—
No sound save the rush of the river;
While soft falls the dew on the face of the dead,
The picket's off duty forever.

—E. E. Beers

"THE SEA ISLANDS"

But while this army is keeping so "quiet along the Potomac," let us take a run out into the ocean, and see what the United States Navy is doing all this time.

At the beginning of the war, the President had ordered that all Southern ports be blockaded. This was very necessary, in order to cut off trade between these ports and foreign countries. You can see how impossible it would be to starve out a prisoner if some one all the while were bringing supplies; so with the Southerners,—the quicker and more wholly they were cut off from all help, the quicker they must give way, and the sooner would the war end. Several vessels were sent to these different ports to blockade them; that is to keep any vessel from going in or coming out. One fleet was sent to the Sea islands, a group of islands south of South

Carolina, that State which had begun the war against the Union. These islands produce the very finest cotton in the world. It is known in the cotton-markets all over the world as the "sea-island cotton." You can see now why it was important to get possession of these islands; at any rate, why it was important to shut them off from foreign trade.

The flag-ship in this fleet was called the "Wabash." Behind her were forty-eight gun-boats and steamers, and twenty-six sailing vessels. Quite a fleet, compared with that of 1812.

The commander formed his fleet into a big circle, and began to steam round and round between two important forts, all keeping up a steady fire as they passed round. Round and round they went, worrying the two forts on all sides, until they gave way—and the richest lands of the South were in the hands of Union vessels.

The owners took to flight, burning their stored cotton as they went, determined that not one shred of it should fall into Yankee hands.

The negro slaves did not flee. They came down to the water side as the vessels drew near,—some of them with the few little things they owned tied up in little bundles,—and begged to be taken away to the land of freedom.

In a few months, great changes were seen on these sea islands. The Yankees were busy learning to raise cotton, and everywhere were schools and teachers for these black people. Think of it! schools for the negroes! Why, the Southerners would as soon have thought of educating their cows as of educating their slaves.

SEIZURE OF MASON AND SLIDELL

The president of the Confederacy, Jefferson Davis, was anxious to get letters to France and England, asking them for help. Of course, with the ports blockaded, it was almost impossible for any one to get away. But some way, two men, Mason and Slidell, did "run the blockade," went to Havana, and from there boarded an English vessel.

A Union sea-captain had heard of the departure of these two men, and, thinking they were up to mischief, watched them. When he found they had gone on board this English vessel, bound for England, he followed, came up with the English vessel, boarded her, and took Mason and Slidell prisoners as traitors to their country.

At first it seemed a very fortunate thing to have kept these two men from going to France and England with their letters asking for help; and the whole North was delighted. No one once thought that the English government had now a chance to say, "You have done to one of our vessels just what you waged war with us for doing in 1812. Have you forgotten that it was because of our taking men from your vessels that that war was brought about? Why can we not wage war upon you now for having done the same thing?"

No one thought of this; but England thought of it, and said it, too, very soon. She demanded, too, that the two men taken from her vessels be returned.

Some Northerners were at first inclined to stand by their deed; but there was an honest man at the head of the Government all this time, you know, and he said, "It does seem a pity to let these men go; but England is right, and it is our duty, not only to return the men, but to make an apology for taking them."

And when the people thought it over, they owned that England *was* right, and the two men were returned.

This was a good, honest, straightforward way to do, and I'm sure England and France both thought so, and respected the North for it. At any rate, the two men had no sort of success in either country, and the South was disappointed and disgusted with the whole affair.

THE MERRIMAC AND THE MONITOR

During the second year of the war, there appeared in the ocean not far from Fortress Monroe, a strange looking monster. Big, and black, and shining—what do you suppose it was?

It was an iron-clad war vessel which had once belonged to the United States Navy. The Confederates at the beginning of the war had sunk this vessel in the harbor; but afterwards some one had thought it would be a good idea to raise the hulk, and fit it up for a fighter.

They found, on raising this hulk, that it was firm and strong; so they had put a great iron roof over the deck, slanting it so that balls would glance off and so do no harm, had plated her sides all over with iron, and put on a great beak of iron and wood, making her indeed a most terrible looking enemy.

Down came this iron vessel straight upon the good old "Cumberland." Of course, no wooden vessel could stand an attack from this iron monster. For two hours these two vessels fought, although the Cumberland knew there was no hope. Bang went the cruel iron beak into the sides of the wooden Cumberland; and at last she sank, carrying with her her brave commander and his men, every one of whom fought to the last, preferring to sink rather than surrender to a Confederate ship.

Even when the vessel had sunk, it is said that the flag still floated above the waves for many hours.

Without a moment's rest, this iron fiend turned upon another Union vessel, and soon she, too, was a wreck. On went the Merrimac, attacking other vessels, until fortunately night came on and put a stop to this day's work; then she withdrew, to rest a while, chuckling no doubt over her day's doings, and planning all sorts of wickedness for the coming day. But to her great surprise, when the sun rose on the following morning, there stood not far away, a funny looking little vessel, dressed in fire-proof coat just like her own.

The Merrimac glared from all her portholes at this funny looking affair, and for a time couldn't seem to get it through her stupid head what it was. It looked like an iron raft with a round iron box in the middle.

What in the world that box could be, and what could be inside the box were a wonder to the Merrimac.

"Does that little Yankee cheese-box on a raft think to fight with me?" said the Merrimac, puffed up with her yesterday's victories.

But the Merrimac did not know that that cheese-box could revolve on a big screw, and that it had within itself some terrible guns which could be aimed almost as true as a rifle.

Up came the little Monitor, much like a little hornet at a great bull. The Merrimac really laughed to see her coming. She did look so funny! But soon bang went one of the great two-hundred pound balls from that little cheese-box, shaking the Merrimac and denting in her iron sides as if she had been made of tin.

The Merrimac stopped laughing now, and went to work. Some one said that the whole affair made him think of the boy David with his little sling walking up to fight the giant Goliah. But you remember Goliah was the one to fall, and in this battle, too, the big Merrimac fell before the little "Cheese-box."

No matter what the Merrimac did, it seemed to harm the Monitor not one whit. The balls from the Merrimac rolled from her like raindrops from a duck's back.

Next, the Merrimac tried her game of running at her with that great iron beak; but only found herself all the more at the mercy of those great guns turning round and round in the cheese-box.

For four long hours this battle went on. At last the Merrimac quietly sailed away, not half understanding yet what this little raft was, and how it had been able to drive her away.

Cheer after cheer went up from the vessels lying about in the harbor; and there was no cause for further dread of the Confederate monster so long as the harbor was guarded by "The Yankee Cheese-box."

THE LAST BROADSIDE

Shall we give them a broadside, my boys, as she goes?
    Shall we send yet another to tell,
In iron-tongued words, to Columbia's foes,
    How bravely her sons say Farewell?

Ay! what though we sink 'neath the turbulent wave,
    'Tis with DUTY and RIGHT at the helm;
And over the form should the fierce waters rave,
    No tide can the spirit o'erwhelm!

For swift o'er the billows of Charon's dark stream
    We'll pass to the immortal shore,
Where the waters of life in brilliancy beam,
    And the pure float in peace evermore.

"Shall we give them a broadside once more, my brave men
    "Ay! Ay!" was the full, earnest cry;
"A broadside! A broadside! we'll give them again!
    Then for God and the Right nobly die!"

"Haste! Haste!"—for amid all that battling din
    Comes a gurgling sound fraught with fear,
As swift flowing waters pour rushingly in;
    Up! up! till her port-holes they near.

No blanching!—no faltering!—still fearless all seem;
    Each man firm to duty doth bide;
A flash! and a "broadside!" a shout! a careen!
    And the Cumberland sinks 'neath the tide!

The "Star-Spangled Banner" still floating above!
    As a beacon upon the dark wave!
Our Ensign of Glory, proud streaming in love,
    O'er the tomb of the "Loyal and Brave!"

Bold hearts! mighty spirits! "tried gold" of our land!
    A halo of glory your meed!
All honored, the noble-souled Cumberland band!
    So true in Columbia's need!

—Elizabeth T. P. Beach.

BATTLE OF MILL SPRING---1862

In the battle of Mill Spring, the Confederates were put to flight by the Yankees.

One gentleman, whose slave had been sent with the Confederates into this battle, was questioning Sambo about what he had seen. Oftentimes these negroes were much brighter than their masters gave them credit for being.

"Well, Sambo, how long did it take you to march to the battle-field?"

"'Bout four days, massa," was the reply.

"That was pretty good marching, I'm sure. How long did it take you to march back?"

"'Bout two days, massa."

Only *two* days! why, that's strange. I shouldn't suppose soldiers after a long battle could march faster than before it."

"Dunno nuffin 'bout dat, massa; but I speck the music make de difference. You see, we marched there to the tune of Dixie; but we come back to tune of Fire! fire! fire! Run boys! Run!"

A BRAVE BOY AT FORT HENRY

Among the wounded in Fort Henry was a young Wisconsin boy, a prisoner, who had his arm shattered by a ball from one of the gun-boats. He was taken into one of the cabins and a Confederate surgeon began to operate upon the injured limb. He had just bared the bone when a large shell came crashing through the hut. The little fellow kept on talking while the bone was being sawed, without showing the least fear. Soon another shot went by them.

"This is getting too hot for me," said the doctor; and taking the boy up in his arms he carried him into one of the bomb-proofs, where he finished the work.

"If you think this hot," replied the boy, "it will be a good deal too hot for you by and by."

"Ah!" said the doctor afterwards, "I should like to see that boy again. He was the bravest little fellow I ever saw."

TAKING OF DONELSON

Let us take a run over into Kentucky and Tennessee, and see what is going on there.

Columbus, at the western end of the Confederate lines, and Bowling Green at the eastern end, together with two strong forts, Donelson and Henry, made for the Confederates a centre that seemed almost too strong to be taken. The Confederates delighted to speak of this as their "Gibraltar," that is their stronghold.

But Grant, you all know who Grant was—was not to be frightened even by this. "It looked risky," he used to say; "but if we *can* get hold of these forts and these cities and break up this Confederate stronghold, think what a gain it will be!"

When Grant had his plans all arranged, he gave them to his chief, and waited eagerly for permission to go on. After a long delay, permission came.

Fort Henry, being the weakest point, was to be attacked first.

"You, Commodore Foote, will take your men down the Tennessee River in gun-boats, and will pepper the fort from that point. When Fort Henry is settled, then comes Donelson."

GEN. U. S. GRANT

Foote did pepper Fort Henry well; and in just one hour and five minutes the fort surrendered.

Six days later, Grant turned toward Fort Donelson. Spreading his forces out in a sort of half circle, he thus approached the fort. Grant made up his mind that the way to get hold of this fort would be to lay siege to it, rather than to try to bring about a battle.

But the Confederate officers knew only too well that they could not hold out against a siege, and so thought it best to give battle at once. The very next morning they came out and fell upon the right wing of Grant's army. Grant him- self was down the river when the attack began; up he galloped to the scene of battle in a "double quick" run you may be sure.

"They have come out prepared to fight for several days, General," said one of the soldiers.

"Why do you think so?" asked Grant.

"Because they have their haversacks filled with rations," was the reply.

"Get me one of those haversacks," said Grant quickly.

One was brought. Grant examined it care-fully, and saw that it was rationed for three days.

"This means retreat, retreat, boys," cried Grant. "Soldiers don't fill their haversacks like this unless they are planning to run away. Now then, one more sharp attack, and we'll finish the fight!"

The men, cheered by Grant's hopefulness, fell upon the enemy hot and heavy. With one grand push, the whole line made the attack. The fight grew hotter and hotter. Over the snow-covered ground everywhere ran streams of blood. Everywhere lay the dead and wounded. Darkness came on at last, thank God, and this awful slaughter was at an end.

The enemy were driven within their own lines. "One more hour of fighting," said Grant, "and the fort will be ours." Inside the fort two of the generals were packing up to get away before daylight. When morning dawned, Gen-eral Buckner sent out to ask Grant on what terms he would be willing to accept their sur-render.

"Unconditional surrender," said Grant, "are my only terms." By that he meant that they should surrender *wholly*, give up themselves and *all they had,* or he would fight them again and *make* them surrender.

General Buckner had little to say. He knew only too well that there was nothing to be done but surrender.

Grant's army marched in and took the fort.

On the same day the commander at Bowling Green saw fit to get his forces out of the way; and a few days later the commander at Columbus did the same. They knew very well that with both forts lost, the cities, too, would have to go. Even in the capital of the State, the governor packed his valuable papers and ran as if from a fire.

The great Confederate stronghold had fallen into the hands of Union troops. Great was the rejoicing in the Northern States. "Unconditional surrender!" came to be the "byword" in every city and town; and Grant came to be called "Unconditional Surrender Grant."

This must be what his initials "U. S." mean, the people said in their joy. And to this day, no soldier hears of U. S. Grant without thinking of "Unconditional Surrender."

A PLUCKY BOY AT FORT DONELSON

A story is told of a little boy about eleven years old, whose father, a Union volunteer, had been taken prisoner some time before.

Having no mother, and no one to care for him, he made up his mind that he would go to fight his father's captors. So he smuggled himself on board of a boat laden with troops for the attack on Donelson. When the troops marched from Fort Henry, he joined the Seventy-eighth Ohio and trudged along with the rest. One of the officers questioned him and tried to turn him back, but he would not go.

On the field of battle he succeeded in getting a musket, and posting himself behind a tree fired at every head he saw above the enemy's breastwork. The Confederate sharpshooters tried hard to drive him away, but he kept himself well hidden all the time.

At last a Confederate soldier on the outside of the breast-work took good aim at him, but the little fellow was too quick and brought him down with a shot from his musket. Knowing that the dead Confederate had a fine Minie rifle, the boy ran out, while the bullets were flying in all directions, and took from the soldier his rifle, cartouch and knapsack. Retreating in safety to his tree, he returned to the Seventy-eighth at night with all his prizes.

THE BATTLE OF SHILOH

After the fall of Donelson, the Confederates had gone down the river to Corinth. Here Beauregard and other commanders came with troops until there were forty thousand of them.

Grant had been closely following, and had halted at a place about twenty miles from Corinth. There had been some rumor that the Confederates were about to attack the Union soldiers, but this did not seem probable; and, hourly expecting more troops, the Union army was quietly sleeping, all unconscious of the terrible day to come. But all this time, the Confederates, forty thousand strong, were hidden in the forests all about, only waiting for daylight to begin their bloody work.

At daybreak, the Union soldiers of one camp were aroused by yells from the enemy. In a moment all was hurry and flurry. The news spread from camp to camp. Grant, who had the day before gone to a town near by for food for his army, heard the firing, and galloped to the battle grounds. Knowing that troops were coming to his aid, and could not be far away, he sent messengers post haste to hurry them up. If only they could hold out till help came, Grant was sure they yet might win.

The aim of the Confederates was to drive the Unionists down to the river, where, as there were no boats, they must either surrender or drown. Beauregard, the plucky little black-eyed general with the white hair, you remember, kept driving up and down his lines, crying, "Drive the Yankees into the river! drive the Yankees into the river!"

All day long this terrible battle raged; but when darkness fell, Beauregard gave orders for his men to rest till morning. A fortunate thing was this for the Union soldiers, for had he kept up the fight, he might indeed have driven the Yankees into the river.

Beauregard instead, however, withdrew to his tent, and there spent the night writing a full account of the brilliant victory so sure to come in the early morning.

But alas for his pretty plan! even while he was writing, the looked-for troops had arrived in Grant's camp. And when the morning sun arose, it looked upon the Union soldiers, fifty thousand strong, drawn up in battle array, ready to renew the fight.

It was plain enough what the end must be. But Beauregard was no coward. He made a brave show of fighting, although he knew he was being driven back with every charge. At noon, he ordered his forces to retreat, and soon the Union flag was waving over the "Battle-field of Shiloh."

THE OLD SERGEANT

BATTLE OF SHILOH (PITTSBURG LANDING), TENN.

*"Come a little nearer, Doctor,—thank you,—let me take the
  cup;
Draw your chair up,—draw it closer,—just another little sup!
Maybe you may think I'm better; but I'm pretty well used up,—
Doctor, you've done all you could do, but I'm just agoing up!*

*"Feel my pulse, sir, if you want to, but it ain't much use to
  try"—
"Never say that," said the surgeon, as he smothered down a
  sigh;
"It will never do, old comrade, for a soldier to say die!"
"What you say will make no difference, Doctor, when you come
  to die.*

*"Doctor, what has been the matter?" "You were very faint, they
  say;
You must try to get to sleep now." "Doctor, have I been away?"
"Not that anybody knows of!" "Doctor,— Doctor, please to
  stay!
There is something I must tell you, and you won't have long to
  stay!*

"I have got my marching orders, and I'm ready now to go;
Doctor, did you say I fainted?—but it couldn't ha' been so.—
For as sure as I'm a Sergeant, and was wounded at Shiloh,
I've this very night been back there, on the old field of Shiloh!

"This is all that I remember: The last time the Lighter came,
And the lights had all been lowered, and the noises much the
    same,
He had not been gone five minutes before something called my
    name:
'Orderly Sergeant—Robert Burton!'—just that way it called
    my name.

"And I wondered who could call me so distinctly and so slow,
Knew it couldn't be the Lighter,—he could not have spoken
    so,—
And I tried to answer, 'here, sir!' but I couldn't make it go;
For I couldn't move a muscle, and I couldn't make it go;

"Then I thought: It's all a nightmare, all a humbug and a bore;
Just another foolish grape-vine,—and it won't come any more;
But it came, sir, notwithstanding, just the same way as before
'Orderly Sergeant—Robert Burton!'—even plainer than be-
    fore.

"That is all that I remember, till a sudden burst of light,
And I stood beside the river, where we stood that Sunday night,
Waiting to be ferried over to the dark bluffs opposite,
When the river was perdition and all hell was opposite!

"And the same old palpitation came again in all its power,
And I heard a bugle sounding as from some celestial tower;
And the same mysterious voice said: 'It is the eleventh hour!
Orderly Sergeant—Robert Burton—it is the eleventh hour!'

731

*"Doctor Austin! what day is this?" "It is Wednesday night, you
    know."*
*"Yes,—to-morrow will be New Year's, and a right good time
    below!*
*"What time is it, Doctor Austin?" "Nearly twelve." "Then don't
    you go!*
Can it be that all this happened—all this—not an hour ago!

*"There was where the gunboats opened on the dark, rebellious
    host;*
And where Webster semicircled his last guns upon the coast;
*There were still the two log-houses, just the same, or else their
    ghost,—*
*And the same old transport came and took me over,—or its
    ghost!*

"And the old field lay before me all deserted far and wide;
*There was where they fell on Prentiss,—there McClernand met
    the tide;*
*There was where stern Sherman rallied, and where Hurlbut's
    heroes died,—*
*Lower down, where Wallace charged them, and kept charging
    till he died.*

*"There was where Lew Wallace showed them he was of the
    canny kin,*
*There was where old Nelson thundered, and where Rosseau
    waded in;*
*There McCook sent 'em to breakfast, and we all began to
    win,—*
*There was where the grape-shot took me, just as we began to
    win.*

*"Now, a shroud of snow and silence over everything was
    spread;*
And but for this old blue mantle, and the old hat on my head,
I should not have even doubted, to this moment I was dead,—
For my footsteps were as silent as the snow upon the dead?

"Death and silence!—Death and silence all round me as I sped!
And behold, a mighty tower, as if builded to the dead.
To the heaven of the heavens lifted up its mighty head,
Till the Stars and Stripes of heaven all seemed waving from its
head!

"Round and mighty-based it towered,— up into the infinite,—
And I knew no mortal mason could have built a shaft so bright,
For it shone like solid sunshine; and a winding-stair of light
Wound around it and around it till it wound clear out of sight!

"And, behold, as I approached it, with a wrapt and dazzled
stare,
Thinking that I saw old comrades just ascending the great
stair,
Suddenly the solemn challenge broke of—'Halt, and who goes
there!'
'I'm a friend,' I said 'if you are.' 'Then advance, sir, to the stair!'

"I advanced! That sentry, Doctor, was Elijah Ballantyne!—
First of all to fall on Monday, after we had formed the line?—
'Welcome, my old Sergeant, welcome! Welcome by that coun-
tersign!'
And he pointed to the scar there, under this old cloak of mine!

"As he grasped my hand, I shuddered, thinking only of the
grave;
But he smiled and pointed upward with a bright and bloodless
glaive;
'That's the way, sir, to head-quarters.' 'What head-quarters?'
'Of the brave.'
'But the great tower?' 'That,' he answered, 'is the way, sir, of
the brave!'

"Then a sudden shame came o'er me, at his uniform of light;
At my own so old and tattered, and at his so new and bright:
'Ah!' said he, 'you have forgotten the new uniform to-night,—
Hurry back, for you must be here just at twelve o'clock to-
night!'

733

"And the next thing I remember, you were sitting there, and
     I—
Doctor, did you hear a footstep? Hark!—God bless you all!
     Good-by!
Doctor, please to give my musket and my knapsack, when I die,
To my son—my son that's coming,—he won't get here till I die!

"Tell him his old father blessed him as he never did before,—
And to carry that old musket"—Hark! a knock is at the door!—
"Till the Union"—See it opens! "Father! Father! speak once
     more?"
"Bless you!" gasped the old, gray Sergeant, and he lay and said
     no more!

—FORCEYTHE WILSON.

BROTHER AGAINST BROTHER

It often happened in the "civil war," that one in a family would fight on the Union side, and another on the Confederate side—each one fighting on the side which to him seemed right.

In Kentucky, where the people were so divided in their opinions of the war, that one hardly could tell whether to call Kentucky a Union State or a Confederate State, it often happened that own brothers would meet fighting face to face in battle.

At the battle of Shiloh, during the hottest of the strife, it happened that two of these Kentucky regiments met and fought each other with the fury and hatred which usually marks civil warfare. One of the Union soldiers happened to wound and take prisoner his own brother; and after handing him to the rear, began firing at a man near a tree. "Hold, Bill," shouted his captured brother, "don't shoot there any more! That's father!"

QUAKER GUNS

But it is about time to hear something from that "Army of the Potomac." You remember I told you a few pages back that this was a large, fresh army, sent from the North. The people expected great things of this army, and were very impatient to see them go to work.

For a long time the enemy had been holding that railroad junction that you heard of not long ago, so that there was no way of getting to Richmond, the capital of the Confederacy. I should not have said there was *no* way of getting to this city—of course there were ways; but here was this railroad running straight to the city, carrying the Confederates food and clothing every day, and so helping to keep them able to fight on and on against their country. "If only this capital could be taken, the war might be as good as ended," every one said. In that city were stored food and blankets, guns and powder—everything that their army could need. "Why *doesn't* McClellan march the Army of the Potomac to take it!" everybody cried.

At last McClellan *did* move. He started his army on to this junction, this stronghold of the Southerners. The troops marched on, expecting, I presume, a terrible fight; but imagine their surprise when on reaching there they found it empty. Every Confederate had fled. More than that, on examining their camp they found that the guns, those terrible guns, which had been so long frightening back the Union Army, were just nothing in the world but big logs, their ends cut out to look like cannon-mouths, and painted black! One of them, even, was only an old stove-pipe! I wonder which this army felt the most—ashamed, or amused, or angry—that all these weeks they had been trembling before these Quaker guns!

Later, McClellan marched his forces upon Yorktown. Here they kept up a siege for more than a month. But one morning it was found that the enemy had run away in the night in the same way they had run away before. This time, too, they left nothing to pay the Union Army for their long work, except some old guns. This Confederate, General Johnston, had a way of retreating in this clever way; and came to be named in time, the "successful re-treater."

DARK DAYS

A long, long time of defeats for the Union army followed. The Confederates were getting themselves together at Richmond, their capital. They knew that was their stronghold and supposed of course the Union army knew it, too, and would before many days bear down upon them.

Down to the banks of the Chickahominy went our "Army of the Potomac." This river was a sluggish, muddy stream, with swamps on every side. The army was set to work digging trenches, and throwing up banks of earth to defend them from the Confederate force in Richmond. This was a sad, sad time. In this damp, unhealthy spot, our soldiers worked on day and night. Unused to the climate, the men began to die as if seized with a plague. Hundreds and hundreds of them sank beneath the poison of the place, and every day our "Army of the Potomac" grew smaller and smaller.

Again McClellan stood still. Johnston, the "successful retreater," not wishing to retreat this time, came out from the city and attacked McClellan himself at *Fair Oaks*. Fortune favored our side in the battle, and Johnston was *made* to retreat this time into the city.

Johnston was wounded in this battle; and so, unfitted for service, he was obliged to give up his command. Robert Lee became the Confederate commander in his place. McClellan still hesitated to push forward and his men were dying off in hundreds.

Stonewall Jackson now arrived at Richmond and joined his forces with those of Lee's.

McClellan still waited, until the enemy again came out and, by attacking him, forced him to act. Now began a series of battles called the "Seven Days' Battles." Every day for a week the two armies engaged in battle, and every day McClellan ordered "retreat, retreat." On the seventh day the Union forces, from a high ridge of land, poured down their fire with such vigor and such success that the enemy, powerful as they were, were driven back broken and confused, having lost greatly in dead and wounded. Even now it is a mystery, explained one way by some, another way by others that McClellan, brave and well-trained as he was should have held his forces back as he did week after week, apparently doing nothing.

Certainly he had some reason for his action (or lack of action) whatever it was. Perhaps some soldier who was in the war can tell you all about it. You and I could hardly form a just opinion regarding it. So, for now, let us go on and read about a battle between McClellan and the brave southern general—Lee.

Gen. R. E. Lee

THE SONG OF THE CAMPS

Far away in the piny woods,
*   Where the dews fall heavy and damp,*
A soldier sat by the smouldering fire
*   And sang the song of the camp.*

"It is not to be weary and worn,
*   It is not to feel hunger and thirst,*
It is not the forced march, nor the terrible fight,
*   That seems to the soldier the worst;*

"But to sit through the comfortless hours,—
*   The lonely, dull hours that will come—*
With his head in his hands, and his eyes on the fire,
*   And his thoughts on visions of home;*

"To wonder how fares it with those
*   Who mingled so late with his life,—*
Is it well with my little children three?
*   Is it well with my sickly wife?*

-J. R. M.

LEE IS KEPT FROM ENTERING PENNSYLVANIA.

HAVING so little success in trying to raise troops in Maryland, Lee next decided to go over into the State of Pennsylvania. There he proposed to have Stonewall Jackson join his army, and together they would go on to the very city of New York.

Now it happened, as Lee's army left Frederick on their march through Pennsylvania, some one of his generals accidentally dropped a paper in the streets, upon which was written the one thing of all others which Lee would not for the world have had the Unionists find out. And that was just what General Lee had planned to do; just the route he intended to take; just how he was going to divide his army; and just where he intended to bring them together for battle.

McClellan at once set out in hot haste to overtake this army. On the 16th of September, both armies lay down to sleep in the beautiful, fertile valley of Antietam, knowing that with the rising of the sun must come one of the hottest contested battles of the war.

THE BATTLE OF ANTIETAM

It was a long bloody battle. Both sides lost, in killed and wounded, large numbers; but neither side could be said to have won the day. It was one of those terrible battles, in which both sides merely held their places, seeming, with all the bloodshed, to gain nothing. The next morning was to have seen the battle renewed; but McClellan, seized again with his over-cautiousness, waited and waited. The next day, Lee escaped over the Potomac. His plans were all broken up by this battle with its terrible losses, and it seemed at the time as if McClellan might, if he had made one bold stroke, have done a great deal more even than that.

GEN. BURNSIDE

But McClellan now again waited and waited, although he had been ordered by Lincoln to march against the enemy. At last, Lincoln ordered that the command be taken from him, and given to General Burnside.

Lee was now encamped at Fredricksburg. Burnside at once marched against him, and attempted to take the city from him. A hot battle followed, but at night Lee was still in the city, and the Union army had again lost hundreds of men.

And now the army was led back to the old camps. There the soldiers built mud huts; and, sick and wounded, their courage all gone, they settled down for the winter.

This campaign in Virginia had been a wretched failure for the Union army.

BARBARA FRIETCHIE

CONCERT READING

Up from the meadows rich with corn,
Clear in the cool September morn,

The cluster'd spires of Frederick stand,
Green-wall'd by the hills of Maryland.

Round about them orchards sweep,
Apple and peach-tree fruited deep,

Fair as a garden of the Lord,
To the eves of the famish'd rebel horde,

On that pleasant morn of the early Fall,
When Lee march'd over the mountain wall,

Over the mountains winding down,
Horse and foot, into Frederick town.

Forty flags with their silver stars,
Forty flags with their crimson bars,

Flapp'd in the morning wind: the sun
Of noon look'd down, and saw not one.

Up rose old Barbara Frietchie then,
Bow'd with her fourscore years and ten;

Bravest of all in Frederick town,
She took up the flag the men haul'd down,

In her attic window the staff she set,
To show that one heart was loyal yet.

Up the street came the rebel tread,
Stonewall Jackson riding ahead.

Under his slouch'd hat, left and right,
He glanced; the old flag met his sight:

"Halt!"—the dust-brown ranks stood fast.
"Fire!"—out blazed the rifle-blast.

It shivered the window, pane and sash;
It rent the banner with seam and gash.

Quick as it fell from the broken staff
Dame Barbara snatched the silken scarf.

She leaned far out on the window-sill,
And shook it forth with a royal will.

"Shoot, if you must, this old gray head,
But spare your country's flag," she said.

A shade of sadness, a blush of shame
Over the face of the leader came;

"Who touches a hair of yon gray head,
Dies like a dog! March on!" he said.

BARBARA FRIETCHIE

All day long through Frederick street
Sounded the tread of marching feet;

All day long that free flag tossed
Over the heads of the rebel host.

Barbara Frietchie's work is o'er,
And the rebel rides on his raids no more.

Barbara Frietchie

THE VIRGINIA ARMY

Now Gen. Pope was ordered to take command of an army of about 50,000, called the "Virginia Army." Very soon it was plain to see that Lee was planning to attack Washington. It was bad enough that our army had not succeeded in taking the Confederate capital; but to have them take Washington!—"No, indeed," said Gen. Pope. "No, indeed," echoed the soldiers.

The two armies met at Cedar Mountain. Here followed one of the most ghastly, most bloody battles of the whole war. Both sides lost great numbers of men, and neither side can be said to have gained much over the other.

Soon more battles were fought, among them another at Bull Run. Bull Run seemed an unlucky place for the Unionists. A second time they were defeated there, but this time there was no shameful running away. At last, Pope's army, called the "Army of Virginia," was ordered to Washington. They were as broken-spirited as McClellan's army had been.

It seemed as if the Fates were against the Union forces. Gen. Pope had been a hero in the West, fighting fiercely, full of hope and daring, a terror to the enemy. Now all seemed changed. Every attack had been a failure.

Now the two armies, the "Army of the Potomac" and the "Army of Virginia" were united—what there was left of them—and Gen. McClellan was again put in command.

Gen. McClellan had been a great favorite among his men, and when he was again put in command, it is said his men received him with shouts of joy; cheers for "Little Mac," as they called him, filled the air.

Gen. Lee meantime was on his way northward. First, he meant to stir up Maryland, and find men there to join his army. Maryland, you remember, had not seceded. Still, Lee knew there were many there who in heart were "secessionists."

So into that State he marched to the old southern tune, "Maryland, My Maryland." It

was a beautiful old song, and was often
played in the Confederate lines, as "Rally
Round the Flag, Boys" was played in our lines.

Some way the Maryland people could not
be aroused, not even by Lee. They refused to
have anything whatever to do with the war. I
think Lee's army at this time would hardly
have inspired any one with a very great desire to join it. Successful though they had
been, they were a wretched looking company.
Ragged, hungry, hatless and coatless, often
shoeless. "Stonewall Jackson" himself, it is
said, was so shabby and worn, that he looked
quite as bad as his troops.

Such brave men as these were, never
shrinking from any hardship, ready to do and
to die, doesn't it seem a pity they were
fighting in such a wretched cause—fighting to
save a government, which as they had said,
should have the buying and selling of slaves
as the corner-stone?

CAPTURE OF NEW ORLEANS

New Orleans, situated at the mouth of the Mississippi, was held by the Confederates. Because it is at the mouth of this great river, you can easily see it was necessary that the Unionists should have it, in order that they might be free to go up and down this great river whenever they chose.

Said Gen. Butler in his usual direct way, "New Orleans should be in our hands, New Orleans can be taken, and I can take it." There were many reasons why it seemed a doubtful place to attack, but Butler usually succeeded in whatever he set out to do; and, as his men often said, could make his hearers believe "the moon was made of green cheese" if he chose.

Soon Butler was on his way to New Orleans. He was very careful to keep his purpose hidden.

On reaching "Ship Island," a low sandy island off the coast of Mississippi, he found it covered all over with little white tents. This was the camp of Gen. Phelps, who, with 6,000 soldiers, was eagerly awaiting Butler's coming. Here Butler was joined by Admiral Farragut, one of the most remarkable naval officers America ever had. Together these two men planned to take New Orleans. Now, this city is a Mississippi sea-port; but it is situated around the corner, up the river a few miles, and was fortified strongly at every point. One could not even enter the river without passing two forts, and then there were many more dangerous points farther on. The only way to get *to* the city even, was either to bombard these forts and make them surrender, or else pass quietly by, letting the forts turn their great guns upon the vessels as they passed along. Neither the one, nor the other was a simple thing to do.

But danger or no danger, both Butler and Farragut were determined to reach that city.

Farragut had forty-eight vessels in all, and they carried three hundred and ten great guns.

Some of the vessels were covered over with a heavy network of iron chains to protect them from the balls from the forts. Their hulks were painted a dark, dull color, so that they could hardly be seen as they lay in the dull, muddy colored river. Then great trees were laced on the vessels' sides; so covering them up, and making them look so much like bits of the forests on the river banks, that, as they stole up the river in the dark night, the soldiers in the forts should not notice them until they were right upon them.

At last all was ready; and at three o'clock in the morning, this strange-looking fleet entered the Mississippi.

The first trouble that met them was a fire boat. This was a great raft, piled up with wood which had been soaked with oil. This was to be pushed up close to some Union vessel, to set it on fire. Of course such a fire as that oiled wood would make, would very soon catch the vessel before anything could be done to save her. And if this pile of pitch and oil were to get in among the tree-covered vessels, there would be a terrible scene!

"A boat! a boat!" cried the soldiers. "Volunteers to tow away this fire raft." "I" and "I!"

and "I!" answered brave men from Farragut's fleet. A boat was lowered and rowed swiftly up to this blazing pile. Grappling irons were thrown and caught fast among the timbers, and away she was towed out of reach of the Union vessels. All by herself, on the water's edge she burned and snapped and crackled, doing no harm, only making of herself a most beautiful bonfire.

Fort Jackson was attacked first. Now followed a fierce siege. For three days the gun boats and the fort kept up the fire. Cannonball and bombshell! Smoke and flash! Roar upon roar, till it seemed as if the very earth did quake! Fish, killed by the shock, floated dead upon the river. Windows thirty miles away were broken in pieces, shaken by the jarring thunder.

A little farther up the river it was found that iron cables had been drawn across, linking together a chain of hulks, and so making passage beyond them almost impossible But nothing seemed impossible to Farragut's men.

These cables *must* be broken. That seemed the only thought. And so again under cover of darkness, two gun-boats were sent to break the cable. With hammer and chisel they worked away, and lo! the cable parted, and down the stream the bulks floated, leaving the passage free.

Up the river steamed the brave fleet, past the forts which threw out a rain of fire and shot upon them, straight through a fleet of confederate gun-boats, sent from New Orleans to prevent their approach to the city. And at last the Union fleet steamed up to the very wharves of the city, demanding its surrender. The people stood aghast! They had believed it impossible to reach their city. All the time the bombarding of the forts had been going on, these people had laughed and joked about it, never once thinking that Farragut could pass the forts, the fire-boats, the cables! But here he was at daybreak, at their very doors!

The people were panic stricken. What should they do? Where should they go? "Burn the city! Burn the city!" cried the men. "Yes, burn the city, and we will help you! The Yankees shall not have our homes!" cried the women.

But now news came that Butler, too, had passed the forts safely and was rapidly approaching by land. This was the last blow;

and the people settled down to their fate with sullen faces, and with hearts full of hatred and revenge.

In marched Butler with flags flying, his bands filling the air with strains of Union music. Can you blame these New Orleans men and women that they hated these Union soldiers?

How the people glared at them! how they muttered and growled! The women, it is said, were more bitter than the men. They were like lionesses aroused to battle. They would not pass a Union soldier on the street. They would go out into the middle of the street rather than to meet one of the officers. The Union officers were insulted on every hand.

Gen. Butler realized how bitter a trial the taking of their city was to them, as we all do. But he could not and would not allow the Union officers, much more the Union flag, to be insulted. He at once took military command of the city, hoisted the "Stars and Stripes" and forced the people to pay, at least, outward respect to his soldiers.

Did you ever read "Uncle Tom's Cabin?" I don't suppose you have—it is too old for you yet—but perhaps you have seen it played.

You remember little Eva, the little girl, who was so good to the slaves. You remember Old Uncle Tom, whose good old heart was nearly broken when he thought he must go away from his "little missus," as he always called the little Eva. And do you remember Eliza, the slave woman with the little baby, who was hunted through the forests and across the rivers, the wicked old slave-owner and his cruel pack of hounds at her heels?

Before the war broke out, Gen. Butler read this story of "Uncle Tom's Cabin;" but didn't approve of it at all. He didn't believe any such cruelty was to be found in the South. But when he left New Orleans, where he lived for nearly a year, he said, "Mrs. Stowe has told the truth in her book. I have seen with my own eyes and have heard with my own ears treatment of slaves here in the South a thousand times worse than anything that Mrs. Stowe has put into 'Uncle Tom's Cabin even.'"

SECESSION WOMEN

Of course, all the women in the United States were not Unionists. You have already heard how the Southern women treated the Union officers whenever they met them on the streets. Do you remember how angry the New Orleans women were when Butler came? But these Southern women, who believed that their side was right, and that the Unionists were but thieves and robbers, were not content with being merely angry. They worked for their soldiers just as the Northern women worked for theirs.

There are some funny stories told of ways in which these bright-witted women used to plan to carry help to the Confederate soldiers.

It was the fashion then for ladies to wear very large hoops; and these ladies soon found it very convenient to fasten packages and letters to the wires of these hoops, and so carry them to the soldiers.

One lady was found to have on a quilted skirt which weighed fifty pounds. What do you suppose she had hidden in this wonderful skirt? You may be sure it was something for the soldiers. It was filled in all among the quiltings with sewing silk for the doctors in the army to use for sewing up wounds, and a medicine, called quinine, which is believed to be very good for fever and chills.

All trunks and boxes and packages that went out from Washington on the train were carefully searched; and sometimes, I fancy, very strange things were found in them.

One story is told of a little red, wooden trunk, marked Mary Berkitt, Wheeling, Virginia. It was a very innocent looking little trunk, looking as if it might belong to some old lady perhaps. But the officers had learned from experience that the most innocent looking people and the most innocent trunks sometimes held the greatest secrets. So Old Lady Mary's trunk was looked into. On the top, lay some clothing, very neatly packed, and under these some dresses.

"Never mind that trunk," said an officer; "there's nothing under there but the old lady's caps."

"Can't be too sure," answered the officer in charge, still pulling out the clothing. Down at the very bottom of the trunk, the caps were found indeed. Hundreds and hundreds of them—more than the old lads could ever wear in a whole lifetime, you will think. Yes, indeed; but you see, boys, they happened to be percussion-caps; and the officer, thinking them more useful for him than for her, emptied them all out, and I fear Mary never saw her trunk again.

THE MOCK FUNERAL

All sorts of ways were invented to carry help across from Maryland to the Confederate states; and you may be sure the officers had to keep their eyes wide open day and night.

One day, on a train, as innocent a looking thing as a lunch basket with a sandwich and a doughnut plainly in sight, was found to be filled with bright brass buttons, on their way to ornament the Confederate soldiers' coats.

But one of the strangest plots for carrying help was by means of funeral processions. One day a very sober looking procession started out from Baltimore over the Long Bridge, into Virginia.

Everything appeared all right. There was the hearse with the coffin within; then came the carriages, their curtains closely drawn to hide the mourners from the people on the streets; the drivers all looked solemn as owls, and to all appearances, it was a very respectable looking funeral procession.

The first sentry at the Bridge, feeling that a funeral procession, of all things, should be allowed to go on its sad way without being interfered with, let it pass—although, as he said afterwards, it *did* flash across his mind that even this might be but another Confederate scheme.

The next sentry on the route, was not so easily fooled. Perhaps he had learned that even funeral processions in those times were suspicious. Stepping forward as the hearse approached, he called "Halt!"

Instantly he caught a look upon the driver's face that told him that something was wrong.

"Open the hearse!" demanded the sentry. The hearse was opened and the coffin dragged out. But by this time, the mourners in the carriages had learned that their plot was discovered; and when the sentry turned to look at them, they were scrambling out of their carriages, and running back to the city just as fast as ever they could go.

On opening the coffin, it was found packed full of muskets, which at that time would have been very acceptable to the Confederate army.

One of the ways the Confederates in Maryland had of getting messages across the river, was by means of kites and balloons. When kites were used, they were made of oiled silk, that the rain might not spoil them, nor the water, should they chance to fall into the river. The bobs of the kites were made of letters and newspapers, fastened on just as you boys fasten the bobs to your kites to-day.

When the wind was in the right direction, these kites were sent up, their strings cut, and across the river they would fly, falling somewhere on the Virginia shore. Some one was always on the watch for these kites; and when the wind turned, back would come the kite laden with letters and papers from the South.

AFFAIRS IN THE WEST

While all these defeats and losses were going on, out in the far West our soldiers were winning laurels for themselves.

Gen. Bragg, a Confederate officer, had cut round behind a part of our army, and had got his forces well into Kentucky. For six weeks this army marched about from place to place, destroying everything and pretty nearly everybody that came in its way.

At last he began collecting his forces with a view to swooping down upon St. Louis. The people of this city were frightened indeed. A panic would surely have followed but for Gen. Lew Wallace. He at once took charge of everything; called for troops, built defences, and, indeed, so quickly did he work, that by the time one of Bragg's divisions reached there, everything was ready for them. The advancing general saw they were ready—indeed, too ready, he thought; so when darkness fell, he turned his troops and marched back to join Gen. Bragg.

I want you to remember this Gen. Lew Wallace; for you are sure to hear of him by and by as you grow older, not so much as a soldier, but as an author. Haven't you seen your mamma or papa reading a book called "Ben Hur?" Or haven't you heard them speak of it? It is a wonderful book, and I fancy Gen. Lew Wallace and his beautiful story will be remembered long after the bugles of this war are half forgotten. Some day when you are older you will read "Ben Hur," and then you will remember that the writer of that book was a general in this Civil War, about which you read when you were little boys and girls.

Bragg had all this time been loading himself with riches in Kentucky. He had fitted out his army with shoes and clothing, had filled his wagons with food, and had seized the splendid Kentucky horses for his cavalry; more than this, he had sent car-load after car-load of these things to the South.

Gen. Buell went against Bragg, but, as usual, fortune seemed to smile on the Confederate side. Gen. Rosecrans then went against a division of Bragg's army. A terrible battle, lasting all one day, took place at Corinth. During the night the Union troops, with their contraband helpers, threw up new defences and strengthened the old one. Early the next morning, with a terrible yell, called in this war the "rebel yell," the Confederates charged upon the Union ranks.

At first the Unionists fell back; but gathering themselves up, they closed round the enemy. Now the field was a scene of terrible slaughter. The Confederates fled, the Unionists at their heels, pouring in their shot upon them as they ran. At last the Unionists had won a victory.

Now Rosecrans was sent to take charge of the "Army of the Cumberland," as this western army was called.

Bragg had settled down at a place called Murfreesboro', and Jefferson Davis had come on to visit him. A grand, good time Bragg and the men were having; giving parties, attending balls, and giving themselves up generally to a good time.

But all this time the wise Rosecrans was laying in a store of provisions, and getting himself ready for a long fight if necessary.

An attack came. A terrible attack it was, too. A hot battle; and much bravery was shown on both sides.

Up and down rode Rosecrans, crying, "We must win this battle, boys!" no matter what he saw or what he heard. For two long days this battle raged, and at last the Confederates gave way, and in a few hours Bragg marched away, bag and baggage, leaving the field to the Union soldiers.

SHARP-SHOOTERS

Do you remember the sharp-shooters who came into Washington's camp during the Revolution? Do you remember how they used to amuse themselves while they were en-camped outside of Boston, by shooting at targets just for the practice?

Well, there were sharp-shooters in the Civil War, too, both among the Unionists and among the Confederates. Their business was to be always on the watch when the armies were encamped near each other; and, if one of the enemy showed himself anywhere in sight, to shoot at him.

John D. Champlain, who has lately written a history of this war for young folks, tells this story of sharp-shooting:

"One of the most skilful of the Confederate marksmen was a large negro, who used to perch himself in a tree and lie there all day, firing whenever he saw a chance for a good shot. He had in this way killed several Union soldiers, and the sharp-shooters had watched a long time for him. At last the Union trenches, which were gradually being dug nearer and nearer, reached a place only about twenty rods from the tree. One morning the darky came out early and took his accustomed place in the tree. The sharp-shooters might have easily killed him as he came out, but they did not want to frighten others who were coming. He was followed soon by several Confederate pickets, on whom the men fired, killing some and driving the others back. The darky, of course, was now "in a fix", or, in other words, was "up a tree," for he could not get back without running the risk of being shot.

"I say, big nigger," called out one of the Union marksmen from the trenches, "you'd better come down from there."

"What for?" he asked.

"I want you as a prisoner."

"Not as this chile knows of," he answered.

"All right. Just as you say," called out the marksman.

In about an hour Mr. Darkey, hearing nothing from in front of his tree, concluded that it was safe to take just one peep; so he poked his head out far enough to get a look at the Union lines. But the sharp-shooter had not taken his eye from the tree for an instant, and no sooner did the head appear than he pulled the trigger of his rifle. A little puff of blue smoke—a flash—the whiz of a bullet—and down came the negro to the ground shot through the head.

STEALING POTATOES

The soldiers often got tired enough of these hard, dry biscuits and the salt meat, and would go out, in the night time, on stealing expeditions. The farmers used to complain bitterly of the soldiers; for they not only would steal everything they could find, but they would trample down the growing vegetables wherever they went.

One day, a good natured old farmer, whose potato fields had been nearly ruined by these half-starved soldiers, came into the camp hoping to find some trace of the thieves. While strolling around among the tents, he saw one of the boys serving up a dish of fine potatoes, which he thought looked very much like his own.

"Have fine potatoes here, I see," he said, halting before the tent.

"Splendid."

"Where do you get them?"

"Draw them."

"Does the government furnish potatoes for rations?"

"Nary tater."

"But I thought you said you drew them."

"Did. We just do that thing."

"But how—if they are not included in your rations?"

"Easiest thing in the world. Won't you take some with us?"

"Thank you. But you will oblige me if you will tell me how you draw your potatoes."

"Nothing easier. Draw 'em by the tops, mostly; sometimes with a hoe, if there's one left in the field."

"Ha! yes! I understand. Well, now, see here. If you won't draw any more of my potatoes, I'll bring you a basketful every morning and draw 'em myself."

"Now will you? Good for you, old fellow!"

And three cheers and a tiger were given for the farmer, who had the pleasure in future of drawing his own potatoes.

JOE PARSONS

At one of the hospitals, was a boy of twenty, who had been shot in the eyes. He used to enjoy sitting by the window, his eyes bandaged, and singing: "O, I'm a sojer boy!"

"What's your name, my boy?" asked a visitor.

"Joe Parsons, sir?"

"What is the matter with you?"

"Blind, sir, blind as a bat; shot at Antietam.

"But it might ha' been worse," he said. "I'm thankful I'm alive, sir."

"You see, I was hit, yer see, and it knocked me down. I lay there all night, and in the morning the fight began again. I could stand the pain, but the balls were flyin' all round, and I wanted to get away. At last I heard a groan beyond me."

"Hallo," said I. "Hallo, yourself," said he.

"Who are you?" said I. "A Gray Jacket?"

"Yes," said he; "and you're a Blue Jacket."

"My leg is broken," said he.

"Can you see?" said I.

"Yes."

"Well, I can't; but, I can walk. Now if you'll do the seeing, I'll do the walking and get us both away from here."

"All right; agreed."

"So that's the way we saved ourselves. And now I'm getting along pretty well."

"But my poor boy," said the visitor, "you will never see again."

"Yes I know that, but—'I'm a bold, bold so-jer boy.'"

"A bold, bold sojer boy"—and the visitor passed on, leaving Joe singing as merry as a lark.

THE HOME SIDE OF THE WAR PICTURE

It would not be fair at all to the women and children of these times, neither do I think it would be a true story of the war if I were to tell you of nothing but the battles. Battles are terrible enough; or if you think so, grand enough, and brave enough. But you must not think that the whole of war is carried on in the battle-field.

Suppose, little boy and little girl, there were a war going on in our country to-day. Suppose *your* father were to go as a soldier to this war. He might look very fine as he marched away in his blue coat, with its gilt braid and its brass buttons. You might be very proud of him, as no doubt you would be; but do you think that would be all, just your seeing him look handsome and brave, and your feeling proud of him?

I am afraid after he had gone and the house was so quiet, and mamma looked so pale and white, and every day when the newspaper came you hardly dared read it for fear you would learn that your papa had been shot dead, or that he had been put into the black prisons—I am afraid you would come to think that there was something more to war than plumes and brass buttons.

And suppose, by and by, you should hear that your papa was starving, that his shoes and stockings were all worn out, and that his feet were lame and sore from marching the hot, rough roads, and that he was sick and dying!

Suppose as the long weeks went on, mamma should have to go out to find some work to earn money to feed you and your little brothers and sisters—would war seem then a beautiful thing, do you think?

But this is what always does come into the homes when the papas and the big brothers go to the battle field. Mamma's heart grows very heavy, I fear; and the little children, too, begin to learn that war is a sad, sad thing.

But in this civil war of ours, I must tell you how brave these mothers and children were.

How generous they were and how willing to work.

The rich sent money and food for the soldiers most freely; but the clothes, the stockings,—these things came usually from the poor who had no money to give. Everywhere societies were formed, called "Soldiers' Relief Societies." The rich would bring to these societies money and cloth and yarn, and the poor people who had nothing to give, would take the cloth and the yarn home to make up into clothes and stockings for the soldiers. In among these wretched battles, I must tell you a story now and then about these good women and children.

LILLIE'S FIVE-DOLLAR GOLD PIECE

A lady at the head of one of these relief societies tells this story:

A little girl not nine years old, with sweet
and timid grace, came into the rooms, and
laying a five-dollar gold piece on our desk,
half frightened, told us its history. "My uncle
gave me that before the war, and I was going
to keep it always; but he's got killed in the
army, and mother says now I may give it to
the soldiers if I want to—and I'd like to do so.
I don't suppose it will buy much for them, will
it?" We led the child to the store-room, and
showed her how valuable her gift was, by
pointing out what it would buy—so many
cans of milk, or so many bottles of ale, or
pounds of tea, or codfish, etc. Her face bright-
ened with pleasure. But when we explained
to her that her five-dollar gold piece was

equal to seven dollars and a half in green-backs, and told her how much comfort we could carry into a hospital, with the stores that sum would buy, she fairly danced with joy.

"Oh, it will do lots of good, won't it?" And folding her hands before her, she begged, in her charmingly modest way, "Please tell me something that you've seen in the hospitals?"

We told her a few little stories—taking care to tell this little child nothing of the horrors of hospital life and death.

Then with tears in her eyes, she said, "Lady, I am going to save every single penny I have for the soldiers; and I'm going to ask all the little girls I know to save theirs, too." Dear Little Lillie! Who can tell what a world of good her five-dollar gold piece with all her love behind it, did for some poor soldier.

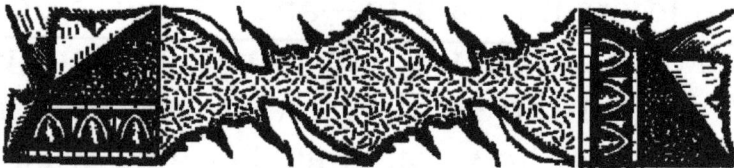

WHAT SOME POOR PEOPLE DID FOR THE SOLDIERS

Up among the mountains, in a farming district, lived a mother and her daughters. They were very poor—too poor by far to buy anything to send the soldiers.

Twelve miles away, over the mountain, was a town in which was one of these "Soldiers' Relief Societies."

"Let us go over the mountain, daughters," said the old mother, "and bring home some work to do for the soldiers. We have no money to give, but, we can find a little time, I am sure, to work for them."

"Yes, indeed," said the daughters; "we can get up earlier and milk the cows, and feed the chickens and the pigs; we can hurry a little with our planting and all the rest of the farm-work, and so make time to sew and knit for the soldiers."

Now, when you think that these three women had all the work to do both in the house and on the farm, and that their farm was all the means of gaining food that they had, you can see that they had quite as much to do as they had time or strength for without taking work home. Nevertheless every two weeks one of these three women used to ride into the village for work. Poorly clad, looking always as if very little of the good things of life had ever come to them, dusty and tired from their long ride, back and forth they came with their little offerings of work.

"I presume you have some dear one in the army," said one of the officers to these women one day.

"No," said they; "none now; our only brother was killed at the Battle of Ball's Bluff. But for his sake, and for our country's sake, we do all we can for the soldiers."

In another little village, lived a widow and her one little girl. Papa had left them to join the army. Mamma worked and the little girl worked for food and clothes till papa should come back to them. But one day the news came that he could never come to them again—he had fallen in the battle of Fair

Oaks. They worked on still; and although they earned so little, they saved enough money, and found enough time, to make a quilt for the hospital, a pair of socks and a shirt. All winter long, these two, mother and child, worked through the long evenings to make these. "Papa died in the hospital," the little girl used to say; "and perhaps he needed these things. Perhaps some other little girl made the quilt that kept him warm, so we will make this one to keep some other good soldier warm."

Many a little girl went without candy in these days, many a little boy went without toys, that they might save their money for the soldiers.

One, little girl, only five years old, knit a pair of stockings to send to the soldiers. Such a little girl! I suspect her mamma had now and then to take a stitch for her on them. But nevertheless the little girl's love was in them from top to toe. On them she pinned a little note, saying, "These socks was nit by a little gurl fiv yers old and she is going to nit lots more for the dere soljers."

I hope the soldier who got these stockings was one who had a little girl at home himself.

Then I am sure he would understand what hours and hours of hard work this baby girl had put into this pair of socks.

Another little girl, Emma Andrews, only ten years old, used to come to the rooms of the Society in her town every Saturday and fill her basket with pieces of linen which had been sent in for bandages for the wounded soldiers. These she would take home, and cut up into nice towels or handkerchiefs, or roll them into neat bandages, and bring them back the next week. Her busy little fingers made over three hundred towels, all neatly hemmed and folded.

It is said that counting up all the money the children saved, together with the value of their work, they as good as sent over a hundred thousand dollars to aid the Union soldiers during this war.

The very old women, too, some of them so old that they could remember the days of the Revolution even, did their part. Thousands of stockings these half blind old grandmammas would knit, while their thoughts, I fancy, ran back over those years so long ago, when they had seen their fathers go away to fight for this same country in 1812, and in 1775.

One old lady, ninety-seven years old, spun a woollen blanket, and carried it a mile and a half to the Society to send to these soldiers. "It is all I could do," said she; "and I had to bring it myself."

Another old lady, Mrs. Bartlett of Medford, Mass., knit over a hundred and ninety pairs of socks for the Union soldiers.

PROCLAMATION OF EMANCIPATION

(PROC-LA-MA-TION OF E-MAN-CI-PA-TION.)

Well, children, those words look big enough to take away your breath! They are bigger than "religious persecution," of which we had so much in the colonial times; or, "taxation without representation", "declaration of independence," of which we heard in the Revolution; or, "impressment of American seamen," of which we heard in the war of 1812.

I wish I were not obliged to use any large words in these little histories; but once in a while it seems impossible to do without them. These phrases, with their long words, have been handed down through all these years of our country's history until they have come to be as settled as the name of a city or the name of a river; and someway it doesn't seem as if they ought to be changed, not even for little folks, any more than the names of cities or rivers should be changed.

And there are not many of them after all.

See if you can repeat these words all together.

1. The early settlers in this country left England to be free from "religious persecution."

2. The cause of the Revolution was "Taxation without Representation."

3. The people of this country drew up a paper in which they said they would no longer be ruled over by the English. This was called the "Declaration of Independence."

4. The cause of the war of 1812 was the "Impressment of American Seamen."

5. And now one more: Abraham Lincoln believed that the negro slaves had a right to be free; so he drew up a paper telling them they *should* be free. This was called the "Proclamation of Emancipation."

You remember Gen. Butler had settled the question of what was to be done with the slaves by saying that they were to be taken as "contraband goods," just like so many cattle, or so many barrels of sugar, or bales of cotton.

But there came a time when it was necessary for some law to be made by the government itself in regard to this matter. There needed to be a law regarding the treatment of these slaves which *all* the soldiers should obey: for as it stood now, one general who believed in freeing the slaves would take them into their camps when they fled from their masters, and shield them from harm; while another general, who cared nothing about the slavery question, and was fighting only to save the Union, would let the slave-hunter come into the camp and carry off the poor, black runaways.

The slaves themselves were growing to feel unsafe. They did not know when they fled to the Union camps whether they would fall into the hands of friends or foes.

And so, on *New Year's Day,* 1863, Abraham Lincoln sent out his "Proclamation of Emancipation," saying that from this time forth no man should *own* another man and call him his "slave." The negro was now as free as the white man. No one had now any right to take him away from his wife and his children to be sold, or to carry away his wife and children from him.

Of course, the Southerners were more bitter than ever; and you can hardly wonder that they were. There were men whose regular business had been to buy and sell negroes, just as men now buy and sell horses. They had invested their money in this business, and now, of course, it was all lost. There were others who owned great farms, or plantations as they call them in the South; the work of which had been always done by the slaves. Now these slaves were all free; and, on those plantations where the master had been cruel to them, you may be sure these slaves did not work very long after the news of freedom reached their ears.

We can afford to be generous to these slave-owners even; when we think what a blow it was to them to have their habits of life all broken up in this way. Many of them were as honest as honest can be in believing those black men and women belonged to them; and that they had a right to use them to work their farms. Then, too, there were thousands and thousands of slave-owners who were just as kind to these black people as they were to their own families. Their slaves had their own little cabins, snug and warm, where they could sit happy as children through the long summer evenings, playing their banjos and singing their funny old plantation songs.

Did you ever hear any of these plantation songs? I wish there were room to put five or six of them in this book; for someway, it doesn't seem as if we can have much idea of these simple hearted people unless we hear their songs.

They were such strange people! Ignorant, because they were seldom allowed to learn to read; believing in ghosts and goblins, fond of yelling and singing and dancing, full of strange ideas of the Bible and God and heaven, either hating their masters, as they hated work, or else loving them as a dog loves his master, ready to die for them and the "missus," as they used to call their masters' wives.

You must ask your teachers to read parts of Uncle Tom's Cabin to you, children. In that book you will get an honest story of Southern life, you will read of kind slave-owners, and of cruel slave-owners, of good slaves and of bad slaves; for I don't want you to think, as I did when I was a little child, that all the Southerners were wicked, wicked people, and that all the slaves were whipped and lashed every day of the year. You must remember the Southerners were just as honest in their opinions during the war as the Unionist soldiers were. They were just as brave too; they were ready to suffer everything for their dear States, just as our soldiers were ready to suffer every thing for the Union. You must remember, too, that very, very many of them were kind to their slaves; so kind, that if it were not that these slaves had souls which had the right to grow, minds which had the right to study and learn about the beautiful things of this world—if it were not for these, one might almost think these slaves, many of them, were better off before they were made free. But, it cannot be right for one person to have the *right* to say he *owns* another man, can it? And so because the *principle* of slavery was wrong, it was a grand thing for Abraham Lincoln to come out fairly and squarely and say, "No person in the United States shall hereafter own slaves!"

NEGRO SONG

This is a funny old song that the "darkeys" used to delight to sing in the days when they believed "Father Abraham" was coming to free them.

1. Say, darkeys, hab you seen de mas - sa Wid de mufstas on his
2. He six foot one way, two foot tudder, An' he welgh tree hundred
3. De ob - er - seer he make us trou-ble, An' he dribe us round a

face, Go long de road some time dis mornin', Like he gwine to leab de
pound, His coat so big he could n't pay de tai-lor, An' it won't go half way
spell; We lock him up in de smoke-house cellar, Wid de key trown in de

place? He seen a smoke, way up de rib-ber, Whar de Linkum gumboats
round. He drill so much dey call him Cap'an, An' he get so dref-ful
well. De whip is lost, de han'-cuff broken, But de massa'll hab his

lay; He took his hat, an' lef ber-ry sudden, An' I spec he 's run a - way!
tann'd, I spec he try an' fool dem Yankees For to tink he 's contraband.
pay: He' s ole enough, big enough, ought to know better Dan to went an' run away.

CHORUS.

De mas - sa run, ha! ha! De dar-keys stay, ho! ho! It

mus' be now de king-dom coming, An' de year ob Ju - bi - lo!

FIRST NEGRO REGIMENT

You have not forgotten how short a time ago it was that the anti-slavery men in Boston had been mobbed; you have not forgotten how bitter many Northerners felt towards black men and women, and towards anti-slavery men and women; you have not forgotten the Run-away Slave Law, which allowed a slave owner to pursue his slaves into the Northern States and take them wherever they were found.

All these feelings had been changing little by little during these two years of war. Nowhere was there quite such bitter feeling, and in Boston it seemed to have died away entirely.

Early in this year, after the Proclamation had been sent forth, there began to be much talk of raising a negro army. "Why not let these slaves fight for their own freedom?" the people began to say.

"Niggers can't fight! Niggers don't know enough to fight!" cried some, who did not quite believe in them yet.

"Whoever saw a nigger soldier?" cried another.

"Fancy a nigger trying to Forward, march! Right wheel! Left wheel! Right about Face!" laughed some of the soldiers.

But for all this the "nigger" regiments were formed; and they proved as effective and as brave as those who laughed at them, I have no doubt.

The first regiment of colored men was the Fifty-fourth Massachusetts, Robert G. Shaw its colonel.

This regiment was to have been sent to the capital by way of New York; but it was found that the feeling against negroes was still strong in that city, so strong that there began to be signs of mobs ready to attack this regiment if they passed through that city.

These troops, therefore, were sent by way of water from Boston.

To show yoy how rapidly the feeling against these black people died out, I must tell you that in only a few months from this time, all New York turned out to cheer a colored regiment that marched down Broadway on its way to the war. Yes, indeed, they were cheered as long, and with as much noise and hearty good-will as had Ellsworth's troops been cheered two years before, when they marched down this same street.

"To every man upon this earth
Death cometh soon or late;
And where can man die better
Than facing fearful odds,
For the ashes of his fathers,
And the temples of his Gods!"

—Indiana's Roll of Honor.

SIEGE OF VICKSBURG.

Now that the North had come out fairly, and had, by freeing the slaves, declared one grand principle of Right, we might well expect success to be found on their side; for although it doesn't always look so to us, Good *does* govern, and it gains the victory in the end. In any struggle the man or woman, boy or girl, who knows that his side is the right side, will feel more courage to go on, more surety of success.

And now we shall begin to hear more about Gen. Grant.

Grant's soldier's were mostly men from States up and down the Mississippi. Now, this river, they said, belonged to them. To shut it up, to cut off their trade, would ruin their part of the country; their farms would be of no value, their flocks and herds, their manufactories would be of no value, all because there would be no way of sending their produce to other markets.

"We will fight for this river," said they, "till our blood flows with it; to the Gulf of Mexico!"

New Orleans you know, had already been taken by Far- ragut and Butler. Not far from New Orleans, up the river, was the city of Vicksburg. This was held by the Confederates, and was said to be so strongly fortified that no army in the world could take it from them.

"But it *must* be taken," said Grant. "Holding New Orleans is of no use, if the Confederates just above can keep us from going up and down the river."

"But Farragut and Porter tried to take it after New Orleans; didn't they batter away at it with cannon ball and bomb-shell until they were tired out?" said the doubting ones.

"That makes no difference," said Grant and his men; "Vicksburg *must* be taken!" The city was built on high bluffs which rose straight up from the low flat river bed. All around it were swampy lands, with creeks and little bays, and muddy places where a man would sink in mud over his head; more than this, there were dense tangled forests of hanging moss and brush, with every where fallen trees lying across each other in a way to make it seem almost impossible for an army to get across.

ADMIRAL FARRAGUT

But Grant, only knew one thing—that the Unionists *needed* to hold that city. He didn't say very much—Grant never did say very much—but he could think, and think, and think; and after Grant had thought, there was pretty sure to be something done.

The year before, when Farragut had tried to take the city, he had begun cutting a canal through towards it. If this canal could now be finished, ships and gunboats could get around behind the city, and so attack it from the rear.

The soldiers began working at this canal. For several days the work went on, the courage of the workmen rising with every spadeful of earth they threw up; but one day, the ungrateful river, which they were working so hard to save from Confederate hands, overflowed, and away went the banks of the canal, the workmen themselves having to run for their lives.

"The good old river will protect us," said the Vicksburg people; but I'm afraid the river neither knew nor cared very much about either Unionists or Confederates; for it seemed always ready to cut its pranks and capers, first on one side, then on the other.

After this, Grant gave up the canal plan. He had another however, and began at once to carry it out. Marching towards the city to attack it from the rear, he learned that a Confederate force was behind him.

"I leave no enemy in the rear," said Grant. "I do not propose to be shut in here like a rat in a trap," said he; so back he marched, to attack the enemy in the rear. The enemy, however, knew too well they could not withstand an attack, so they fled. The Union soldiers ran up the Union flag on the state-house of the city which the Confederates left, sang a good old battle-song, and then marched back again to meet the enemy coming from the opposite direction.

Half-way between Jackson and Vicksburg, the armies met in battle. The Confederates, driven back into the city, shut themselves up, and waited to see what Grant would do.

Grant made one attack on the city, but it was useless. Now if that other army did not come and attack them, Grant was sure that he could in time starve out the city. So he settled his army round about, and the whizzing of bombs and shells into the city was the only sign of war.

Inside the city the people had dug caves, and had taken their food and furniture into them, that they might be safe from the shells.

In time, however, provisions began to grow scarce. The people had already begun to eat horses, and rats even. Their only hope was that some Confederate force would come and attack Grant. Grant's only hope was that some Confederate force would not come to attack him.

No force came; and in July a white flag was seen floating from the walls of the city. This of course meant, "We can hold out no longer."

On the Fourth of July, the Confederate army marched out, each man throwing down his gun and knapsack as he passed. The Union soldiers stood quietly by as the beaten army passed; but when later they marched into the city, and ran up the Union flag, then cheer on cheer rent the air. This was the happiest "Fourth" the country had seen for a long time.

All this time Gen. Banks had been besieging Port Hudson, just below Vicksburg. But as soon as word came that Vicksburg had surrendered, the commander within Port Hudson knew that all was over. He, too, surrendered; and now the Mississippi was free from its source to its mouth. Every point was in the hands of Union soldiers; and from every fort and from every city floated the Union flag.

"STONEWALL JACKSON" IS KILLED.

I almost dread to take you back to see what the army of the Potomac has been doing all this time. While this Army of the West had been so full of success, the Eastern army had met only with defeat.

McClellan, you remember, had been taken from the command, and Burnside had been put in his place. Burnside had made that one unfortunate attack upon Lee in Fredericksburg, and had then settled down in huts by the river side for the winter. Burnside had never felt that he was equal to the guiding of such an army, and now at the beginning of this year, 1863, he resigned his position; and Gen. Hooker—called "Fighting Joe"—was given the command.

Gen. Hooker was wide awake. He began at once getting the army in training for a new start.

His first move was to quietly cross the river, and creep up to Lee's army in Fredericksburg. This he did with such success, that Lee knew nothing about it, till he heard the army at Chancellorsville, just outside of Fredericksburg.

Lee did not care to he attacked in the city; so he marched out to meet Hooker. This attack was managed by "Stonewall Jackson," the General whose very name the Union soldiers had learned to fear.

All day long the battle raged; and a sad day it was for the Union soldiers. Just at its close, Jackson, who had been the very life of the battle, was hurrying towards a company of his own men, when they, mistaking him in the smoke and fire of the battle for a Union man, fired upon him. He was terribly wounded; but, lived on for several days, full of hope to the very last that he should yet be able to take his place again in the battle field.

When Lee heard that Jackson had lost his left arm he wrote to him, "You have lost your left arm; but I, in losing you, have lost my right arm."

Indeed, the loss of Stonewall Jackson was a death blow to Lee, and to the Confederate cause. Gaining ten battles could not make up for it. Jackson, sturdy old soldier that he was, believing fully in the Confederate side, loving his State flag with all his heart, was indeed the General of the Confederates. Wherever he was, rallying his men, there was sure to be victory. Powerful, honest, brave soldier that he was, it seems a pity that his life should have been lost in fighting for a wrong cause.

STORY OF STONEWALL JACKSON

Stonewall Jackson's victories in the Valley had won him great renown. Everybody was anxious to see him, but he was so retiring in his habits that he shunned the public gaze. His dress was generally so shabby that many did not know him, even when they saw him on his old sorrel horse. Once, about the time he joined Lee's army, he was riding with some of his officers through a field of oats. The owner ran after them in a rage, demanding Jackson's name, that he might report him at headquarters.

"Jackson is my name, sir," replied the general.

"What Jackson?" inquired the farmer.

"General Jackson."

"What! Stonewall Jackson!" exclaimed the man in astonishment.

"That is what they call me," replied Jackson.

"General," said the man, taking off his hat, "ride over my whole field. Do whatever you like with it, sir."

BATTLE OF GETTYSBURG

We now come to the battle of Gettysburg. It is the battle of which you will hear, I think, more than all the rest put together. There is a writer who has written a book about the fifteen greatest battles in the history of the whole world; and he has called this battle of Gettysburg one of those fifteen.

Now, it is not that this battle was of itself so very different from any other battle; it was not that the armies were so very much larger; not that the soldiers were so very much braver, or the generals so very much wiser. Still it is spoken of as *the* battle of the Civil War.

Let me try to help you to see just why, then, this was such a great battle.

Lee had now defeated the Union soldiers so many times that he began to think his own army was equal to anything. And well he might; for had he not defeated McClellan and

Pope and Burnside and Hooker—four of the greatest generals of the Union army.

"Now," said Lee, "it is time for us to start again up through Pennsylvania, to New York, and on to Boston if we see fit." Again the Southerners began to make their threats of how the New York streets should soon be rivers of blood, and how proud old Boston should bow before the Confederate army.

BATTLE OF GETTYSBURG

The people of Pennsylvania were filled with fright. There was the great Potomac army, made up of the bravest of the North; but never yet had a General been found in whom the people trusted. Nothing but defeat after defeat had been their share. Now, indeed, had come a time when if ever a wise leader was needed, it was needed now. Lee was setting out upon his march into the very heart of the North! What if no one could stop him! What if he went on and on, burning the towns as he passed and taking the people prisoners! When would he stop! What would be the result!

Suppose, children, a great fire should start in the fields and forest outside your town, and come leaping on, burning the grass, the bushes, the trees, the fences—everything in its track, until it reached the rows of houses just on the edges of your town. Now suppose the flames were no redder, the fire no hotter, the smoke no blacker than when it all came rolling over the hills and across the fields. Still, can't you see why just here you would be more frightened, why the firemen would work harder than ever, why the peril, the danger, would be greater than at any time be-

fore? Not that the fire is any wilder, but because it had reached that point, where, if it
isn't conquered at once and there, the whole
town will be lost.

GEN. MEADE

This is just the condition the North was in
at the time of this battle of Gettysburg. Gettysburg was like the rows of houses along the

edges of the town. Lee's fire had come on and on, sweeping everything before it up to just this point. He was now upon the border-land of the North. A battle was at hand! He, *must* not be allowed to come one step farther! "If we only had a leader!" cried the people. "If we only had a leader!" cried the soldiers. And a leader came. Hooker and another General had a quarrel just about this time over some war question; Hooker threw up the command, and Gen. Meade was put in his place. Meade, with new forces from the North, started on in pursuit of Lee.

When Lee found that so large an army was at his heels, he thought the best thing he could do would be to stand still, and let Meade overtake him. A battle was sure to come sooner or later, and Lee was wise enough to know that the sooner it came, the better; for in case of his own defeat, he would not be far from his own part of the country, and therefore not far from help.

So it happened that Meade came upon Lee at Gettysburg. Gettysburg was a pretty little village, nestling down among the hills; its people so quiet and peaceful—its farms so broad and green—doesn't it seem a shame to fill this beautiful valley with the roar of cannon and the fire and smoke of battle?

The battle began on the morning of the 1st of July. For two days it seemed as if again Lee was to win; but on the third day the tide turned. More than forty thousand men lay dead and wounded on the field. At the close of this third day, Lee began to draw away his forces. Lee was at last defeated. And on the Fourth of July, the same day that Grant's men were cheering within the walls of Vicksburg, Lee's army, what there was left of it, was marching away towards the South, broken, discouraged, defeated; and the North once more was saved.

JOHN BURNS: JENNY WADE

Most of the people of Gettysburg left their homes on the approach of the Confederates, but among the citizens was one old man named John Burns, a veteran of the war of 1812, who had no notion of running away. When he heard that the enemy was marching on the town, he took down his old State musket and began running bullets.

"What are going to do with those bullets?" asked his wife, who had anxiously watched his movements.

"Oh," replied he, "I thought some of the boys might want the old gun, and I'm getting it ready for them."

When the Union troops passed through the streets, he seized his gun and started out.

"Where are you going?" called the old lady after him.

"Going to see what's going on," he answered.

Going to a Wisconsin regiment, he asked the men if he might join them. They gave him three rousing cheers and told him to fall in. A rifle was given him in place of his old gun, and the old man fought bravely in the first day's fight, and received three wounds. When the Union troops fell back, he was left with the other wounded on the battle field, where he was found by the Confederates. Being in citizen's dress, he knew they would shoot him if they found out that he had been fighting against them, so when they said to him, "Old man, what are you doing here?" he replied:

"I am lying here wounded, as you see."

"But what business had you here, and who wounded you, our troops or yours?"

"I don't know who wounded me; I only know that I am wounded and in a bad fix."

"Well, what were you doing here? What business had you here on the field in battle time?"

He told them he was going home across the fields, and got caught in the scrape before he knew it. They asked him where he lived, and carried him home and left him there; they suspected him, for they asked him many more questions; but old Burns stuck to his story, and they finally left him.

There was a heroine as well as a hero among the people of Gettysburg. Before the battle, Jenny Wade was baking bread for the Union soldiers. She was in a house within range of the guns. When the Confederates drove the Union troops through the town, and forced them to take refuge on Cemetery Hill, they ordered her to leave.

But she refused and kept at her work even while the battle was going on. While busy with her baking a Minie ball killed her almost instantly. She was laid in a coffin which had been prepared for a Confederate officer, slain about the same time, and now lies on Cemetery Hill, where the battle raged hottest that day.

"DRAFTING"

How many Northern men had already fallen on the battlefield, do you suppose? I am sure I don't know; and you would have no idea of what the number meant, if I could give it to you. More men, than all the people you ever saw in all your lives, children. If you were to count every man and every woman, every boy and every girl in your city, all the people you ever saw on the cars, all the people you ever saw in the stores at Christmas time, or at the beach in the summer time—if you were to count them every one, even then you wouldn't have, I think, more than a handful compared with the thousands and thousands of Northern men who had gone to join the army.

And for two long years they had been fighting, with no success of much importance until the taking of Vicksburg and the driving back of Lee from Gettysburg.

Do you wonder, then, that at the beginning of this third year of the war, there were so few men left in the North and many of those so discouraged that Lincoln could no longer depend upon volunteers. Do not forget, children, that up to this time, all these brave men had joined the army of their own free will. They need not have gone had they not wanted to—nobody had made them go. They had gone bravely, because they thought it was *right*, and because they so loved their country that they were willing to give up friends, home, family—everything, and die, if need be for their Flag.

But now, in this third year of the war, the President was forced to "draft" these northern men—that is, he had to say to each town, you *must* send so many men.

This draft was made as mild as possible. No men over forty-five years of age were drafted, and no boys under eighteen. No son who had a widowed mother depending upon him, nor a father who had motherless children. You see, every attempt was made not to be unjust or cruel in this drafting.

There was in the North, at this time, a party who called themselves the peace party. They were tired of the war, had lost their courage by these two long years of defeat, and said the best thing that could be done was to declare peace, and let the Confederate States do as they pleased. This sounds all very well; but I am sure even you children can see that it was too late to talk that way then, and it was by far too early to say to the South, "You have beaten us; we give up the struggle."

These "peace-party" men, managed to stir up a good deal of anger among the low, ignorant classes in the city of New York, and a terrible riot followed. On the day the "drafting" began in that city these low people formed themselves into a mob—as they had done once before per- haps you remember—and, half drunk, armed with clubs and knives, they surged up and down the streets, killing policemen, stabbing and trampling upon black men and women and children, burning their bodies, or dragging them through the streets. Houses were entered, stores were robbed, and buildings burned.

For three whole days, this horrible riot went on—till, at last, a band of soldiers arrived. Then the mob, cowards, as such people are, slunk away to their dens and their grog-shops, and the riot, one of the most terrible and most disgraceful events of the war, was at an end.

ATTACK ON CHARLESTON

From the very beginning everyone knew that if Richmond and Charleston could be taken, and the Mississippi be freed from the control of the Confederates, the war would be at an end. The Mississippi was already free, and it seemed high time that something be done towards taking Richmond and Charleston.

Charleston is a sea-port on the coast of South Carolina. It has a fine harbor, just outside of which are many small islands. The Confederates knew this was one of their strong-holds, and they had taken great pains, therefore, to guard it. On each of these little islands was a fort; and right in the middle of the entrance to the harbor stood old Fort Sumter, its Confederate flag flying, as proud and grand as you please. This fort, you remember, had been taken by the Confederates at the very beginning of the war.

You can see how impossible it would be to enter that harbor, with all its forts ready to aim their guns upon any vessel that should dare attempt it. Indeed, one might as well have tried to enter a hornet's nest as to enter this harbor with any common kind of vessels.

It has always been a wonder to me that after that little Yankee cheese-box did such wonderful work, there weren't twenty more of them built and sent straight down to this harbor. But all this time nothing of very much importance had been done, and Charleston had good reason to suppose that it would not be taken.

Early in this year of 1863, an attempt was made to enter this harbor. Commodore Dupont, with five gun-boats and nine "Monitors," steamed in between two of these islands, and began pouring their fire upon Fort Sumter. But with all these forts filled with soldiers and guns as they were now, it is hardly to be wondered at that the attack was a failure. Even the nine little Monitors steamed back out of the harbor as fast as ever they could, while the Charleston people from the tops of their houses looked on with delight at the whole proceeding. They were sure their harbor could not be taken now!

Later, another attack upon the city was made. This time with double forces. While a fleet was to attack them from the waterside, land forces were to attack them from the rear. On Morris Island was Fort Wagner, one of the strongest of the Charleston forts. Here a force of two thousand landed, and quietly creeping toward the fort, made an attack upon it. They were driven back; and, hiding in the swamps, waited for more troops to come. A few days later, another attack was made. This time, six regiments went against the fort—among them this first colored regiment, with brave Robert Shaw as its leader.

"Now, my good men," said he to his colored soldiers, "now has come a time for you to prove that freedom is worth the price we pay for it."

On the half-run these regiments advanced. Out came a volume of deadly fire upon them from the fort. On they pressed, leaping the ditches, until at last, scaling the walls, the "Stars and Stripes" were placed upon the ramparts. But only for a second did they stand; the storming column of men fell back, dead; and into the ditch below, fell, too, the flag.

Colonel Shaw had fallen close under the walls; and, when the Union soldiers had all been driven back, and the Con- federates came out to bury the dead, they found his body covered over by the dead bodies of his brave colored soldiers whom he had loved so well.

The Confederates boasted that they had "buried him in a ditch under his own niggers;" but no ditch was deep enough to bury the memory of this brave young hero.

This unfortunate attack had proved that Fort Wagner was not to be taken in this manner. The only way now was to try to bombard the fort. But where should they set their cannon, you will ask? Surely not in the water, in front of the fort; and it seemed almost impossible to think of setting up cannon in such a swamp as that in the rear. In a swamp, where, before their eyes, many a workman had sunk out of sight in the slimy mud, seemed hardly a place to plant a cannon.

Still, this they tried to do. Night after night they worked, digging here, and piling up there, until at last they had advanced close upon the fort. Here they drove piles one on top of the other, until a place was made so firm and strong, that a cannon could stand with safety. Upon this firm floor, they built ramparts, and set up their cannon.

The soldiers called this their "swamp angel." Bombardment began, and on the 8th of September this plucky little band of workers marched into the fort and set up the Union flag. One fort in Charleston harbor was ours; one step had been taken towards entering the city.

THE GUERILLAS

Out in Kentucky were bands of horsemen called "guerillas." One of their chiefs, John Morgan, had made his name a terror to loyal people.

During this year of the war, he planned a raid into neighboring States, which was worse than any he had ever before attempted. Crossing the Cumberland river with his two thousand men, he marched to a little encampment of two hundred Union soldiers.

"Surrender!" cried Morgan, riding up to the camp.

"If it were not the Fourth of July," said an officer, coolly, "we might think about it; but Union men never surrender on their nation's birthday." And turning to his men, he ordered an attack on Morgan's men. So fierce and quick was the attack that, in spite of their numbers, Morgan thought best to ride away as fast as he could ride.

Morgan then went on to a little fort commanded by Col. Hanson. Here, too, Morgan was met with a volley from the little band within. In this, Morgan's brother was killed. Then Morgan, wild with fury, set fire to the little fort, and Hanson was forced to surrender.

On went Morgan from town to town, and from village to village, stealing, burning, destroying the crops, tearing up railroads and cutting telegraph wires, wherever he went.

But this could not go on forever. When he had gone up in this way to Ohio, the people began to think it was time that something should be done. Troops were raised and sent against him, and when he was all ready to cross over into Virginia to join Lee's army, he found himself hemmed in by Union soldiers. He was made to give up his arms and be led away a prisoner.

He and his men were taken to a prison, and there, as Morgan himself said afterwards, they were shaved and washed and scrubbed, and put into their cells by a "nigger."

There was another guerilla raid after Morgan's capture. This one was led by a ruffian named Quantrell. He went over into Kansas and fell upon the town of Lawrence, the favorite town of "free state" people, since the days of John Brown.

It was a pretty little village, with its churches and school-houses; lying there so peaceful and quiet on this Sabbath morning!

Into this town rode the ruffian band, Quantrell at its head. This was a most brutal and cowardly attack. Worse than Morgan's even; for his had been upon soldiers usually. This was upon a quiet little village of unarmed men and women. The ruffians burned the houses, robbed the stores, killed men, women and children. It was a disgraceful affair, a cowardly, mean attack upon defenceless people. I am glad, however, that this was not done by any order from the Confederate officers or the Confederate government. It is supposed to have been done by this rough band of men, merely for the sake of plunder, and for their own amusement, if doing such things can be amusement.

BATTLE IN THE VALLEY OF CHICKAMAUGA

The only stronghold now left to the Confederates in the West was Chattanooga. They had been driven from place to place by the Union army, from Kentucky, through Tennessee, until they are now on the very border of Georgia.

You remember, in the first stories of this war, you were told that there were many Unionists in Tennessee; and that it is believed that the State would never have seceded had the Unionists been allowed to speak in the convention which was held there.

You can imagine, then, the delight of these Tennessee Unionists, when Gen. Burnside marched into one of their largest cities, and planted there the Union flag.

It had been a long time since they had seen the good old Stars and Stripes, and it is said that many a one cried for joy when once more they saw the "red, white and blue." On every side, the people crowded around Burnside and his men, offering them food and drink— many of them robbing their own poor homes, that they might bring something to the Union soldiers.

Meantime, Rosecrans, our Union general, followed Bragg, the Confederate general, on to Chattanooga, a little town, lying in a sort of gateway between the mountains, and very nearly on the border line between Tennessee and Georgia.

Both Bragg and Rosecrans knew that here would be a final battle, which would decide who should hold Tennessee—the Confederates or the Unionists. Bragg, therefore, had sent for help to all the other generals round about; and now he had an army far outnumbering the Union army.

A terrible battle was fought here in this beautiful valley of Chickamauga, in which our army was sadly defeated. Rosecrans retreated, leaving 16,000 dead and wounded upon the field.

Rosecrans, although he was a brave general, and had been very successful before, was blamed for having lost this battle, and General Thomas was put in command.

Grant, the quiet general who smoked so much and talked so little, was now in command of all the Western forces. He came to Chattanooga now to see for himself how matters stood. Before he could go to Thomas, he telegraphed, "Hold Chattanooga." The reply that Thomas sent will show you somewhat of the firm character of the man. "I will hold it or starve."

JOHNNY CLEM

Johnny Clem was an Ohio boy, twelve years old. At the battle of Chickamauga, Johnny was in the thickest of the fight. Three bullets went through his cap, but Johnny didn't care for that.

After the battle, when every one was hurrying to and fro, Johnny became separated from his comrades, and was running, gun in hand, across an open field.

A Confederate officer, seeing him, sprang upon his horse and rushed after him.

"Stop! you little Yank!" called the Colonel.

Johnny, seeing that the Colonel was sure to overtake him, halted, faced around to meet the Colonel, and set his gun ready to shoot.

"You are my prisoner, young chap," said the Colonel as he rode up.

But instantly Johnny drew up his gun and fired. The colonel fell dead, and Johnny ran on to join his comrades.

Johnny, for this deed, was made a sergeant, and was put on duty at headquarters. He must have been a very odd-looking little sergeant, I think, dressed in a full sized man's uniform. But perhaps he did have a uniform that fitted him after that; and very likely he made a very spruce-looking sergeant.

"BATTLE IN THE CLOUDS"

THOMAS'S army had now grown quite large. Sherman had joined him, and Hooker had joined him—both able generals, and both in command of brave soldiers.

Bragg's army lay on Missionary Ridge and on Lookout Mountain. They had enjoyed their position up there greatly. Those on Lookout Mountain could look down upon the Union soldiers, and, with their field glasses, tell every move they made.

This was all very well in pleasant weather, under a cloudless sky; but there came a day, so "misty moisty" that the Unionists could not look up the mountain, neither could the Confederates look down.

Did you ever see a mountain with its summit all lost to sight in a big cloud of mist and rain? The little boys and girls who have lived all their lives close to the beautiful hills, have seen this hundreds of times. It is nothing new to them; but I hope they will never grow to be so used to it that they think it not worth noticing. It is, I almost think, the most beautiful sight in nature. I shall never forget the first mountain I ever saw. It was away down in Maine, up close to the New Hampshire line. As our train steamed out of the forests round a curve, we came all at once upon a broad clear place, with the mountains straight ahead. It was a heavy, cloudy "dog-day" in August;—one minute it would be dark and rainy, with big black clouds overhead, and the next minute, perhaps, the sun would be shining out from the rifts in the very blackest of the clouds. It was in one of these sunshiny minutes that I caught this first glimpse of the mountains. On one of them, settled way down half-way to its base, was a black, black cloud. Above this cloud, the mountain peak stood out bright and clear, in the sunshine. On the side of the mountains, in the cloud, was a rift. Slowly this opened, letting in the sun-light, and showing a little white cottage, nestling there among the trees. Then it closed again, and nothing was to be seen but the black circle of cloud. The light from the top slowly died away, the rain fell, and all was dark again. For a few minutes I felt dazed; it seemed as if I had been dreaming; indeed, it seemed almost as if I ought to rub my eyes to see if I really were not half asleep.

Now, it was just such a day as this, I fancy, that the Battle of Lookout Mountain, or, as we call it, the "Battle in the Clouds," took place.

Hooker started up the mountain to attack Bragg's force. It must have been a strange sight from the valley to watch these men go up, up, higher and higher, until they were lost to sight in the mountain mist.

It was a strange sight to Bragg's army, too, I imagine, when, on the other side of the mist, these blue-coats suddenly came into view.

We often hear people say, "Why, where did you come from? Did you drop from the clouds?" I never heard that Bragg said this to his unexpected visitors, but I'm sure he was surprised enough to have said it.

Grant, from a hill near by, watched the troops climbing up the mountain side until they were lost in the mist. After that, now and then, the clouds would break away, as if to give the watcher a peep at the battle going on. But little use was that after all, for no one could tell which side was winning. It was an anxious time indeed. At last, out burst the gray-coats from the cloud; down the mountain, pell-mell over the river they went—the blue-coats close at their heels. "The gray-coats are running! The gray-coats are running! The Union soldiers are driving them down the mountain!"

The gray-coats were indeed running; and they did not stop until they were safely over the river, and had joined their comrades on Missionary Ridge.

Night had now fallen, and Hooker must wait until morning to follow them farther. When morning came, it was found that the enemy had destroyed the bridge, and were now centered on Missionary Ridge.

Sherman advanced first upon them, and had a sharp fight of it for eight or nine hours. Then Sheridan came to his aid. Again they charged up the mountain side, and again the enemy fled into the valley below. Now Lookout Mountain, Missionary Ridge (so called because there had once been an Indian mission school on its brow), and Chattanooga Valley, all were in the hands of the Union soldiers.

On the following morning, again Sherman and Hooker set out in pursuit of the flying enemy. The contest for Tennessee was now over,—the Confederates were indeed driven beyond its limits, and far into Georgia.

Quite a difference, children, between the quick, active following up of battle after battle under these generals, and the slow, crawling movements of the Army of the Potomac under McClellan.

"We don't propose," these generals used to say, "to give the enemy time to get rested and fed—and so ready to fight us again the next day. No! we are upon them *at once*—before they have time to get back their breath from running."

LIBBY PRISON

I wish there were no need of my saying anything to you children about the horrible life of our soldiers in this Southern prison. If not telling it to you would make it any less a part of the history of this war, I would gladly leave it out of our stories; but it *is* a part of it, and one view of the war would be wholly lost to you if I were not to tell you of these "prison pens," as they were called.

When any of the enemy are captured in a battle, they are, as you know, called "prisoners of war." We say, in a certain battle, so many soldiers were killed, so many wounded, and so many taken prisoners.

In the city of Richmond, that capital of the Confederates, which months and months ago some of our Union generals ought to have "taken prisoner,"—in this city of Richmond stood the "Libby Prison."

It was a large brick building, which, before the war, had been used as a storehouse. It was large, to be sure; but no building is very large when you think of packing thousands and thousands of men into it.

I am afraid these men, packed into this prison like cattle into a freight car, suffered more than you or I can imagine from filth and bad air, and hunger and starvation. When this building was full, prisoners were confined, on a small island in the James River, called Belle Isle, where a kind of camp was made, surrounded by a wall of earth and by ditches. It is said that the prisoners were penned up there like sheep, without any shelter even in winter, and that many were frozen to death. It is also said that all the prisoners were given poor food, and that they were starved by the Confederates so as to make them unfit for further service. Southern writers say, on the contrary, that these stories are untrue; that the prisoners on Belle Isle were furnished with tents like those of the soldiers who guarded them; and that the food furnished to them and to those in Libby Prison was the same as the rations of their soldiers in the field. They also say that the healthfulness of the place and the good care taken of the prisoners is proved by the fact that out of more than twenty thousand prisoners confined on Belle Isle, only one hundred sixty-four died between June, 1862 and February, 1865, or about five each month.

Whether this charge was true or not, we do not know, but it was believed to be true then. In the early part of 1864, there was an attempt made by Gen. Kilpatrick and Col. Dahlgren, to free these prisoners. It was an unfortunate sort of a plan—one that did more harm than good. With a small band of mounted soldiers they started on a raid to Richmond. They tore up railroads, cut telegraph wires, and did all the mischief they could. When Kilpatrick was within three and a half miles of the city, he halted, expecting to hear Dahlgren's signal from the other side. But he waited in vain. Dahlgren had met only with misfortunes on his march, and was at that moment lying dead in the forests not far distant.

There was great excitement over this affair throughout the country. The Confederates declared that papers were found on Dahlgren's body, showing a plot to free the

Union soldiers, and then with their aid, to burn the city and to kill President Davis.

The Unionists declared that this was all a lie, made up by the Confederates to excuse them for treating Dahlgren's dead body as brutally as it is said it was treated when found by the Confederates in the forest.

How much or how little was true on either side, we cannot judge from what was said about it at that time. During a war like this, we should hardly expect to find the people very just in their judgments of each other. The "golden rule" cannot live in war time; and when that is trampled under foot, and hate gets the upper hand, the good angels of peace and truth and justice go away in sorrow, I fear, and leave the field to the bad angels alone.

TRAMP! TRAMP! TRAMP!

In the prison-cell I sit, thinking, mother dear, of you,
*   And our bright and happy home so far away,*
And the tears they fill my eyes, spite of all that I can do,
*   Though I try to cheer my comrades and be gay.*

*   Tramp, tramp, tramp, the boys are marching,*
*   Cheer up, comrades, they will come;*
*   And beneath the starry flag we shall breathe the air again*
*   Of the freeland in our own beloved home.*

In the battle-front we stood when their fiercest charge they
*   made,*
*   And they swept us off, a hundred men or more;*
But before we reached their lines they were beaten back dis-
*   mayed,*
*   And we heard the cry of vict'ry o'er and o'er.*

*   Tramp, tramp, tramp, the boys are marching,*
*   Cheer up, comrades, they will come;*
*   And beneath the starry flag we shall breathe the air again*
*   Of the freeland in our own beloved home.*

So within the prison-cell we are waiting for the day
*   That shall come to open wide the iron door.*
And the hollow eye grows bright, and the poor heart almost
*   gay*
*   As we think of seeing home and friends once more.*

Tramp, tramp, tramp, the boys are marching,
Cheer up, comrades, they will come;
And beneath the starry flag we shall breathe the air again
Of the freeland in our own beloved home.

OLD VIRGINIA

At the beginning of the war, the governor of South Carolina had said to his people, "In this State we may as well go ahead with our cotton and tobacco planting; for if there is a war the battles will be fought, most of them, up there in Old Virginia on the border line."

This speech of Governor Pickens had come true. As we know, the deadliest warfare had been carried on in the "Old Dominion State," as it is called.

ON TO RICHMOND!

This was the war-cry for 1864. On to Richmond! had been the cry of the Army of the Potomac ever since the war began; but, as we know, that army had never succeeded in getting there.

Now the Army of the West, having swept the enemy all out of Kentucky and Tennessee over into Georgia, set up as their cry, "On to Atlanta!"

Grant, during this time had come to be spoken of in the papers as "that General in the West who talks little, but does much."

"I should like to talk with that little Western General," said Lincoln. "He seems to be the sort of a man to DO." And so it came about that in the spring of 1864 Grant was made Lieutenant-general of the United States armies, and called to take command of the Army of the Potomac.

Grant came. He knew that it was no easy task he had before him; but he knew, also, that this wretched war could be brought to an end speedily if only some one was wise enough to know the way.

After looking over the ground, Grant said, "Our armies have been acting like balky horses—never pulling together. Now I propose to keep close at Lee's heels. I'll hammer and hammer at him until he is all worn out."

Having visited all the armies to know just what sort of soldiers, and what sort of officers he had to deal with, on the 3d of May, 1864, Grant started out to "hammer" Lee. At nearly the same, time Lee started out. The armies met at a place called "The Wilderness." A terrible battle followed,—one of the bloodiest of the war. Grant had begun his "hammering." All day long the armies fought, and when darkness came, fell back, tired indeed; still neither side was ready to yield. During the night aid came to Lee; but, at the same time, Burnside came to the aid of Grant. Lee planned to make an attack upon Grant's army at two o'clock in the morning; Grant also had planned to make an attack upon Lee's army at two o'clock in the morning.

Another day of terrible slaughter followed. Again night fell, leaving two bruised and broken armies, neither willing to admit itself defeated.

After such a battle as this had been the Army of the Potomac had been in the habit of falling back; so, when the order came from Grant to break up camp, the army supposed they were to fall back as usual. But that was not Grant's way. Although he had not defeated Lee, Grant knew that he had greatly shattered his forces. He therefore proposed to go on—the quicker the better.

When it was understood that Grant intended to go on, the soldiers, tired as they were from the long battle, sent up such a chorus of shouts, that you would have thought the very skies would have fallen.

I wonder what Lee thought when he heard those cheers. Surely it didn't sound as if the army was preparing to slink away like whipped dogs.

On the army went, with faces toward Richmond. "Richmond, Richmond, Richmond," was all Grant seemed to think of. If an officer asked, "What for tomorrow, general?" he said, "Richmond." If an officer came to him full of hope and eager to go on, Grant gave him a good hearty handshake, and said, "Richmond, my man!" If an officer came discouraged and doubting, Grant still said, "Richmond."

It was at this time that Grant sent the telegram to Lincoln which became so famous: "*I propose to fight it out on this line if it takes all summer.*"

On the 2d of June another terrible battle was fought at Cold Harbor. Lee, who was now no longer strong enough to make an attack, fell back towards Richmond.

After this battle, Grant decided to take his army across the river, and find the weakest point for attack upon the enemy's forces.

He formed a plan of attack on Petersburg, a place only a few miles from Richmond. As soon as Lee knew what his plans were to be, he poured his army into the city to defend it, and made the fortifications doubly strong.

Grant made one attack upon it, but it was a sad failure. He did not, however, retreat, but settled down before the city, determined to wait for another chance.

Meantime Burnside's soldiers set to work digging out an underground tunnel to one of the strongest forts of the city. For a whole month they worked, planning to undermine it and blow it up with gunpowder. On the 30th of July the mine was exploded. A terrible roar was the first warning to the people in the city. Stones, guns, and pieces of cannon were thrown high in the air. The earth shook as from an earthquake.

When it was over, a great hole like the crater of a volcano was seen in the very middle of the defences. Now came the order to "charge!" But so slowly could they advance over the ruins and heaps of rubbish, that before they were upon the defences the Confederates had rallied from the shock, and were ready to fight like madmen. The crater became to the Union soldiers a "pit of death." The great pit was filled with human bodies, black and white; men, trying to climb from the pit, were driven back with muskets and clubs. It was a scene of horror; and, as Grant himself said, "a needlessly miserable affair."

After this, Grant did little more during the fall and early winter than to hold what he had gained. All this time Sherman had been steadily "marching through Georgia," and on towards Richmond from the South. Everywhere the enemy had retreated before his brave army, and Grant was holding Lee firmly in his grasp at Petersburg.

When January of 1865 dawned, the Southern Confederates knew their end was at hand. Grant, with his persistent "hammering," and Sherman, with his brilliant marching, had indeed drawn their snares close around the Confederate Army.

In March, Lee resolved to make one more attack upon Grant's forces. He hoped to get through Grant's lines and join Johnston's forces in North Carolina. Accordingly, a sudden attack was made, and Fort Steadman, the principal point in all Grant's defences fell into Lee's hands.

Grant was indeed surprised. But soon the Union soldiers rallied, and the Confederates were driven back with great loss of men.

Grant, now that the weather was growing warm, and the muddy bogs and roads were becoming firm and dry, sent word to Sheridan that he had now made up his mind to end this matter. Sheridan, always full of hope and bravery. and quick to move, hastened to Grant's quarters with fresh troops from West Virginia.

Lee's forces were stretched in a circle forty miles around Richmond; but the lines were very thin, and Grant made up his mind that it was time to attack them. Sending Sheridan with horsemen to a place called "Five Forks," where Lee's force was especially weak, he himself began his "hammering," as he still called it, on Petersburg.

Lee was in a fix! He needed all his forces at Petersburg. and he needed them all at Five Forks. At four o'clock in the afternoon of April Fool's Day, the charge was made. The Confederates fought bravely enough. Had their cause been a just one, they had certainly deserved to win. But there was no hope! Soon they were in full flight, Sheridan's cavalry at their heels.

Lee was a brave, wise general. He was a hard man to conquer, but he knew when he was conquered. "Leave Richmond at once," he telegraphed to Jefferson Davis, when his soldiers came flying into Petersburg with the news of their defeat.

The telegram reached Davis the following morning, Sunday, and was carried to him at church. Davis rose and quietly left the church. No one knew what the telegram had told him; nor did he intend they should until he had satisfied himself there was no help. Not until afternoon did he allow it to be generally known that the city was lost. The people knew a battle had been going on; but battles as near as Richmond had gone on before when McClellan was in command, and no harm had come to their city from it.

SHERIDAN'S RIDE

Up from the South, at break of day,
Bringing to Winchester, fresh dismay,
The affrighted air with a shudder bore,
Like a herald in haste to the chieftain's door,
The terrible grumble and rumble and roar,
Telling the battle was on once more,
And Sheridan twenty miles away.

And wider still those billows of war
Thundered along the horizon's bar,
And louder yet into Winchester rolled
The roar of that red sea, uncontrolled,
Making the blood of the listener cold
As he thought of the stake in that fiery fray,
And Sheridan twenty miles away.

But there is a road to Winchester town,
A good, broad highway, leading down;
And there, through the flush of the morning light,
A steed, as black as the steeds of night,
Was seen to pass as with eagle flight;
As if he knew the terrible need,
He stretched away with his utmost speed.
Hill rose and fell; but his heart was gay,
With Sheridan fifteen miles away.

SHERIDAN'S RIDE

Still sprung from those swift hoofs, thundering south.
The dust, like the smoke from the cannon's mouth,
Or the trail of a comet sweeping faster and faster,
Foreboding to traitors the doom of disaster;
The heart of the steed and the heart of the master
Were beating like prisoners assaulting their walls,
Impatient to be where the battle-field calls.
Every nerve of the charger was strained to full play,
With Sheridan only ten miles away.

Under his spurning feet the road
Like an arrowy Alpine river flowed;
And the landscape sped away behind
Like an ocean flying before the wind;
Swept on with his wild eyes full of fire.
And the steed, like a bark fed with furnace fire.
But lo! he is nearing his heart's desire;
He is snuffing the smoke of the roaring fray,
With Sheridan only five miles away.

The first that the General saw were the groups
Of stragglers, and then the retreating troops.
What was done—what to do—a glance told him both;
Then striking his spurs, with a terrible oath,
He dashed down the line, 'mid a storm of huzzas,
And the wave of retreat checked his course there, because
The sight of the master compelled it to pause.
With foam and with dust the black charger was gray.
By the flash of his eye, and his red nostril's play
He seemed to the whole great army to say
"I have brought you Sheridan all the way
From Winchester down to save you the day!"

Hurrah, hurrah, for Sheridan!
Hurrah, hurrah, for horse and man!
And when their statues are placed on high,
Under the dome of the Union sky—
The American soldier's Temple of Fame,—
There, with the glorious General's name,
Be it said in letters, bold and bright:
    "Here is the steed that saved the day
By carrying Sheridan into the fight,
    From Winchester, twenty miles away!"

-T. Buchanan Reed,

SHERIDAN TURNING THE TIDE OF BATTLE

EVACUATION OF RICHMOND

A Richmond newspaper at that time, writing of this day, said:

"It was late in the afternoon before the people really began to know that their city was indeed lost to them. Wagons on the streets were being hastily loaded with boxes, trunks, etc., and driven to the Danville depot. . . . Carriages suddenly, arose to a value that was astounding; and ten, fifteen, and even a hundred dollars was offered for a carriage. Suddenly, as if by magic, the streets became filled with men, walking as though for a wager, and behind them excited negroes with trunks, bundles and luggage of every description. All over the city it was the same— wagons, trunks, band-boxes, and their owners, filling the streets. The banks were all open, and people were as busy as bees removing their money. Hundreds of thousands of dollars of paper money were destroyed, both State and Confederate. Night came, and with it came only worse confusion. There was no sleep for human eyes in Richmond that night.

"The City Council had met in the evening and resolved to destroy all the liquor in the city, to avoid the temptation to drink at such a time. About the hour of midnight the work commenced, under the direction of citizens in all the wards. Hundreds of barrels of liquor were rolled into the streets and the heads knocked in. The gutters ran with liquor freshet, and the fumes filled the air. Fine cases of bottled liquors were tossed into the street from third-story windows and wrecked into a thousand pieces. As the work progressed some straggling soldiers, retreating through the city, managed to get hold of a quantity of the liquor. From that moment law and order ceased to exist. Many of the stores were robbed, and the sidewalks were covered with broken glass, where the thieves had smashed the windows. The air was filled with wild cries of distress or the yells of the robbers.

An order had been issued from Gen. Ewell's headquarters to fire the four principal tobacco ware-houses in the city. The ware-houses were fired. The rams in the James River were blown up. The Richmond, Virginia, and another one were all blown to the four winds of heaven.

"The bridges leading out of the city were also fired, and were soon wrapped in flames.

"Morning broke upon a scene such as those who witnessed it can never forget. The roar of an immense conflagration sounded in their ears, tongues of flame leaped from street to street."

By seven o'clock, Monday morning, the Confederate troops were out of the city, leaving Richmond in flames. The streets were still filled with crowds of men and women, black and white, loaded down with their plunder from burning houses and stores.

Here was a negro with a bag of coffee or of sugar upon his back; another with a bag crammed with shoes or hats; a third with several pieces of cotton or woollen cloth on his head, or with an armful of ready-made clothing; a woman with a dozen hoop-skirts; and even children with boxes of thread, ribbons, and other small goods. The Babel of their voices was almost drowned in the roar of the flames and the explosion of gunpowder. Capitol Square was crowded with frightened women and children, huddled among piles of furniture and household goods saved from their burning homes. The Confederate rear-guard had scarcely left when a cry of "The Yankees! the Yankees!" arose in Main Street.

In marched the Union troops. As they entered the city, bursts of cheers went up from each regiment. "Richmond was taken!" and the war was really over.

Lee at once left Petersburg, hastening with his forces towards the West. Grant followed close upon him. There was little need to pursue them; for so broken and exhausted were they, that thousands threw down their arms, too weak and ill to carry them. On the 9th of April, Grant and Lee met, and agreed upon the terms of surrender. It did not take them very long. The "Army of Virginia" was to disband and go home, each man promising to fight no more against the Union.

Lee rode back to his camp, sad and silent. His men received him with a cheer. He looked at them sorrowfully and said, "Men, we have fought the war together; and I have done the best I could for you."

On the 12th of April, the Confederate army came out for its last parade. Grant generously kept his troops out of sight, while Lee's men stacked their guns, and covered them over with the Confederate flags, in sign of surrender.

GUN PRACTICE

FROM ATLANTA TO THE SEA

1. Bring the good old   bu - gle, boys! we 'll sing an-oth - er song—
2. How the dark-ies shout - ed when they heard the joy-ful sound!

Sing it with a   spir - it that will start the world a - long—
How the tur - keys gob-bled which our com-mis - sa - ry found!

Sing it as   we used to sing it, fif - ty thous-and ; rong,
How the sweet po - ta - toes e - ven start-ed from the round,

CHORUS.

While we were marching thro' Georgia.   Hur-rah! hur-rah! We

bring the ju - bi - lee! Hur - rah! hur - rah!   the

flag that makes you free! So   we sang the cho-rus from At -

lan - ta to   the sea, While we were marching thro' Georgia.

ON TO ATLANTA

When Grant took command of the United States' armies, he put William T. Sherman in full control of the "Army of the West."

On the day following the one in which Grant started out for Richmond, Sherman began his march toward Atlanta.

"On to Atlanta!" was their watch-word, just as in Grant's army, "On to Richmond!" was the watch-word.

I shall not try to tell you of the battle after battle in Sherman's Great March. At Atlanta the enemy drew up all their forces, determined that this place should be fought for inch by inch. It was a hard, close fight, both generals equally wise and brave; but after several days, the Confederate general gave way, and Sherman telegraphed to Grant, "Atlanta is ours, and fairly won."

GEN. WILLIAM T. SHERMAN

Hood, the Confederate general wild over the loss of Atlanta, made a desperate dash back towards Nashville, hoping to cut off Sherman's supplies.

Sherman was brave as a lion, but he was also wise as a serpent. He saw at once what Hood was hoping to do. Gen. Thomas, called by his men, "Old Reliable," saved the city. For two days the battle raged: but twilight of the second day saw the Confederates in full retreat. On they went throwing away as they ran, their guns, knapsacks, all that would hinder their flight. Our troops pursued till darkness stopped the race. Next day the pursuit was continued. Thomas strongly hoped to capture all Hood's army. On this point Hood disappointed him. Gathering his troops together, he formed now an orderly retreat, and crossed the Tennessee with what was left of his army. The flight had been indeed Bull Run over again; only this time the Confederates were flying and the Unionists were pursuing.

Sherman feeling sure that Thomas would be equal to any battle with Hood's army, had kept straight on with his plan of marching now "from Atlanta to the sea."

His object was to destroy the railroads, and cut off the supplies of food, clothing, powder and cannon of the Confederate army. This seems almost cruel; but it wasn't half so cruel, in reality, as it would have been to let the war drag on for many months more.

Taking only twenty days' provisions, Sherman told his men they must find their living in the country over which they marched. The men understood what their General meant, and about the middle of November, while Grant was holding Lee's army in Petersburg, Sherman started across "from Atlanta to the Sea."

Just before Christmas, Sherman's army marched into Savannah, and hoisted "Old Glory," as they called their flag. At once he telegraphed to Lincoln, "I beg to present to you as a Christmas present, the city of Savannah, with one hundred and fifty guns, plenty of powder, and twenty-five thousand bales of cotton."

After a long rest, which Sherman's army so greatly needed, and which they so richly deserved, they next moved towards Charleston. The North stood breathless when word came that Sherman was marching towards Charleston. Charleston! the centre of the whole secession country! Charleston! the city that was said to be unconquerable!

But Sherman conquered it, and once more the Union flag waved over old Fort Sumter.

And now the Union Army felt their journey was nearly over. In a few days they would join forces with Grant's own.

Goldsboro' was the next place to fall upon.

Here Gen. Joseph Johnston was straining every nerve for a final battle. It was like a drowning man catching at a straw. He had with him, Bragg from Wilmington, Hardee from Savannah, Beauregard from Charleston, and Wade Hampton, with his cavalry. The shattered remnant of Hood's army from Nashville had joined him.

But affairs looked dark for the Southerners. Their army in Tennessee had been broken up, Lee was held by Grant in Virginia; Sherman had conquered Georgia and South Carolina; if he now joined Grant, Lee's army would be captured. The only hope was that Johnston might defeat one or all of the armies marching on Goldsboro', and prevent their junction with the Army of the Potomac; then go north and help Lee drive Grant from his post near Richmond. It was a desperate last chance, and might be successful.

A bloody battle followed, but when night fell, Sherman's soldiers had not fallen back one inch. During the night several fresh divisions had come and joined the Union soldiers, making our lines now too strong to be broken. Johnston retreated during the night and Goldsboro' was won.

It was not long after this that Johnston surrendered to Sherman, knowing that since Lee had surrendered to Grant, the war was indeed at an end. Johnston accordingly wrote to Sherman asking that there be no further bloodshed between their soldiers, and offering to surrender his whole army.

TORPEDOES

Some very cruel work was done during the war with torpedoes. When Richmond was evacuated, the troops were sent into the city with orders to move very carefully for it was reported that the streets had been filled with torpedoes. You can easily imagine what the explosion of one of these under foot would do. Fortunately, however, when the Confederates had put these torpedoes into the ground, they had marked the location of them all with little red flags, that they themselves might know where *not* to step. In the rush and hurry of leaving the city, these flags had been entirely forgotten. It was very fortunate for the Union soldiers that they had been left standing there, warning them as well as the Confederates where not to step.

Torpedoes were put in the harbors, too. Did you ever see a three-tined prong attached to a torpedo in the water? The prong is fastened to the torpedo in such a way that when a vessel comes sailing along, it would strike against those little hooks. That would move the lever connected with the trigger of the pistol within, and a fearful explosion would be the result. Thousands of brave men's lives have been lost in this cruel way; and if it is a good thing to kill off thousands of men and blow them in pieces, then torpedoes are, I suppose, a very good thing. They are spoken of as one of the improvements of modern warfare. What do you think, boys?

SIGNALS

DURING the war it was often necessary to signal from place to place.

During the night, signalling was done by torches, during the day, by flags.

Suppose there were two signal parties, on two different mountains, five or ten miles apart. Suppose there is a battle going on near one signal party, or a bridge has been burned, or the enemy are coming near. The other signal party will need to know of all this. So first of all the flag-man sets up his flag. The officer gets his field glass in position, and watches until he finds that the signal party on the other mountain has seen the signal, and is waiting to receive the message.

Now the flag-man begins to signal. He waves his flag to the right, or the left, or the front.

Suppose to the right means 1, to the left 2, in front 3. Now, if the flagman should dip twice to the right, once to the left and once in front, that would make the number 1,123.

When the officer on the other mountain had got the whole signal, he would look in a book he carries, called a "signal code." and learn what 1,123 means. Perhaps he would find that it meant "railroad bridge burned," or "send us troops at once," or "we have defeated the Confederates," or "Grant is only five miles away."

Of course these books have to be kept very secret; and if in any way one of them should fall into the hands of the enemy, a new set of numbers would have to be made out for it wouldn't be a very nice thing to have the enemy know what the signals meant.

THE WAR IS OVER

PICTURE to yourself if you can, the joy of the people in the North when the news of these surrenders spread over the land! The telegraphs flashed it over the wires from city to city and from town to town, until the news reached the lonely homes away out on the prairies and away up on the mountains.

Our "Union boys," the "boys in blue" tossed up their hats for joy. Faces in the homes—even in those whose soldier boys would never come back to them—shone with thankfulness that this cruel war was over.

But nobody was happier than Lincoln himself. Washington was all one blaze of light; fireworks were shooting, bonfires were blazing, and bands were playing.

President Lincoln came out upon the balcony of the White House, and asked one of the bands to play the tune of "Dixie." This had been the favorite tune of the Confederates all through the war, just as "John Brown's Body" had been the favorite with our soldiers.

"I have always thought Dixie one of the best songs I ever knew. Our enemies over the way tried to make it their own; but I think we captured it with the rest; and I now ask the band to give us a good turn on it."

This was Abraham Lincoln's last public speech.

Next evening, the 14th of April, the president went to the theatre to see an English play, called "Our American Cousin." For four years the heavy duties of his great office, the sorrow which he had felt at the horrors of the war, had made an evening of amusement almost impossible for him.

But the war was over; he could lay off some of his cares. There was now to be a little time for laughter and enjoyment; a holiday for the nation and its president. So Mr. Lincoln went to the theatre, sitting in a box just above the stage. About half-past ten o'clock in the evening, as the play drew near its close, a man named John Wilkes Booth, wrapped closely in a cloak, entered the box. He came up behind the president and shot him in the back of the head. The ball entered the brain, Lincoln's head drooped forward, his eyes closed, and he never spoke afterwards. It is hoped that he felt no more pain, though he lingered until next morning, and then quietly passed away.

After the shot the murderer with the cry, "Thus may it be always with tyrants," leaped over the box railing down upon the stage. Rushing hastily through the frightened actors, hardly conscious of what had been done, he escaped through a back entrance, mounted a horse made ready for him at the theatre door, and rode rapidly away.

This news of horror so quickly following that of joy, spread over the country, filling it with gloom. This good, simple man, Abraham Lincoln,—this gentleman of the people,—had won to himself all loyal hearts. His face, so full of pathos, winning in spite of its rugged plainness, his manly, truthful nature; his noble humanity; had gained him the regard even of those who at first sneered at the "vulgar rail-splitter." Across the ocean in England where he had been held up to ridicule, his name was now mentioned with reverence.

The assassin, as he leaped from the box upon the stage, had caught his foot in the

American flag, which draped the front of the President's box. He fell forward and broke his leg in the fall. A party was at once sent in pursuit of him. On the 21st of April he was found in a barn near Fredericksburg. Defiant to the last, he stood at bay, like a hunted wild animal, with loaded weapon, prepared to take the life of any one who attempted to take him alive.

The barn was set on fire, and, as he attempted to escape, he was shot at by one of those in pursuit, and so captured. He died soon after from the effects of the wound, and his body was buried secretly.

Andrew Johnson, the vice-president now became president, and the people set to work to bring the country back into its old condition of peace and prosperity. Since then the country has grown very rapidly, and we are to-day the freest, the happiest, the richest, the best nation, I hope you all think, on the face of the earth.

Peace shall unite us again and forever,
  Though thousands lie cold in the graves of these wars;
Those who survive them shall never prove, never,
  False to the flag of the Stripes and the Stars!

WHEN JOHNNY COMES MARCHING HOME

1. When John - ny comes marching home a - gain, Hur - rah, hur-
2. The old church bell will peal with joy, Hur - rah, hur-

Solo.   Chorus.

rah! We'll give him a heart - y welcome then, Hur - rah, hurrah! To wel - come home our dar - ling boy, Hur - rah, hur-

Solo.

rah! The men will cheer, the boys will shout, The
rah! The vil - lage lads and las - sies say, With

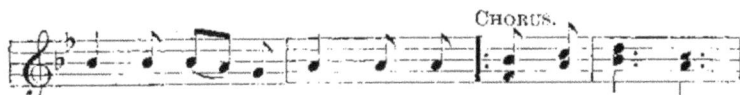

Chorus.

la - dies, they will all turn out, And we'll all feel
ro - ses they will strew the way,

gay when John - ny comes march - ing home.

BATTLE HYMN OF THE REPUBLIC

1. Mine eyes have seen the glo - ry of the com - ing of the Lord: He is trampling out the vintage where the grapes of wrath are stored; He hath loosed the fateful lightning of His ter - ri - ble swift sword: His truth is march-ing on.

2. I have seen Him In the watch - fires of a hun-dred circling camps; They have builded Him an al - tar in the even-ing dews and damps; I can read His righteous sentence by the dim and flar - ing lamps: His day is marc-ing on.

BATTLE HYMN OF THE REPUBLIC

Glo - ry, Glo - ry, Hal - le - lu - jah,

Glo - ry, Glo - ry, Glo - ry, Hal - le - lu - jah, Glo - ry

Glo - ry, Hal - le - lu - jah! And we are marching on.

3 He has sounded forth the trumpet that shall never call retreat;
He is sifting out the hearts of men before His judgment-seat;
Oh, be swift, my soul, to answer Him! be jubilant, my feet!
    Our God is marching on. — CHORUS — Glory, etc.

4 In the beauty of the lilies Christ was borne across the sea,
With a glory in His bosom that transfigures you and me;
As He died to make men holy, let us die to make men free,
    While God is marching on. — CHORUS — Glory, etc.

HUMMING BIRD.

The Adventures of Sajo and her Beaver People
Grey Owl
Benediction Classics, 2011
164 pages
ISBN: 978-1849024655

Available from
www.amazon.com,
www.amazon.co.uk

Grey Owl's children's story,
first published in 1935. This
delightful novel comes complete with Grey Owl's original
drawings, chapter head-pieces
and a glossary of Ojibway Indian words.

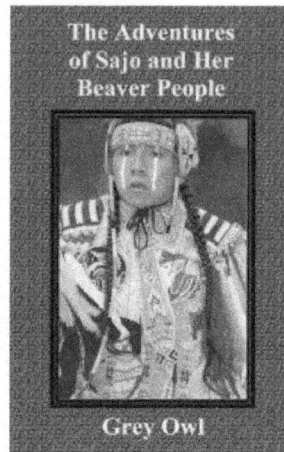

Hurlbut's Story of the Bible
Unabridged and fully illustrated in
BW
Jesse Lyman Hurlbut
Benediction Classics, 2011
976 pages
Size 11 x 8.5 inches
ISBN: 978-1849024556

Available from www.amazon.com,
www.amazon.co.uk

In the tradition of parents telling
their children stories from the Bible, this new edition of a delightful
book presents a continuous narrative of the Scriptures that brings the
great heroes and events from the Bible to life. It is unabridged and features 168 stories from the Old and New Testaments, copious BW
illustrations, a presentation page and a retouched version of the 1904
cover. Since it was written in 1904 by an American Methodist Episco-
pal Clergyman, Jesse Lyman Hurlbut, over 4 million copies have been
distributed.

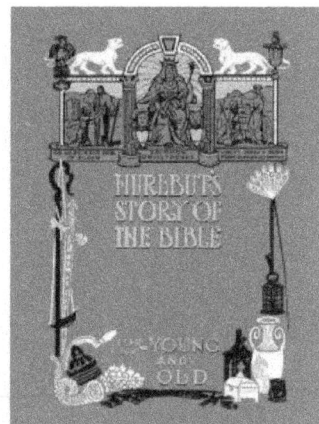

Collected Stories for Children
- 17 short stories
Walter de la Mare
Oxford City Press, 2011
280 pages
ISBN: 978-1-84902-436-5

Available from www.amazon.com,
www.amazon.co.uk

Collected Stories for Children was first
published in 1947 and is a collection of
the best seventeen short stories written by
Walter de la Mare. The stories cover a range of subjects, but are all
dreamy and poetic, captivating both adults and children. The book was
awarded the Carnegie Medal in 1947, the first time a collection of stories had won this award. It was unexpected, as none of the stories were
new, spanning the previous two decades, but the award acknowledged
him in this way: "the achievement of the most gifted writer of the century who had dedicated his finest powers to delighting children".

The stories contained in the collection are
☐ Dick and the Beanstalk
☐ The Dutch Cheese
☐ A Penny a Day
☐ The Scarecrow
☐ The Three Sleeping Boys of Warwickshire
☐ The Lovely Myfanwy
☐ Lucy
☐ Miss Jemima
☐ The Magic Jacket
☐ The Lord Fish
☐ Mr. Bumps and his Monkey (also known as The Old Lion)
☐ Broomsticks
☐ Alice's Godmother
☐ The Maria-Fly
☐ Visitors
☐ Sambo and the Snow Mountains
☐ The Riddle

Also from Benediction Books …
Wandering Between Two Worlds: Essays on Faith and Art
Anita Mathias
Benediction Books, 2007
152 pages
ISBN: 0955373700

Available from www.amazon.com, www.amazon.co.uk

In these wide-ranging lyrical essays, Anita Mathias writes, in lush,
lovely prose, of her naughty Catholic childhood in Jamshedpur, India;
her large, eccentric family in Mangalore, a sea-coast town converted
by the Portuguese in the sixteenth century; her rebellion and atheism
as a teenager in her Himalayan boarding school, run by German missionary nuns, St. Mary's Convent, Nainital; and her abrupt religious
conversion after which she entered Mother Teresa's convent in Calcut-
ta as a novice. Later rich, elegant essays explore the dualities of her
life as a writer, mother, and Christian in the United States-- Domestici-
ty and Art, Writing and Prayer, and the experience of being "an alien
and stranger" as an immigrant in America, sensing the need for roots.

About the Author

Anita Mathias is the author of *Wandering Between Two Worlds: Essays on Faith and Art*. She has a B.A. and M.A. in English from
Somerville College, Oxford University, and an M.A. in Creative Writing from the Ohio State University, USA. Anita won a National
Endowment of the Arts fellowship in Creative Nonfiction in 1997.
She lives in Oxford, England with her husband, Roy, and her daughters, Zoe and Irene.

Anita's website:
    http://www.anitamathias.com, and
Anita's blog Dreaming Beneath the Spires:
    http://dreamingbeneaththespires.blogspot.com

The Church That Had Too Much
Anita Mathias
Benediction Books, 2010
52 pages
ISBN: 9781849026567

Available from www.amazon.com, www.amazon.co.uk

The Church That Had Too Much was very well-intentioned. She wanted to love God, she wanted to love people, but she was both hampered by her muchness and the abundance of her possessions, and beset by ambition, power struggles and snobbery. Read about the surprising way The Church That Had Too Much began to resolve her problems in this deceptively simple and enchanting fable.

About the Author

Anita Mathias is the author of *Wandering Between Two Worlds: Essays on Faith and Art*. She has a B.A. and M.A. in English from Somerville College, Oxford University, and an M.A. in Creative Writing from the Ohio State University, USA. Anita won a National Endowment of the Arts fellowship in Creative Nonfiction in 1997. She lives in Oxford, England with her husband, Roy, and her daughters, Zoe and Irene.

Anita's website:
    http://www.anitamathias.com, and
Anita's blog Dreaming Beneath the Spires:
    http://dreamingbeneaththespires.blogspot.com